A Gardener Obsessed

A Gardener Obsessed

OBSERVATIONS, REFLECTIONS, AND ADVICE

FOR OTHER DEDICATED GARDENERS

Geoffrey · B · Charlesworth

DAVID R. GODINE · PUBLISHER
Boston

First published in 1994 by
DAVID R. GODINE, PUBLISHER, INC.
Horticultural Hall
300 Massachusetts Avenue
Boston, Massachusetts 02115

All photographs taken by the author.
Black and white illustrations reprinted from *Henderson's
Handbook of Plants and General Horticulture,* courtesy of the
Library of the Massachusetts Horticultural Society.

Library of Congress Cataloging-in-Publication Data
Charlesworth, Geoffrey B.
A gardener obsessed / Geoffrey B. Charlesworth. -- 1st ed.
p. cm.
1. Rock gardens. 2. Gardening. 1. Title. SB459.C415 1994
635.9´672--DC20 94-15375 CIP

ISBN 0-56792-002-0

First edition, 1994
Printed and bound in the United States of America

For
❧ *Norman* ❧

Acknowledgments

Without Norman Singer's encouragement, I would never have thought of publishing this collection of pieces, and without his help I could not have finished the work. Without the Berkshire Chapter of the North American Rock Garden Society as an audience I would never have written the pieces in the first place. So I want to thank Norman and all my gardening friends for forcing me to learn new things and to think through (partially) the meaning of life.

Thanks are also due to the many friends who have been quoted with or without permission. Sometimes a good phrase resonates so well you think you have coined it yourself. In particular the catalog quotes of our eloquent nurserymen and seed collectors deserve special thanks.

Contents

Part One

᪷

A GARDENER OBSESSED

Introduction

ঙ ঙ EVERY GARDENER NEEDS a library of reference books—books written by experts on the technical aspects of gardening, books on the names and origins of plants, books on garden design and history. This is not such a book. Rather it is meant to be a sharing and an entertainment. I want to say: You are not alone in your madness. Whether you are a timid soul who thinks that twenty dollars spent on seeds each spring is not only an extravagance, but a too revealing statement about an unbecoming preoccupation with gardening, or whether your expenses cover the salaries of several gardeners and you think transplanting the right tree to exactly the right spot on your estate is worth every effort, there are thousands of others who can understand your obsession with this absorbing activity. To make my point I may have to expose my own weaknesses, excesses, and prejudices. If you don't already share them, perhaps you will either forgive them or learn from them.

I also want to say: Gardening is fun, serious fun possibly, but always an antidote to the idiocies of Politics, Sex, and Religion and the pretensions of Art, Science, and the Humanities. Gardening is an activity that constantly reveals to us our beliefs, emotions, and character, and sometimes, in the process, we reveal them to others. Gardening is itself an outlet for fanaticism, violence, love, and rationality without their worst side effects. One is at one's most serious when engaged in fun because without optimism and joy we face an abyss.

My third "message" is: Gardening requires you to use mind as well as body. Learning is part of the activity and if you reject the intellectual stimulus offered by this close contact with Nature and Life you will misunderstand most of the true relationship of humans with the Earth and see life only in terms of the six abstractions already listed.

My main obsessions are with rock gardening and growing

plants from seed. These are not universal concerns. Only a small minority of gardeners would describe themselves as rock gardeners, but it is, perhaps, the most compelling form of gardening. Certainly gardeners of all kinds seem to gravitate towards rock gardening either casually or obsessively as a kind of climax to their gardening lives. But they rarely lose interest in their earlier horticultural activities. Also relatively few rock gardeners are ardent seed growers, though most have dabbled in it. So my final message is that it is not my intention to convert you to rock gardening, nor to bully you into seed growing. These are both life-transforming interests for which no garden writer would wish to take responsibility.

❧ ≈

Serious Rock Gardening

❧ ❧ RECENTLY I HAD to write a brief biography of a friend who was to be a speaker at a national meeting of the North American Rock Garden Society, so I asked him to give me a few sentences that he would like to see included in a description of his background. One of these was: "I want to be thought of as a serious gardener." Well, I wrote it but I thought it was rather an odd thing to confess and I began to think about whether *I* was a "serious" gardener and if I was, did I want other people to *think* I was; and if I wasn't did I want other people to think I *was*. The question of seriousness in gardening has continued to haunt me quite a lot since then. I spend twenty-four hours a day thinking and dreaming of gardening and depending on the season from eight to twelve hours actually doing it. I *could* persuade myself that I am serious. But if serious means professional then I must admit that I am not. I do not make my living gardening. I would not do your gardening for money. Also "professional gardener" is not a title of great distinction. Very little cachet there. People who work for you in the garden want to be called garden designers, landscape architects, tree shapers, and nurserymen—anything but gardeners. Lesser titles and you might as well be one of the two hundred anonymous members of Miss Willmott's staff. And "professional" isn't quite the word that would describe either a serious gardener or me. I know from my days in Academe that it isn't always the professional who is most passionate about his or her discipline. Professions seem to have more to do with initiation rites and exclusions than with passions. Have you ever seen Rosenkavalier? What do you think the Marschallin is doing during the second act? She is not listening to Strauss's deathless music. She is playing Canasta in her dressing room. In fact she doesn't need to hear it again—it is already etched in her brain, vocal chords, and soul. She is doubtless passionate about her performance, but it is quite possible she is not at all passionate about the Beautiful Art. Is every Historian passionate about History? I am sure you know a few who are blasé, a few who are cynical even among otherwise irreproachable professionals. And certainly nurserymen have been known to look at a plant and see a dollar sign. Sometimes ease of propagation is a plant's most attractive feature. Landscapers may do a job and not love either plants or gardens. In fact their knowledge of plants may be limited to a hundred or so reliable familiar favorites. Love doesn't come into it.

Possibly I am serious but don't want to be thought of as serious. Serious can mean obsessive yet no one wants to be stigmatized as bordering on neurotic. Yet I do spend all my time with plants, plant parts, or plant fantasies. Instead of writing about gardening I would prefer to be transplanting some of the seedlings that have germinated from the two thousand pots I sow between December and March. As the weather improves I would prefer to be starting a new bed, dividing perennials, moving overcrowded plants, clearing up the mess I failed to clear up last fall. Every activity that takes me away from it creates a conflict. The next best thing to gardening is talking about plants to other gardeners and even looking at their gardens. Writing is only a substitute.

I would certainly prefer to be sowing seed, transplanting, or weeding to writing about it, so maybe I should explain how I began writing. There is a society in the United States now called the North American Rock Garden Society, and being chairman of one of its chapters gave me an excuse and an opportunity to describe my rock gardening experiences in newsletters and bulletins. In any event, first let me explain what a rock garden is. A rock garden is a place where you grow rock plants. What are rock plants? Plants that appeal to rock gardeners. What kind of plants appeal to rock gardeners? I shall list a few.

1. First and foremost they are alpine plants; *not* plants necessarily from the European Alps but plants from above the tree line. The tree line in Alaska can be at sea level so essentially we are talking about plants growing in nature on tundra. Plants adapted to strong wind, large fluctuations in temperature, harsh winters and unreliable summers, heavy snow, heavy rain, or drought. They can cope by forming low mats, hemispherical mounds, deep roots, silver leaves, hairy leaves; forms that protect the plant from sun and wind. Rarely would they be annuals. A poor season might wipe out a population of annuals if no seed could be produced. Examples of alpine plants are *Silene acaulis* with a circumpolar distribution; *Diapensia lapponica,* found on Mount Washington, *Gentiana verna,* from the high Alps of Europe.

2. Subalpine plants and montane plants; i.e., from the scrub and wooded areas of the high mountains but not necessarily from exposed situations. Examples would be *Dianthus, Lupinus, Delphinium.*

3. Plants which look as though they could grow on mountains even though they don't. *Houstonia caerulea* (Bluets), *Viola pedata* (Bird's Foot Violet), *Morisia monantha* (a yellow crucifer from Corsica). These are lowlanders but have the tight cushionlike growth habit most desired by rock gardeners.

4. Plants from woodland areas. *Trilliums, Sanguinaria canadensis* (Bloodroot), *Hepatica, Primulas.* Everybody in the Northeast United States has a few trees and fancies a woodland gar-

den. This is partly because they refuse to cut down the trees, but mostly because the woodland flora of the Northeast is glorious.

5. Species plants of all descriptions. Because we like them. *Kniphofia galpinii* from the mountains of South Africa, *Liatris spicata* from the American prairies, *Coryphantha vivipara* from the Arizona desert, *Aster linariifolius,* also called Stiff Aster, of the Massachusetts roadside. If we like a plant we can find room and the right conditions for it (we think).

6. Dwarf conifers. Dwarf rhododendrons. Dwarf so that they are in scale. Notice how aesthetics creeps in insidiously.

7. Plants that are selections of good forms found in the wild. These would be propagated vegetatively. The idea is to grow the best looking plant of the species. Such clones are given names like *Phlox* 'Miss Lingard' or *Saxifraga* 'Winifred Bevington'.

8. Interspecific hybrids. Even rock gardeners do some breeding. Hybridizing runs in waves of popularity. Porophyllum saxifrages and *Lewisia* hybrids have been popular subjects for decades. There are even hybrids of two different genera. One excuse for hybrids is that natural hybrids exist in the wild. The other is we like them.

9. Etc.

And what plants do not appeal to rock gardeners?

1. Petunias, marigolds, zinnias, and cosmos. (Bedding annuals)

2. Bearded iris, day lilies, hybrid lilies. (These have their own devotees and societies.)

3. Hybrid peonies, Oriental poppies, *Phlox paniculata.* (All these are man-made and rather flashy.)

4. Selections of tall wild flowers: *Helenium autumnale* 'Moerheim Beauty', *Sedum spectabile* 'Autumn Joy'. (Less "graceful," less "ingenuous," less "noble" than the species)

But what am I saying? None of this is true. I know rock gardeners who grow all of these things. I do.

So I extend my apologies to all herbaceous border fanciers for posing as a plant snob. You must read into this the confessions of a schizophrenic personality. Hardly anybody is pure: a one-hundred-percent rock gardener is a fiction. All our gardens are hybrids, chimeras. Rock gardening is but one of many horticultural interests. Most gardeners will incorporate a rock garden into a more generalized landscape. But inside every gardener, there is a rock gardener trying to emerge. If you don't love rock plants you haven't really looked at them. Once you have seen *Edraianthus pumilio,* a small relative of *Campanulas,* once you have seen *Hymenoxys grandiflora,* the Old Man of the Mountains growing on Independence Pass in Colorado, you know you must grow these plants, possess them, fuss over them, and photograph them before you die.

And what is a rock gardener? A rock gardener must be a good gardener. A serious gardener. Good gardeners are not obsessed with weeds and definitely don't point them out in other people's gardens. (One's own garden is far too vulnerable to risk it.) Good gardeners don't criticize other people's gardens. (There is always a perfectly good explanation for the mess.) Good gardeners don't "put down" a plant except in the presence of other gardeners who share the same taste in plants and even then they do it gently. For instance, you are standing in front of a large patch of bearded iris that you happen to dislike, and you feel you should comment. What do you do? Well, you can say, "I don't grow bearded iris." "I don't know bearded iris." "I don't care for the kind of bearded iris that need staking." But if you sound off about how bearded iris have been overbred for color, height, flower size, degree of frilliness, flounciness, spottedness, and streakiness, you risk alienating your dearest friend whose secret pleasure is to collect twenty-four new bearded iris every year. She may even long to breed them herself. So however much you may dislike or think you dislike a species, a genus, a color, or a smell, please don't talk about it in front of the plant while its owner stands by politely, seething at your insensitivity.

I ought to conclude by reminding you what a rock garden is. A rock garden is the kind of garden a rock gardener makes. It has to accommodate the plants he or she likes. The traditional one consists of large rocks and boulders arranged to imitate or distill some aspect of Nature, especially Nature as seen on a mountain. In England you might see a garden with rock laid in strata, in the Czech Republic you might see a crevice garden where every plant is planted between tilted, closely set blocks of rock. There is a scree garden in Edinburgh, and in Kew and the Denver Botanic Garden there are monumental boulders arranged in cliffs and chasms. Wisley has a replica of a mountain face with paths ascending. In the United States with its vast spectrum of climates and garden locations there are bog gardens, desert gardens, woodland gardens, and prairie gardens that extend the rock garden mystique to include all aspects of Nature. Ordinary people can try a modification of these themes, sometimes a debasement if looked at without a sympathetic eye. Some alternatives are raised beds, greenhouses and cold frames, pavement gardens, wall gardens, and containers and troughs. There is no inviolable canon. Everyone must face his or her own piece of property and decide what to do. Gardens are individual constructs that mirror the idiosyncrasies of the gardener. There is really only one criterion: does it grow the plants you want it to grow? There will always be something you want to grow that hates your conditions but you keep trying. Gardening is a process and you should never think of any garden as finished. If you do, Nature will quickly step in and prove you wrong.

⌒ ⌒

The Private Memoirs and Confessions
of a Justified Seedaholic

⌒ ⌒ IT IS APRIL. We have spent two weeks visiting Ireland and England. Too early in the year to collect seed even on the west coast of Ireland, but in Dublin, Charles Nelson, taxonomist at the National Botanic Garden, tantalizes us by giving us their bulky seedlist. It doesn't seem polite to try to read it as we sit in his office talking about gardens and eventually it is pushed into my luggage unread. I promise to indulge my fantasies as soon as we return to Massachusetts. At a meeting in Warwick, John Watson, noted plant explorer, is selling seed from his expedition to South America. The arrangements for buying are primitive—crowded and with a whimsical schedule that nobody seems to understand with any certainty. After lining up nose to neck for several minutes we got to look at one of the two seedlists available. There were a few rosulate violets on the list so it was worth the wait. Pushing my way back to fresh air I noticed Sally Walker selling seeds collected in Arizona. I had already ordered, received, and sown these seeds, but I glanced again down her list to see if there was anything I had missed.

We got back to Massachusetts with a couple of packets from Jack Elliot, whose garden we had visited in England, a few seeds from Joan Whillans, a New Zealander at the conference, and a packet of "blue sweet pea" from my sister Margaret, who had been given them by a friend who had just visited the Garden of Gethsemane. This was a curiosity but one never rejects an unusual acquisition. By mid-April I had already sown over two thousand pots of seed (mostly in winter), the outdoor tables were full of trays of seed-pots, my computer list was longer than ever, and I was feeling inundated by pots and loaded with anxiety. Germination had already begun before we left for England, but when we got back hundreds of pots were showing green. To sow more seeds seemed excessive. So I made a dramatic decision—I would sow no more seeds this year. Everything from now on would be saved until the fall and another season.

There was a mountain of mail to read and as usual a few of the letters contained seed. We had been extraordinarily fortunate in contacting Ron Ratko, a genius from the West Coast. He collects selectively—he decides where to go to collect what. Ordinary people decide where to go and collect whatever. There are no adequate names to describe all the different kinds of emotional involvement people have with seed and Ron's may be unique. Other seed collectors have their own agenda. There was a fat package of seed from Ron and another large package from the Botanic Garden at Vacratot in Hungary. They send out a large chunky seedlist with a list of collected Hungarian wildflowers separated from the seed collected in the botanic garden. Like Ron's, the seed envelopes come labeled with names, not just numbers, so you can enjoy reading plant names as you open the package and thumb through the seed envelopes. Some of them I couldn't remember ordering: four centaureas, some tall umbelliferae and things like *Dianthus giganteiformis* and *Fumana procumbens* that I knew I had grown before. I was puzzled but only for a moment until I remembered that Norman Singer, who gardens with me, had also ordered seed and these were meant only for him. Another dilemma: Should I also sow these seeds or leave them strictly for Norman? Well, having decided not to sow any more seeds this season, that decision could be postponed until November at least. Cambridge Botanic Garden also sends out seed quite late. I suppose botanic gardens favor each other and send sister institutions their requests before those of private individuals. It is hard to accept this. How could the botanic garden in Lausanne get even half the pleasure at receiving seed from Cambridge that I do? The crumbs that fall from the rich man's table are still very welcome and resentments must be put aside.

The American Primrose Society is also very late this year. What do you do with primula seed in late April? Also Vaclav Plestil in the Czech Republic and Gert Boehme in Germany, who send their bounty all through the winter, have sent their final offerings. David and Deidre Tomlinson, who garden in Toronto, are a week later than usual and our recent trip makes it later still but there is a packet from them of mostly border plants including three species of phlomis I want to test for hardiness. There are also two new mertensias and a repeat of *Morina longifolia,* which I loved but lost three years ago. Gert is sending another collection of Russian plants carefully taped to a short note in English. His English (like my German) is dictionary English. Vaclav's package contains twenty-two differ-ent campanulas and six species of aubrieta. His message says that since we are going to have a plant sale at the end of August these would be the kind of good rock plants that everybody wants. True, but they must be put on one side; April is too late to sow if you want large enough plants to sell by August. At least I think so. Anyway the tables are full so I have nowhere to put them. Anyway I can't keep making the same decision over and over again. So I put all the incoming seed into a shoebox in a closet until I can record it and finally sow it.

Around this time, just as everything is sown and germinating and transplantings are well advanced, the new seedlist season starts. It is June and the New Zealand Rock Garden Society seedlist ar-rives. This is a real jolt. In May the garden is running smoothly and you think you know what it is all about. Transplanting is proceed-ing well, and by June the garden is full again and you can literally see hundreds of seedlings in the cold frames with thousands to fol-low. The garden is at capacity. I could open up another half acre and fill it with ease if I had the time and energy. Besides, I ordered too many plants by mail and they are crowding the frames too. And yet as this new seedlist arrives I hear seductive voices urging me to grow celmisias, to try notothlaspi again and finally succeed with aci-phylla. There is little point in thinking about greenhouse space and how I would get these temperamental plants through the winter. The important thing is that if I pass up the opportunity to order seeds now I shall lose the option of trying. So I order. As though to cement the decision, a letter arrives from Joan Whillans contain-ing fresh celmisia seed and a few days later a seedlist from the Otago Alpine Garden Group with even more celmisias to choose from. At the back of my mind is the conviction that these are poor germinators at best and there is little danger of being crowded out with celmisia plants. In any case I would rather like that. What is surely overloaded is my game plan, my ambitions, and my shoebox of seeds. I break my resolution here too and sow a little of the celmisia seed, partly as an insurance policy.

It is midsummer and already the seed is ripening on the drabas, the townsendias, and a few androsaces. Ideally I should go around the garden every day with a trayful of empty margarine containers, some used labels, a pair of scissors, and a pencil, collecting seed as it ripens and leaving it to dry off in the greenhouse before storing it in envelopes. It remains an ideal. Most of the time you notice ripe seed when you have nothing to put them in and no earthly way of remembering what they are. A trip back to the greenhouse to get the paraphernalia is an expenditure of energy that has to be carefully weighed against the benefits. Perversely, if I make a special trip around the garden with gathering tools in hand, in the cool of the evening but before the dew forms, when I am too tired to do any other kind of gardening (in other words when the timing is perfect), nothing is ever ready—the pulsatilla feathers don't detach easily, the aster heads are squashed black balls, the lupinus seed have dispersed from their curled up pods, there are no phlox seed in sight, and I come back with a trayful of empty plastic containers. One journey back to the greenhouse I willingly make. I had been watching the seed of *Adonis vernalis* ripen and was prepared for the exact moment to take it. Not as you might think when the exposed seed was brown, but while it was still green and just ready to fall off with a light touch of the finger. Then sow immediately. This method succeeded phenomenally the year before and I ended up with three pots of germinated seed. Unfortunately it was October when I noticed them and I had to consider how to get them through the winter. They survived well in a closed cold frame, and in late April after they started growing again I transplanted them all. Wrong decision! Every one of them died within a couple of months.

Gradually though, the little plastic margarine bowls accumulate in the greenhouse and just as they get out of hand I start the job of cleaning the seed and putting it in envelopes ready for sending away. Meanwhile other gardeners in other gardens are doing just this and one feels part of a gigantic worldwide gleaning operation.

Visitors to the garden are alert to plants in seed and beg a head of centaurea or a pod of papaver for their own garden.

In August, stories circulate of seed collecting expeditions; some are organized to see flowers but hoping for a little seed, some are arranged just to collect seed with only a faint hope of seeing a few flowers. We went to Switzerland in early September and were almost too late to do either. Collecting seed in other people's gardens gives the double pleasure of growing a plant one has admired and having it sentimentalized by taking it from a person you like or from a location that is important in some way. So we not only got seed from Hedi Schott and Bruny Monney whom we visited, but also from the garden of a man who calls himself "gardener of the Lord" and decorates his garden with verses from the Bible in wrought iron. We also got a pinch of seed surreptitiously from a botanic garden high in the mountains that displayed a plaque screwed on to a rock commemorating a visit by an American Rock Garden Society group. Our daily hikes into the mountains were punctuated by stops to collect seed of *Saxifraga oppositifolia* and *Dryas octopetala*. If we found a primula or a campanula, we could rarely identify the species so most of the time the seed was anonymous but its provenance was precise and memorable.

Back at home after two weeks away, a mountain of mail and a million jobs are waiting, most pressing being cleaning seed, packing it, and sending it off to societies and friends. A dozen sieves, three sheets of clean paper, pencils, coin envelopes, good light, and lots of patience are the tools. You have to be careful at mealtimes not to eat any of the poppy seeds that appear to have fallen from rolls on to the table. They could be leftover aconitum seeds or something else poisonous. If you are an incorrigible crumb eater you shouldn't work on the dining table. Ours is a kitchen table and we do and Norman is, but so far everybody is alive. The kitchen floor is littered with chaff and dry stalks for a couple of weeks. Several magnifying glasses and flashlights sit around waiting to help distinguish seed from chaff. Surprisingly this is not always straightforward. The round, hard, shiny spheres of alliums and poppies are the exception rather than the rule. You forget from one year to the next exactly what seed looks like, though it helps to realize that most seed of species of the same genus are similar. Occasionally capsules that look full are empty and not everything that rattles is seed. The "blow and see if it blows away" test often fails. Then there is the moralistic/pragmatic decision about whether to take the parachutes off the composites (moralistic because some seed directors deplore parachutes on daisy seed; pragmatic because it doesn't really affect anybody else). Whether to strip the seeds from the rock hard heads of *Anacyclus depressus,* whether to extract the seed from hard to handle astragalus pods, how far to go in trying to separate campanula seed from dust exactly the same size as the seed. There are also challenges to one's instinct for self protection: What to do with the prickly seed of cirsium, onopordon, acanthus, the hostile hard pointed seed capsules of penstemons, and the bristly hairs of onosma? You also have to decide what seed to keep for yourself and what to give away. Is there enough to send away? Do seed exchange directors really mean it when they say "any amount no matter how small"? Would anybody want *one* seed of *Arnebia echioides?* I decided to keep that one for myself. Next you have to decide what the correct name for the seed is. Are you going to follow *Hortus Third?* Are you going to look up every single name? If, like me, you usually keep the name that was on the seed packet when you received it years ago, you face quite a problem. Both your credibility and sophistication are at stake if you send in an obsolete name. Then you must separate the packets of seed into helpings for each society, deciding which is their best destination. Seed from North American plants is especially valuable because you imagine that is what they most want in England, the Czech Republic, Canada, and New Zealand. The best non-American seed goes to the North American Rock Garden Society (NARGS) but always you try to keep back a helping to sow yourself or for friends, especially if it is something unusual.

Meanwhile commercial seedlists are arriving. It is almost an insult to call them "commercial" even though you have to pay for the seed. These are my favorite seedlists. They come from dedicated people who go on arduous and sometimes hazardous trips to bring back seed in relatively small quantities. I suppose they are depriving some alpine mice of a couple of good breakfasts, but the effect is negligible compared with the wholesale removal of plants from the Alps in the bad old days. Maybe even this minimal activity will be frowned on by the next century, but at the moment we have the responsible and the knowledgeable performing a service for the dedicated and appreciative. This seems to be an acceptable interim situation in these transitional times. I feel a little anxious about committing even this tepid point of view to paper remembering that the name Reginald Farrer, the holy messenger of rock gardening, now brings shivers to one's spine as we contemplate his ancient sins, collecting plants in the mountains of Europe.

So we are indebted to Jim and Jenny Archibald, Sally Walker, Gwen and Panayoti Kelaidis, Joseph Jurasek, Josef Halda, Ron Ratko, Alan Bradshaw, Mojmir Pavelka, Vojtech Holubec, Ota Vlasek, Zdenek Zvolanek, and anyone I have forgotten for going to inaccessible places and bringing back enough seeds so that they can sell minuscule quantities at high enough prices to pay their expenses and keep them through the winter. I shall not even complain about the price— I remember the cost of a plane ticket, a car rental, and a wretched motel, and most of all the fact that I really don't know where to go to find the plants whose seed I want. We are also indebted to the people who go on expeditions to places with no motels at all and not even gas stations every twenty miles: Chris Chadwell and John Watson and their kind. We know that expeditions are less daunting now than the historic forays of Forrest and Farrer, because many of our friends have done something similar, but it is all too bumpy, rainy, hungry, and weary for most of us.

In October a new book arrives from Norman Deno describing his experiments with seed germination. A lot of the information is invaluable but the methodology seems rather remote from my own and I have to interpret the results to fit my own experience. I get a terrific lift from his comment about *Adonis vernalis:* "More seed of these have been planted without success than any other genus." Again this year I have three pots of flourishing seedlings sitting in the cold frame. Oh well, that is only the first step after all. Last year was a fiasco. But the book convinces me about drabas. I tried sowing seed from my *best* drabas fresh and got miserable results. The secret is that crucifers need dry storage for a few months before sowing.

In November, seed is accumulating fast from the commercial sources. Seed of lewisia has arrived from Ashwood. Gardening friends have almost stopped gardening so they have time to write letters. Seed arrives from Gert Boehme in Germany, Bedrich Parizek, Josef Stibic, Anna Jilkova, Vladimir Jane, Maria Korizkova in the Czech Republic, Hedi Schott in Switzerland, Charles Cresson in Pennsylvania, Harry Jans sends a seedlist from Holland, Bruny Monney from Switzerland, and Olga Duchakova from the Czech Republic. Everybody lists something familiar, something new.

There is so much seed by now that I decide to save time later on by writing labels now. Tomorrow I could start sowing again. The tables are clear, there is no snow yet, the greenhouse is relatively warm. Gwen Kelaidis always sows her seed on January first but why wait until Gwen's magic date?

The first two club seedlists have arrived and the orders have been mailed. Northern Nevada Native Plant Society has mostly plants from the arid southwest but this year there were several donors from Washington state. The British Columbia seedlist emphasizes North and South American plants and always includes a large proportion of wild collected seed. As December and January progress the other major seedlists will arrive from North American Rock Garden Society (NARGS), Alpine Garden Society (AGS), Scottish Rock Garden Club (SRGC), Hardy Plant Society (HPS),

Northwestern Horticultural Society (NHS), and Royal Horticultural Society (RHS). There will be a lot of looking up of names in
Hortus, the RHS dictionary, *Ohwi's Flora of Japan,* and other reference works. If you could just pick out the twenty or thirty species
you most want, there would be no problem, but in order to get your
allowance you have to select close to a hundred species from the list.
My philosophy is not to worry about getting first choices, just to be
sure I really want all of the hundred kinds I am listing. First choices
then become a bonus instead of a right. I have to admit it is becoming harder to find a hundred plants I want and don't already
have, so my next ploy is to choose seeds collected in the wild (you
might get different forms from different places), or from a known
"good grower" (on the theory that they wouldn't be likely to send
seeds of something not worth growing), or seeds of just a limited
number of genera (seeds of plants you are willing to learn to like). I
have exhausted some genera in the sense that I have grown all the
species you are likely to find in a seedlist. You can go through quite
large genera in a few years; for instance silene, dianthus, androsace,
primula, saxifraga, draba, and even penstemon have a hard time
producing more than one new species in a given year. Of course I
always try to get that one but so does every other seedaholic. So next
you ask for repeats of seeds of your favorites. You can't have too
many plants of *Androsace vandellii,* and in some genera such as cyclamen, erythronium, and fritillaria, seed of any species is useful
even if you already have that species. If you like these genera you
could order the same species time after time and build up a colony.
Of course most bulbs take a long time to flower so do this while you
are still young. None of this is true of symphyandra or campanula.
One happy plant will almost certainly give you more selfsown
seedlings than you want without ordering more seed from a seed exchange. But some campanulas are so elusive that you can try every
year and still end up with only a couple of plants that flower and die
without progeny. So ordering from a society seed exchange requires
a strategy. Never imagine that you can order exactly ten numbers

and no more and expect to get them. If you try this you will inspire an emotion close to hate in the person who tries to fill your order. You have put them in a moral quandary. On the one hand they do not want to deprive you of your rights (to get some seed for your money); on the other hand they do not want to deprive other people of their rights. (You doubtlessly ordered only aretian androsaces or unusual hostas or Japanese violets and if you get only the "best" seed, what will be left for the others?) This dilemma may be without merit but your strategy should anticipate the worst case. So use a seedlist to broaden your taste in plants, to transform your garden instead of consolidating your prejudices. Include new species and genera, plants you could grow to love as you certainly would if you grew them yourself from seed. At least for the first year.

We must be grateful to the seedlist people too. True they are probably enjoying themselves socializing and eating cookies as they package seed and fill orders. But volunteers for good deeds never get the right kind of gratitude. The satisfaction is mostly internally generated. The applicant for seed sees himself not as a supplicant satisfied with anything that providence brings but as a purchaser who has requested something specific, paid the asking price, and has perhaps received something else. So if you cannot be grateful to the people who donate seeds and the people who give their time for the exchange you should find a commercial source for exactly the seed you need. It will cost a little more but you can usually find a source. Seed exchange workers and the rest of us who are merely applying for seed are like motorists and pedestrians who often complain about each other but are in fact the same people.

It is March and the seed exchanges are closed. The garden is still wintry but the first signs of life are stirring. All seed should have been sown by now except possibly tender annuals. The first seedlings will be up before April begins. And still there are seeds arriving by mail. Edith Ordille in Germany finally has her seedlist ready, Mark McDonough the Onion Man sends out his list of alliums. The Bevingtons write from England about their next trip to the Pyrenees and include a few narcissus seeds. The plant catalogs have also been arriving since the beginning of the year. I always order a few plants whose seeds I have just sown—to be on the safe side. We have heard from other botanic gardens, from Denver, Lausanne, North Carolina, and the seeds are steadily mounting. The final hard copy run on the computer list of this year's seeds has been made. Anything new that comes in is still welcome, even thrilling, but it also has a certain nuisance value. Either it gets left off the computer list completely, or it is handwritten out of alphabetical order at the back of the list, or worst of all there is so much of it I have to run an addendum to the seedlist. Never do this if you can help it. You can never remember to look at it. An alternative to these unpleasant possibilities is to save the seed until the following season. This seems like sacrilege, but the tables are full again and I know I won't have time to do all that transplanting if they all germinate.

When does the seed season start and end? I don't know. When does spring begin? It is September for *Colchicums,* June for *Roscoea*—every month is spring for something. Intoxication with seeds knows no season. Should seedaholics be allowed to drive? Only in cities. Do you want them in your garden? They do less damage than photographers, dogs, and children. Should they be encouraged? Yes. It is the most self-interested thing you can do. (Cast thy bread upon the water...) Are there any societies to cure this disease? Yes, but so far their only effect has been to exacerbate the symptoms. Is there a danger that seedaholics will use up the world's seed supply? No. It is estimated that there are fewer than a hundred gardeners suffering from severe cases of this affliction. If each of them sowed fifty seeds of two thousand species, they would consume fewer seeds than a single plant of *Verbascum thapsis* produces in a season. Are seedaholics a danger to others? Not if your only contact is kissing or using the same hand towel. Too much listening and reading may lead to aberrant behavior. Entering a roomful of seedaholics may be dangerous; on the other hand this is often the best inoculant against infection. Whatever the locus, sight and sound are more to be feared than inhalation or bodily contact. Can the sickness be cured? Most sufferers need external suppliers to support their habit. Monetary considerations are of secondary importance since most suppliers are interested only in making converts. Apprehend the supplier and the battle is half won. There is a move to advocate the prohibition of seed across state lines, but so far most "cures" of this drastic nature would be declared unconstitutional, being contrary to the guarantees of the eighth amendment. Should we foster seedaholism in children? No. Children display every other form of greed. Leave this one to people of voting age.

This completes the Justification of seedaholism.

⌇ ⌇

Members of an Organization:
Obsessive Behavior Patterns

ॐ ॐ ALTHOUGH I DETEST being pigeonholed (and more than likely stereotyped), I am going to take the liberty of categorizing seven main modes of obsessive behavior exhibited by members of the North American Rock Garden Society (or of any other gardening society for that matter). You may feel you fit into more than one category or you may not feel you belong to any of them. Beginners especially may feel excluded, but without doubt there is a category waiting for you if you garden long enough. And those people in two or more categories usually fit into them one at a time—a particular one at a particular time in their gardening career, or switching compartments and changing modes through the gardening year. Each box has its permanent residents, and though I have tiptoed into nearly all the boxes, I belong mostly in the last box, the seventh box whose joys and sorrows I have experienced most fully.

First the *Activators*. These people make things happen—the organizers, presidents, chairpersons, editors, treasurers. By the time you have listed their names and their activities you might well believe you had encompassed the whole Society, since they put on meetings and plant shows, run seed exchanges, journals and newsletters. They nominate and second and think up new bylaws, run raffles, and give slide talks; they lead tours, decide policy and "implement" decisions. You can also include in this group gardeners who open their gardens to the public and botanic garden directors. There are also the people who win prizes at plant shows even if only because they brought plants just "to fill up the tables." Include too, nurserymen and commercial growers who service our needs and slake our passions. Without them some of us would have nothing to grow. Without activators very little of consequence would happen.

The second type of gardener is *Contemplative.* These are the Nature lovers, the people who have benches in their gardens they actually sit on, and probably sundials and animal statues that complement the horticultural display with man-made symbolic objects. They include gardeners who value dormant plants and dead stalks in winter as much as the flowers of spring or the festive fruits of fall. They make wreaths, bouquets, and potpourris with dead plant parts. They fill bowls with peonies in early summer. They may be mystics or religious, pagans or pantheists. Historians, too, fall into the contemplative mode as they seek to evaluate the universals of gardening, the extraordinary and the obsolete in past gardens, and how they themselves continue history. Then there is the Romantic who understands the intent of a garden and is willing to overlook unfinished business, seeing a mountainside where prosaic neighbors only notice a pile of misplaced rocks.

The third group is *Cerebral:* people who look at a garden as a handy laboratory or as a model or a museum. Garden writers and designers who garden on paper, scientists—botanists, geologists, entomologists, ornithologists—people whose impact on gardening is indirect but fires the intellect and enthusiasm of gardeners enough to make them look up from their plants. They are the authorities who identify wildlife, change names on labels, criticize flawed rockwork, diagnose disease, establish gardening almanacs and hardiness zones. Their information is usually at a level once removed from the gardening ordinary folks do.

The fourth type are the *Arcane:* hybridizers, people who understand tissue culture, rooting hormones, pruning techniques, gibberellic acid, and when to spray fruit trees. They keep a refrigerator just for seeds and cuttings and do experiments on germination without necessarily raising plants later. They know which plants are calcifuge and understand the needs of plants growing on serpentine. They belong to specialist societies and know the lineage of hybrid auriculas and rhododendrons, the shape of penstemon seed. They specialize in alliums, cyclamen, heathers, lewisias, sempervivums, and saxifrages. They form societies and send out newsletters. Each section of a genus could be thought worthy of a new society with its own by-laws. They grow cactus and orchids in warm greenhouses, conservatories, and other effete surroundings. They know the best time of year to take cuttings and whether to use hardwood or half ripe and if a heel is essential. They mutilate bulbs to increase stock and know which daphnes are hardy in Zone 6.

Group five could be lumped together as *Artists,* though they might quarrel among themselves about who should be included: garden designers and flower arrangers both work out their designs based on principles that can be codified and justified. For them a garden doesn't just grow haphazardly, it is planned; a bouquet of freshly cut flowers stuffed into a vase of water is wanton waste. Their work has an authenticity that must be acknowledged even if the theories are debatable. Include also photographers who capture mists, dew on spiderwebs, sunlight through trellises, and frost on *Sedum spectabile;* a flower close-up staged with cunning may leave you guessing about its true size or wondering what the rest of the plant looks like, but in the process you are made to see beauty in things you had previously ignored. And there are those people who are constantly transplanting in quest for the perfect plant association. For them the point of a garden is color combination, texture contrast, and the grouping of plants for effect. Season of bloom assumes a major importance and foliage may be more valuable than flowers. For them colchicum leaves and bright red flowers are "difficult to place." Chartreuse and variegated foliage are either favored or condemned. A garden is an exercise in taste and design that the artistically-deprived gardener is too insensitive or busy to worry about.

The sixth major category consists of *Technicians:* rock garden builders, moraine designers, terrace layers, wall builders, irrigation experts. People who understand artificial streams and waterfalls, who make pools that don't leak, people who understand drainage, bogs, berms, and ditches. They can make you a trough that doesn't fall apart in winter, a cold frame with windproof lids, they erect greenhouses and plastic tunnels. When they stake delphiniums you know they will survive the next hurricane, their dwarf conifers are properly protected in the winter, they love using a chain saw. When a rock needs to be placed they understand fulcrums and levers. They built the Pyramids and the Eiffel Tower. Such people are often spouses, spouse equivalents, or spouse substitutes. If two people garden together one of them is usually more of a technician than the other and as you look at the garden you don't know whose garden it really is. Does a garden belong to the person whose *idea* it is or to the person who did most of the *work?*

Finally, in the seventh group, there are the *Seedlovers:* those who find seed irresistible both on the plant, ready for picking, and in the envelope, ready for sowing. This strangely obsessive group earns its own special category because they are most closely associated with rock gardening as opposed to the many other manifestations of flower gardening. You could go a step further and say they are the heart of rock gardening because ultimately they are the source of most new plants in our gardens. You may want to separate out the people who only collect seed in the wild—they may not even have a garden but if they do, growing from seed will surely be a major part of their activity. As for the gardeners who prefer to see their seed neatly packaged in small envelopes, cleaned and ready for sowing rather than on a wild plant on a cold mountain side in September, they form a specialized subset of seedlovers. In winter they garden by mail. Letters fly back and forth across the world to a network of seedaholics, carrying seedlists and packets of seed. Sometimes the seed envelopes are neatly taped across the accompanying letter, sometimes they are stuffed haphazardly into a flimsy envelope with no message, but always they are welcome. Even seeds of plants you have already in the garden are welcome. In December who knows what will survive the winter? So you grow it again in case it doesn't, or in case it is a different form or a better color. And even if you end up growing the same old weedy campanula again it will have the special virtue of coming from a plant friend. The obsession rages for a full six months. Category seven mode peaks for most people in January. The euphoria may fade in March as seedlings freeze or damp off. By mid-April the consequences of the disease are unfolding. Hundreds of pots of seeds have germinated and the world of seedaholics splits abruptly into those who plan to take care of seedlings and those who plan to take a vacation or conjure up some other excuse for imminent horticultural disaster. By May or June all categories blend into a horticultural rainbow of obsessive behavior as the spell of gardening switches on all seven possible modes.

But whatever the upshot of last season's infection, by mid-October the letters, the seedlists, and the little packets are flying again and there is a fresh outbreak of seed fever, that blessed disease. Also by October thousands of new plants have entered the rock gardens of the Northern hemisphere as a direct consequence of the affliction. Some of them will be weeds, most of them will be on probation in the gardens of the wary. A few will be new gems to enrich the gardens of all of us.

⌁ ⌁

Envy Overcome

❧ ❧ YOU CAN BELIEVE in the seven deadly sins without being

unduly burdened by religion. They are the emotional attitudes that spoil our lives but somehow have to be dealt with either by expressing them or suppressing them. Envy is one of these insidious sins and, like all of them, is double-edged: in excess, destructive and unproductive, but in moderation useful in getting things done you hadn't thought possible, rewarding in bringing unlikely pleasures and insights. Excess in the opposite direction from Envy is, I suppose, some aspect of the many-faced demon, Pride. This could manifest itself either as hubris or smugness. A trifle of each usually gets one over debilitating Envy. Anyway, as far as gardening is concerned, Envy and its opposites are facts of life. Very few of us can claim an immaculate record.

There is an explanation we in New England use for nearly all our horticultural failures—the weather. We bemoan the fickle ups and downs of temperature and the erratic rainfall. Especially we blame our zone number. Being in Zone 4 or even Zone 5 seems to explain fully and completely why we fail to establish *Veronica bombycina* or why it is impossible to flower *Potentilla nitida rubra* or *Soldanella alpina.* Thoughts about such failures that seem to be shared by all our gardening friends within a fifty mile radius could provoke a quiver of envy for those places where everything seems to grow and where zone numbers skyrocket up to 6, 7, or even 8. Beyond 8 we start thinking of Florida and Louisiana and common sense takes over. We realize that envy has bounds. In the United States you may have to couple a high zone number with high temperature in summer. If you multiply the zone number by 10 and add 40 you get what could happen to the temperature on a really bad summer day. The moist West Coast might be different. There the zone number plus 4 might indicate the length in inches of the longest slug of the season, while zone number times 10 could be the number of inches of rain in a bountiful year. As we listen to our distant American gardening friends blaming their own zone number for not being able to grow *Veronica bombycina* nor flower *Potentilla nitida rubra,* our envy turns us in a different direction.

How is it that the English are so successful? They have zone numbers in England, too. Most of England has a winter low of 14°F (-10C), the coastal region of Wales, Cornwall, Ireland, and south and east England has a low of 23°F (-5C). This places them in Zones 8 and 9 respectively! Like Georgia and central Florida without the humid summer heat, or California and Oregon without the slugs! A rush of envy flushes the base of my scalp as I visualize mats of *Veronica bombycina* stretching from Land's End to Dover. How can we do in our gardens what they do in theirs? Why should we even try? What a pleasure their winters must be with year-round gardening and nonstop flowering.

We visited England in January 1991. This was my first midwinter there for forty-five years or more. As expected, the grass was green and the gardens either growing or poised for growth. Helleborus and galanthus were in flower; by early February my sister was reporting hepaticas and eranthis in bloom. But what I had forgotten was the gloom of the daylight hours. The days were short in any case since Great Britain is at the same latitude as Labrador. By 3:30 p.m. evening was already descending. The most striking aspect of the English winter is the low sun. Even at midday the sun doesn't get above the car's windshield. You might expect people here to be ardent sun-worshippers as they wait for its rebirth at the solstice. Perhaps when the smog problem has been solved they will revert to ancient beliefs that acknowledge the sun's wanderings. Meanwhile it is hard to distinguish between man-made gloom and astronomical events. The sun looks as though it is recuperating from a sickness rather than beginning a new life.

The upshot of my visit was to dispel any lingering Envy and its close relative, Nostalgia. We returned home to the blue skies and bright sun of a Massachusetts January. The "promise" of our garden is not that it is trying to grow but that it is trying to sleep. I walked around the garden on frozen ground and saw the dormant buds on bird's-eye primulas, saxifrages, and drabas. It somehow seemed more appropriate that alpines should be in retreat from winter and not trying to be too precocious. For a few days I was content (=smug) that the cycle of seasons in Zone 5 is more pronounced than in Zones 8 and 9. Then we had a February thaw while England had a crippling snowstorm and heaven knows what was happening in Georgia and Oregon. It became obvious that nobody in the temperate zone—that ribbon of gardens that runs round the world—is proof against weather anomalies. Envy is a nonproductive emotion, but Smugness is also a sin which brings certain retribution. After all our boasting and squirming to explain our deficiencies, we are subject to forces that can defeat all our feeble efforts. But isn't it wonderful when the effort pays off? Isn't it wonderful when we get *Veronica bombycina* to stay with us over a winter for *whatever* reason?

We paid a second visit to the British Isles in April of the same year. We arrived in the early morning, and with a whole day ahead of us, even though we hadn't slept on the plane, we went to Wisley to inspect the work being done on the rock garden there. Wisley had fallen from its past glory and had a slightly neglected, shabby air about it. The rock garden was depressing with half of it "under construction" and the other half unweeded showing great gaps where plants used to be. The splendid shrubs that used to adorn the higher levels of the garden had vanished and left blocky rocks looking like rows of decayed molars. Above the rock garden, things were better with the patio of troughs in good shape and the alpine house planted at ground level looking fine.

The heather garden was sad too, and storm damage in the woodland area had also left its mark. It was still fun to be there because Wisley's structure and topography is essentially beautiful and certain features, such as the "alpine lawn" of *Narcissus bulbocodium,* are unmatched.

Next day we went to Kent to stay with gardening friends and finally saw their garden (mostly perennials) in its glorious setting without the floods of two years previously. And although you couldn't call it an alpine garden, there were raised beds, greenhouses, and a marvelous iris frame at waist level used for all kinds of interesting plants that get some overhead protection in winter. Our host's garden was enclosed by an ancient wall with oast house, barn, greenhouses, and an ancient house as congenial as Sissinghurst on a slightly smaller scale. Every plant had character, and different sections of the garden were separated by walls, buildings, and gates making every part "secret."

We were taken to a local alpine plant show and to a very interesting nursery specializing in hellebores; also we visited the garden of a prominent authority on bulbs. I felt little surges of envy during these three days. The gardens were a good deal further advanced than ours; they talked about the yearlong drought, but nothing we saw looked stressed. The show plants were *superb* and quite beyond the abilities of any American gardener I know; the expertise of plantsmanship, showmanship, and horticultural know-how is so concentrated. Kent is smaller than Rhode Island and yet we had met one of the world's experts on bulbs, some of the best alpine and perennial nurserymen anywhere, and locally there were world-famous gardens to be visited in which you could happily spend a day or more without exhausting their interest. At this wonderful nursery the hellebores we saw were all the way from buttery yellow to almost black and there were five or six outstanding clones of pulmonaria as well as a few new corydalis.

The bulb man's coldframes contained rare fritillarias and other bulbs overgrown with grass. Here was a different way to garden. Start with an eighteenth-century house on a beautiful property with pond, ditch, springs, and orchard, grow what you want to grow and refuse to be distracted by the weeds. Ultimately I suppose you would have to rescue some of the less vigorous plants, but the interim effect was quite pleasing.

The gardens we later saw in Ireland were also very fine. One garden had been revitalized during the past ten years or so by the owners, now in their seventies. The dog kennels had been in an enclosed yard and this was now converted into a garden of raised beds.

New Zealand plants were flourishing with celmisias and raoulias as good as any we saw in New Zealand. Another celebrated garden was in Dublin. A Georgian mansion with enormous windows overlooked charming lawns, beds, allées, and a graceful *Cornus alternifolia variegata*. You leave the living room down a flight of steps and find troughs and a greenhouse full of well-grown plants. The garden is a collection of plants chosen for rarity, beauty, and interest but so well placed that it looks like a well-designed gardenscape and no plant is either lost or out of place.

Back in England we went to the plant show at the Alpine Garden Society's international conference. The show was another tour de force of horticulture. The dionysias, androsaces, fritillarias, and rhododendrons were perfection. One entry of twelve different fritillarias all in perfect bloom was alone worth the trip. But picking out one entry gives the wrong impression—there were hundreds of perfect plants.

So how can I say: Envy is no longer in charge? I think it is because I really like doing what I do and my gardening activities do not overlap with anything I saw. I cannot say our weather is the best in the world for growing plants or for anything else, but I see other gardeners with their own weather problems. The floods and droughts of Kent, the persistent rains of Ireland. We spent a lot of time in gardens shivering and sneezing and I quickly added up the amount of "quality time" I could squeeze out of our hometown of Sandisfield, Massachusetts, in a year and concluded it wouldn't be all that different from either England or Ireland. One gardener in Ireland confessed she rarely did any work in the winter. It seems the "promise" is just that—cold winds, soggy ground, poor light do not add up to a good day's gardening. I will stick with my occasional crisp, blue winter day with pruning shears, saw, and leaf rake.

And what about the plants themselves? Well, the celmisias and the hellebores are just more plants I can't obtain or grow. They join the ranks of *Kniphofias, Silene hookeri, Calochortus,* and *Hebe*— wonderful plants that I leave for other gardeners to grow. There are many plants that we can grow in Massachusetts and points north. We don't need to envy any gardener his or her range of possibilities.

As for the plants on the show tables, I have to confess to having strangely ambivalent feelings—well-nigh sinful feelings about these paragons. The glorious *Dionysias,* the perfect *Androsace vandelliis,* the rare *Clematis marmorias,* the fat flowered trilliums totally unlike our own wild *T. erectum,* and especially the flamboyant rhododendrons all begin to look like hothouse orchids or tea roses. They seem too remote from the happy-go-lucky gardening I want to do and very remote from the mountains, woods, and deserts that their ancestors came from. This is not a complaint so much as an acceptance. I could never aspire to growing these lovely things, but I don't want to grow them. However I think we have to be grateful there are gardeners who want to take a plant and reveal what a glorious thing it can be, given the right care in the isolation of a pot.

If I had a complaint it would be that the plants brought to the shows are the same year after year so that a perfectly grown specimen no longer makes us catch our breath. I think the judges must share a little of the same jaded feelings as they try to select the single best of a dozen perfect plants on the basis of such irrelevancies as a dead leaf that hasn't been removed, a couple of flowers that have gone over or are not yet fully opened. As in the heyday of Auricula shows, whenever people have learned to grow plants to this degree of perfection the rules for judging become as artificial as the plants themselves. I think it is this aspect of showing that reduces horticulture to sport. Dog shows have little to do with owning your own family dog. As laymen we are grateful that these competitions exist, otherwise we would never see these exquisite results and would fail to understand the ultimate possibility of a plant.

And so with apologies to Milton:

> *Hence loathed Envy!*
> *Of Celmisia and blackest Hellebore born,*
> *In Dionysian cave forlorn,*

'mongst perfect shapes, and forms and sights.
Leave Shows that wrinkled Care derides
Join Gardeners planting far and wide.
Come and rake it as ye go
Use a light fantastic hoe
And in thy right hand take with thee
Mountain avens, plant with glee
Herbs and other country messes
Which neat-handed Phyllis dresses.
Haste thee Gardener, bring with thee
Zest and youthful jollity,
Seeds and cuttings, gardeners' wiles,
Change thy frowns to wreathed smiles.

❧ ❧

Part Two

❧

IDEAS ABOUT GARDENING

What Is a Garden?

❧ ❧ A GARDEN IS the *Interface* between the house and the rest of civilization. It acts as the protective skin of the house deterring a stranger from entering. This seemed especially true in Alexandria, Egypt, when I lived for some time as a paying guest in a convent, whose entrance from one of the main streets was a high wrought-iron gate. The street had clanging street cars, beggars, and the raucous noises of a cosmopolitan city. Through the gate there was a small garden of palms both beautifying the street and protecting the convent from it. The paved driveway through the garden was neither part of the city nor yet an integral part of the stark black and white and institutional cream of a German convent. The garden represented a cultural separation as well as a physical one. Many people living in the row houses of northern England don't have this luxury and step out from their living quarters into the public street. Without the protective skin or interface that a garden provides, privacy is at a premium and sometimes not attainable. Living in New York City, we had hallways, foyers, and stoops that perform a comparable function less successfully than a garden. However, resourceful people use windowboxes and planters as ways of excluding the casual glances of strangers as much as for their decorative effect.

Even in the isolation of the country, a garden mutely prohibits strangers from treating the house and grounds as public land. But also in the country a garden is the interface of the house with nature. It seems important to mark off an area where Nature is excluded or modified and where "humanness" begins. A garden has this effect. We emerge from our rough woodland into the cleared area around the house with a sense of escaping from a certain kind of danger: the vulnerability of ill-equipped humans when confronted by brush, bog, and the pointless but primitive fear of wild animals. Nature hasn't been excluded by making a garden but it has been modified— animals and birds seem to know this is shared territory and either take advantage of it or avoid it. Plants may or may not be aware but the net effect is the same. Local weeds romp in the good soil; precious introduced wild flowers cannot be persuaded to grow.

Between city and country are innumerable exercises in the creation of interfaces ranging from the fenceless (and defenseless) lawns of suburban Long Island to the walled and hedged fortresses you find in England and France. There is a sociology lesson to be learned from the garden as separator, a lesson more about the community than the individual owner who might be unwilling or unable to express his own concept of what a garden should be. In the suburbs, Nature is adopted as a property or simply ignored. The birds we feed become part of the garden; they are *our* birds and *our* squirrels. The proprietary feeling is intensified if a bird actually nests in the garden. The dandelions and goldenrod in our neighbor's neglected backyard become *their* weeds.

At a more conscious level, a garden is an extension of *Living Space*, an outside room, a place to hang laundry, cut firewood, wash cars, shake a blanket. We use it to sit in, to eat in, to cook in, even to get married in. It is used for a tea party or a major celebration. In summer when chronic neglect has settled over the little used rooms inside the house, the garden becomes the only elegant reception room available. Many an otherwise hospitable and generous gardener denies visitors access to the kitchen and dining room for this reason. But visiting gardeners who forgive disarray in a garden will by extension of this courtesy choose not to notice the disarray in a fellow gardener's kitchen when for some reason (heavy rain) the garden visit ends up indoors. Good visitors bake cookies to take on garden visits knowing that the gardener has spent hours in the garden preparing for the visit and couldn't possibly have had time to bake. But there are so many compulsive personalities who garden that most of one's friends are not in the least ashamed of their dining room, kitchen, or bathroom even in May.

You could even sleep in a garden. It would not be recommended in New England without protection from mosquitoes before retiring and black flies before rising. You would certainly need a tent and only a child or a romantic city dweller confusing the discomforts of primitive living with frontiersmanship would want to spend a night on the lawn. If you lived in the country and not on a main highway you might want to install an outdoor shower as I did hoping to enjoy the sensuous freedom of a hot shower in the open. Against this idea—you don't usually need the shower until you have finished working by which time the sun is sinking and a cool breeze makes it a disadvantage to be wet. But, you may say, a cold shower is exactly what you need in the middle of a hot day to get you through the afternoon. Yes indeed, but a garden hose is just as good. Moreover a major reason for not having an outside shower is the gnawing fear of forgetting to remove the water from the pipes at the end of the showering season. Broken pipes in January will probably not be noticed until the following June at which time the plumber is on vacation in Italy.

Breaks in pipes are a nontrivial problem of all outside plumbing including that in a greenhouse. Horizontal pipes are quite likely to sag with use and misuse. They require a good strong stream of air blown through them (with your mouth) to eject the water that settles in pools at the lowest points of the pipes. Our greenhouse is heated by hot air from a gas heater activated by a thermostat set at 40F. This is insufficient heat to keep cold water pipes leading to the faucets from freezing. Consequently we don't use running water during the winter and the pipes must be emptied completely by blowing down a hose attached to the faucet. One year before we knew about the sagging we had seven or eight breaks. The breaks themselves were not nearly as bad as the end-of-the-world feeling you get when something mechanical goes wrong in the country. Armageddon will take place in winter after a heavy snowfall before the roads are clear. The refrigerator will be off and the phone lines down, it will probably be in March when the firewood supply in the porch has been used up and of course it will be late on Saturday afternoon. The roof of the greenhouse will collapse and it will suddenly become clear that the plants you have cosseted through the winter will be there to greet you after the Last Battle.

A garden is an *Intrusion* into the living space of animals; it is that part of the world we share willingly or not with animals. Porcupine, deer, chipmunk, raccoon, woodchuck, skunk, mole, vole, mouse, squirrel move freely in and out. Following the surprise at seeing wild animals in the garden, other unexpected emotions follow in quick succession: delight, awe, indignation, anger, patriotism, resignation, tolerance, and then groups of several emotions together. In New England animals are "varmint." Snakes, efts, newts, toads, and turtles are rarely seen but always present. Robins, grosbeaks, chickadees, wrens, turkeys, jays, and fifty more species of bird nest in, feed in, or fly over the garden. Insects from the abominable black flies and mosquitoes to the useful ladybugs and gorgeous butterflies go through their life cycle with the regularity of the flowers. A garden would have interest enough if it were cultivated just for the spiders in it.

A garden too is a *Natural History Museum.* I don't mean only the exasperating footprints that might be a challenge to identify for a boy scout, nor the piles of scat; though it is a fascinating exercise to recognize an animal by its droppings. (The raccoons leave enough cherry stones to give the average human acute appendicitis.) But we also get dead birds to examine, sometimes half consumed. By a hawk? Occasionally one flies into the glass of the greenhouse or porch; hummingbirds never do this although they are the swiftest flyers, slow birds like chickadees are dazed for a few minutes and then fly away. But a nonresident warbler is sometimes a victim. Birds' nests too can be examined after the young have left; we find the twiggy conglomerate of a wren stuffed between the vertical boards of the lathhouse, the mud goblets of the barn swallow, and the tiny nests of warblers and hummingbirds, usually after they have been blown down by autumn gales. Robins drop their discarded shells in the beds fooling you into believing you have an unexpected turquoise flower in bloom. Last November I found a complete turtle shell, empty except for some elegant bones too large to drop out of the cavity. Feathers of jays and flickers, shed skins of garter snakes, and porcupine quills are summer delights. Every episode leaves Nature more mysterious than ever since a gardener is too busy to be sidetracked into trying to decode the life story of the creatures that share the garden. It's as though somebody came into the garden with a travel brochure for Peru. Intensely interesting but a deflection of purpose.

A garden is a *Gymnasium:* an outlet for energy, a place where accidents can occur, where muscles develop and fat is shed. A place where the body is used and used up. A place where we test our health and strength, where age arrives stealthily, and the body retreats more or less gracefully into less and less demanding activity. At least that is the ideal; most of us test our luck at some time and lose a month or a year over some idiotic "accident." The gymnasium is nonsexist and nonageist—no one need ask which chores are suitable except the gardener. A garden is a *Playground,* a ball park, a frisbee range, a kite launch pad. People with ponds and pools swim or expose their bodies to the sun. People with children have swings. People with dogs throw sticks and look sporty. In midwinter our lawns and fields become a cross-country ski run. In summer we put chairs and benches at strategic viewing points intending to relax there after a hard day's work. This never happens. On the way to the seat you notice a patch of weeds or a branch that needs pruning or a broken label or seed that has to be collected. It would take a very determined gardener to either play or rest in a garden.

A garden is a *Medium for Self-Expression.* It is the equivalent of a blank canvas or the clay of a sculptor. Or you can think of it as the studio itself. The materials are soil, rocks, and plants. Whether you call what you do a hobby or an artform is only a matter of attitude. To succeed, though, means to collaborate with nature. Do you spend winter nights with paper and pencil making designs for beds?

Five of this and seven of that in neat little shapes with flowering time, color, and height given careful consideration. It is a nostalgic exercise, a way of waiting for spring, a way of retaining contact with the garden intellectually and emotionally. By April the design is forgotten. You had neglected to take into account that large immovable daphne that you can't even cut back, and the two dwarf conifers in slightly the wrong position for your scheme, and there is a host of precious and semi-precious plants with roots too long and deep to transplant, and you find you have nowhere to put them even if you could dig them up. Half the plants you ordered by mail are not available and the ones that arrive in mid-May are so small you daren't give them that generous oval space you had in the diagram. You settle for a modification of the original plan and wait a year for the plants to bloom. They are not the color or height you had in mind, they bloom at the wrong time, and you don't really like them as well as you thought you might a year ago. Another way to make a plan is to use plants you already have in the garden. The realities of spring are exactly the same as before—not quite enough of this, divisions of that perish in the coldframe, two colors planned as neighbors now seem bland, the shape and size of the bed are totally at variance with our winter scheming.

How do beds get planned then? Well, "planning" is mostly done on an *ad hoc* basis. We move a plant for one reason or another and replant it where it fits in best. I don't want to ridicule this process, it is both sound and practical. We correct faults and try to leave the garden improved in a particular way, keeping some general aim in mind. Often the process is intuitive and is best not verbalized, but if a friend is watching it is better to have a theoretical justification handy or you will be showered with embarrassing questions and objections. If a landscape designer can claim more success than an ordinary hands-on gardener with his or her presketched plans, it is probably because the design makes use of plants the designer has in his backyard waiting to sell to you; otherwise common sense tells you that he would face the same problems as we do ourselves. The second year of anybody's garden bed has to be an exercise in improvement and modification. Don't be too gullible about plant associations, though obviously there *are* plants that look well together and even bloom together one particular year. We know this because we have seen photographs of such triumphs taken by professional photographers in well-known gardens. One year our own garden provided one of these pictures—a magnificent pairing of hydrangea 'Annabelle' with a smoke tree and a variegated cornus as back-up. Alas, that year was the climax of the grouping. Since then the height and girth of the plants increased year by year and while there is nothing wrong with the present thicket, the photographed scene was never duplicated. Thus it is with every garden and every garden picture.

A garden is a *Process*. There are the seasonal changes: the reawakening each spring, the rapid greening and flowering followed by summer's voluptuous sloth, fall's beautiful sad flurry, and the gradual sinking into another dormancy. As this process takes place another kind of change is happening; growth and decay of plants ensure that a garden is never the same two years running. And superimposed on these natural events is the development due to human input, the changes brought on by changes in interest and in one's perception of the garden's purpose. We started our garden with annuals bought from a local nursery the week the contract on the house was signed. Then came perennials, shrubs, and trees. Later we became interested in particular perennials and bought collections of Oriental poppies, irises, and daylilies. Then followed summer bulbs: gladiolus, cannas, galtonias, and ismenes, with frantic digging in the fall usually after the weather was uncomfortably cold, storage in baskets and boxes filling half the floor space in the cellar, and counting, cleaning, and dividing of the harvest. It was as much fun as the first bumper harvest of summer squash. But there were usually too many of the easy ones and the ones you really wanted to propagate ended the winter dried up or rotten. Lilies seemed a better road to follow and we planted dozens of hybrids to

give a succession of those glorious bowls, bells, and goblets upfac-
ing, outfacing, and pendent, orange, red, and white. These were
shared over the next three years with the mice and after they had
found them all we stopped planting them. It was worth it, though;
nothing is more sumptuous than lilies and if you can find a way to
keep them I would recommend growing all the species you can find.
The hybrids too, but keep them separate; mixing them makes the
hybrids look gross and the species look dim.

Meanwhile we were collecting shrubs, crab apples, dwarf
conifers, rhododendrons, and "weeping" trees. These have all con-
tributed to the gradual change that has crept over the landscape.
Ten years is not long in a garden's life but in that time a rooted cutting passes through the cute adolescent stage until it has a presence
that affects the shape of the entire garden. As trees grow you have to
correct many errors of placement. Sometimes the only solution
may be to cut down a fast growing tree or shrub. Handling hostile
berberis, chaenomeles, and species roses can be a nightmare. By the
time your fingers have been pierced a hundred times in the process
of removing a twig or a branch you become a merciless slasher and
chopper, eager to get revenge and impatient for the coup de grace.
Berberis will have the last word and prick you all the way to the trash
heap.

Herbs and edible plants have also been introduced up and
down the garden. One season we tried a thyme garden, but that was
for as long as it took for thymes to show their predilection for con-
quest of all free and occupied territory, even of lawns. A single plant
under stern discipline can give yearlong pleasure; a bed of thymes
without restraint is a mess. Before you try to prove otherwise remember one more thing about thymes: bees love them and at no
time during their flowering season will you get close enough to a
whole bed of thymes to keep them in order. Maybe on rainy days.
Thymes, lavenders, sages, asparagus, blueberries, and rhubarbs are
all decorative and useful. I never make much use of food from the
garden. A few side dishes of asparagus and one rhubarb pudding a

year. Catbirds and robins get the blueberries, they like them a little less ripe than I do. After fifteen years of weeding asparagus beds with bad grace and a guilty conscience at being late again, I dug up the bed and now enjoy with a clear conscience asparagus from the supermarket—a good bit earlier than my own crop. Anyway I needed the space to grow grasses. Some of these retain their beauty for weeks. They are still "experimental"; I haven't tried to find a strategic location for the tall ones or a rational way to show off the shorter ones. If they begin to selfsow they may face banishment. An overgrown bed of grasses looks like a meadow.

The main interest in the garden is the alpine plants, and as the collection grows the face of the garden is pockmarked with raised beds. Perhaps beauty spots would be a kinder term. Mountain plants can be grown in many situations. If you can only associate them in your mind with rocks arranged to simulate miniature mountains and cliffs, no doubt you will build a rock garden. And no doubt will leave yourself with nowhere to expand. So it is important to free your mind of this prejudice if you intend to increase your collection beyond the confines of the "rockery." Rock work is as difficult to change or extend as it is to build in the first place. Much of the "process" in my garden has been installing and discarding rocks for one reason or another, and one well-placed, good-sized rock can take up a day's labor—both getting it in and getting it out.

The idea of *Process* also means that each part of the garden has a history. The character of one particular bed in our garden illustrates this. It passed through the following stages: trash heap for the broken plates and bed springs of previous tenants, overlaying a base layer of saddle parts and horse shoes; after much labor, vegetables; then successively, annuals, thymes, lilies, heathers, and finally rock plants. During this period, paths have changed position and surface, rocks have been introduced and cleared, raised beds have been made. But remnants of all the former ideas are still there. The changes are brought about by changes in taste, development of skills, and because Nature wants it that way.

A garden is a *Landscape*. It may contrast with nature or merge with nature. It may contrast with its urban setting or merge into it. My present garden is embedded in Nature. There are open views of wooded hills, hidden places, formal and wild areas with a maze of paths and suggestions of paths to get you from one place to another. A neatly designed area and a more "natural" area need not be at odds; the one intensifies the response to the other. Nature is always part of the landscape. Sometimes it dominates the picture. The fall of the leaves reduces the garden to triviality and in winter the garden may hardly have an existence separate from Nature. Then we imagine ourselves students of Capability Brown and visualize a tree moved ten feet to the right and a small lake that would enhance the landscape. In spring and summer many visitors never see the landscape. Their eyes go instantly earthward to examine the plants. Others don't even glance at plants but may remark on the beautiful view of the hills or the wall of trees—some phrase that mollifies our indignation at having our beloved plants ignored. Occasionally a visitor can only see the garden as a potential building site. A good place to build a larger garage.

A garden is a *Picture Frame* for a house. A setting for a building. Many suburban dwellers see a garden only in these terms. Their shrubs are grown specifically to hide an ugly foundation. Their lawns set off the house, keeping it visually separate from the neighbors. A planting close to a building seems to decorate the building rather than having an independent existence.

A garden is a *Fantasy*, a repository of memories, a place to indulge sentimentality. This explains garden sculpture, romantic nooks and crannies, antique implements, sundials, seashells, and gnomes. Many of our plants have associations with friends and relatives. We have a *Cornus mas* donated by a sister, a *Cornus kousa* by a friend. Kattles gave us this lonicera; this path is Henry's Walk; this bed is Garry's Garden and this one George's. Fake ruins and grottoes are now out of style and too expensive to construct, but the romantic feelings of gardeners will not be denied and are often expressed in defiance of common sense. Collections of obsolete farm equipment, cherubs, or glass balls can foster the illusion of an active imagination.

A garden is a *Collection* of plants. This is usually the visitor's second impression after the landscape has been absorbed. There are both wild plants and plants developed by Horticulture. We admire the triumphs of the propagators: the dwarf conifers, the grafted fruit trees, the weeping pines and larches, the hybrid lilies, the selections of bearded iris, the many cultivars of narcissus and tulip, the incredible strains of annuals. Perhaps even more we marvel at the diversity of species, the variations of form and color. A garden is both a feast for the eye and a challenge to the intellect. Plants invite questions—biological, philosophical, ethical, mathematical, historical, and, at the obvious level, horticultural.

The plant collection is most often displayed with aesthetic considerations dominant. But plants could be arranged by genus or family, by geographic origins or by habitat requirements. I have tried all these with only partial success. Possibly these arrangements are all doomed to be compromised if only for practical reasons.

A garden is a *Workplace*. A place where plants are produced, a nursery. Central to any garden that does not rely on outside sources for its plants and labor are two locations. One is a toolshed, the other a propagation area. These might be the same place, a barn, greenhouse, bunker, coldframe, kitchen, vestibule, shed, or garage. Whatever the physical location it is part of the garden. It is not a place to be ashamed of though it may well be a place one wants to hide. From this central place all useful, noncontemplative activity originates. Seeds are sown, seedlings transplanted, cuttings rooted, labels written, logbook kept, boxes of plants packed for friends; this is where water comes from, where spades and trowels are stored, where compost, weedkiller, pesticides, and fertilizers are kept. It bears the same relation to the garden as the kitchen and cellar do to the house.

A garden is a *Laboratory*, a place where experiments are performed. These are mostly on a trial and error basis—neither statistically nor genetically sound, though there is often an aspect of the experiments that resembles science. We experiment with winter protection, pest control, soil improvement, irrigation, hybridization, and control of growth. If we see visible results we estimate by intuition whether the experiment has been a success and whether it is worth repeating. This aspect of gardening raises one's status from dabbler to craftsman and makes the epithet "gardener" one to aspire to.

A garden is a *Display*. The arrangement of plants can be a preoccupation as absorbing and demanding as a stage set, a display window on Fifth Avenue, or a museum. We pay attention to color combinations and combinations of texture and form; we try to arrange that no plant is invisible or overpowered by its neighbors. The situation is complicated by time and line of sight. A stage set is a dead object meant to be viewed from the front, but a garden changes with time and has an infinite number of viewing points. Both are strongly influenced by lighting. A garden more nearly resembles a "happening" where the viewer enters the work of art and experiences sounds, smells, and variation of position. Perhaps the comparison is with the interior of a cathedral. Or should the comparison be made in reverse? A cathedral is like a garden with its odd smells, colored glass and banners, scurrying figures, and the sound of swishing garments with occasional bursts of music and distant theatrical voices distorted by echoes. The display can ignite a spark of reverence or simply set in motion down-to-earth discussions of techniques related to the display. Labels can be seen as plaques honoring the donor and stating acquisition date and provenance or simply as tombstones.

But unlike a cathedral, changeless over the years, a garden offers a succession of effects like a parade in slow motion. And as the year progresses and the light changes we are struck by special snapshots that we carry in our memory or record as a photograph. A garden becomes a picture postcard, a picture of a flowering shrub in a glossy catalog, a Christmas card, an Impressionist painting or a Minimalist painting. In fact every school of painting is represented in a garden: Renaissance, Expressionist, every mode of abstraction. It needs only the right viewer at the right time to recognize the influence of gardens on art. Gardens distill nature and neaten up the chaotic in nature ready for the artist's eye.

A garden is a *Haven,* not just for people escaping from stress and noise, but for the plants themselves. You cannot go into a wood or a meadow, dig a hole, and drop in an alpine plant from the Himalayas and expect it to grow. You cannot even move a plant from a natural woodland to a woodland garden fifty feet away without giving it some encouragement and protection. A garden implies care. Care implies skill and knowledge. Some people appear to have green fingers. This means they are willing to take a little trouble, apply a few principles and experiment. It may mean that they hide their failures. If your garden is to be a haven for difficult plants you have to make special arrangements for them, just as you would for a panther or a peacock. You find that some plants need the winter protection of a greenhouse or an unheated alpine house. One of the biggest decisions is what to grow, where to set limits for the amount (in expense and time) of care you want to give a plant. Low maintenance gardens are usually low in interest. Usually if you build a greenhouse or a coldframe you test it to its limits to see what kind of plants will grow with the amount of heat you can afford and the amount of attention you can spare. We reject plants like orchids, bog plants, and tender trees if we can't provide an adequate home.

A garden is part of *History.* Gardening is as old as mankind— at least once humans got beyond nomadic life. It is because of gardens that we are civilized (urbanized). Agriculture is only gardening on a large scale. Most gardeners have used their plot of ground to produce food at one time or another. Growing only food in a garden wastes an opportunity and could either indicate a very needy person or someone role-playing as provider or survivor. On the other hand vegetable growing provides an outlet for competitiveness and aesthetics as well as producing superior food and sometimes income.

Above all a garden is a *Privilege* and a *Treasure*. Bloody revolutions occur when people do not have gardens of their own. Caste systems evolve when people allow or enforce others to tend their gardens. Industrial revolutions force people to abandon their gardens. If you own a garden it is because at some time your country, your family, or your position in society made it possible. Gratitude may seem an inappropriate response, but it has to be clear that owning a garden is not a right but a privilege. Maybe it should be a right. What is equally clear is that a garden is very precious. It is a badge of physical fitness, responsibility, civilized behavior, love of beauty, and love for the Earth.

⚓ ⚓

Rocks in a Rock Garden

⚓ ⚓ WHEN WE LOOK at a rock garden, especially our own, we can ask a lot of needling questions. We could question the aesthetic aspect of the rocks—their size, shape, color, and texture. We could question their horticultural value: Are they placed correctly for the health of the plants? Are they deep enough? Do they have the right slope? Are we using limestone for the lime lovers and granite for the acid lovers? Are the crevices well designed for the crevice plants? We could question their value in the miniature landscape we are attempting to create: Are they placed convincingly to represent an outcrop, a boulder field, a moraine, or whichever aspect of a mountain we are trying to imitate? We can also question the positioning of the rock garden relative to the rest of the garden. We would like part shade without rain drip from nearby trees, we want a mulch of course but not a blanket of leaves every fall. We want the aspect to be well chosen with a north-facing slope for some plants and perhaps full sun on a south slope for others. We can't usually control this aspect of the garden but we can always blame the inadequacies of the site for our failures. We also want to feel we are obeying some immutable law of design (even a spurious one) so we place the rock garden away from the house (so it doesn't conflict with the perennial border); close to the house (so that the rockwork complements the masonry of the foundation); hidden by a hedge of shrubs (because the garden shouldn't be visible in its entirety); behind a wall (so that it comes as a surprise to a visitor), in a separate "room" (because that's the way they do it at Sissinghurst).

We are in a quandary if there aren't any slopes and we have to build a mound in the middle of the lawn. It becomes a matter of *trompe l'oeil* to make the mound look natural, and we sometimes end up defying common sense instead of fooling our eyes. We don't really care if our whole garden is a rock garden and the "room" concept is inappropriate. We easily shrug off rules that don't apply.

But what about questioning the rocks themselves? Could there be a rock garden without any rocks? This seems like heresy. Yet my experience with rocks has made me question this basic premise of rock gardening. Well, we know about sand beds and container gardens and all the other alternative garden styles practiced by people in penthouses and people with an axe to grind, but if you could have rocks, isn't it mandatory to want them?

Everybody knows that New England soil is full of rocks of all sizes. This is not the rocky soil you get on a typical mountaintop in the American West or the European Alps. There is little real, deep loamy soil on a mountaintop above the tree line. In the bad old days when gardeners thought it proper to dig for plants in the mountains, there were endless stories about roots impossible to extricate from the rocks and plants unable to survive the mutilation. Nobody does that nowadays, but just poking your finger into Mount Evans will convince you that the soil is mostly stone chips of various sizes. The soil in our garden on the other hand can be deep, sandy loam, mildly acid, and sometimes leafy. In most places this apparent perfection is deceptive, because as you dig you hit boulders of all sizes at all depths with your spade. At the first ring of steel on rock your heart sinks a little. Will it be a 10" by 6" by 3" stone that can be extracted with the next spadeful of earth or will it be an eighty pound monster that will take you the rest of the morning? If you suspect a monster you must decide whether it is really worth the trouble of getting it out, if indeed you can. Sometimes this takes two days and requires crowbars, planks, elementary knowledge of the laws of mechanics, and possibly a few buckets of sand to pour under the rock to aid its elevation. And what do you do with the rock when you have it exposed and sitting on the lawn challenging you with surly defiance: Do something with me. If you don't I shall sit on your lawn all summer and kill the grass. You could load it into a cart if you have one big enough and strong enough; you could load it into a wheelbarrow if you are skillful and strong enough; you could arrange a series of logs and planks and start an undignified rolling operation to the nearest stone wall. There you would add one more untidy lump to an already precarious structure. This is a last resort though and the easy way out. Your first duty is to use the rock as part of your rock garden.

Rocks come in an infinity of shapes and your first observation must be to count the number of flat surfaces. Place the rock on one of these planes. Is it stable? Is there a second flat surface that you can stand on? Even if the rock is roughly the shape of an asteroid, one of its sides may still be suitable for sinking into the soil leaving you with a stable object. If stability is unachievable and the rock is unsuitable for standing or sitting on under any circumstances, perhaps you had better consign it to the stone fence. Most rocks though have some potential.

My first attempt at using almost usable rocks was to create a *boulder field.* Each rock would be sunk into the ground and meet only the one strict criterion of stability. I knew by experience the hazards of badly placed rocks that jiggled unexpectedly. The second criterion was desirable but not essential—rocks should function as stepping stones. There is no point in being too strict about this. The exposed side of these glacial boulders is sometimes round, sometimes glassy smooth, and often both. I had to learn which rocks were safe, which were safe even in wet weather, and which had surfaces so slippery that I could only balance on them for a split second as I leaped from one safe rock to another. The rocks were laid more or less in rows along the contour lines of a slope. Boulder fields are statistical and not in the least geometrical but my thinking was that the rocks should not be a hindrance in getting around the garden. They had to act as *paths* and the *boulder field* idea was to be my rationalization of the *natural* garden idea. In a vague way there was even some slight resemblance to a zigzag mountain track.

A second use for boulders was building the walls for raised beds. Here you need rocks that have much stricter requirements. You can use a very few large rocks with all convex surfaces, but most rocks have to have two flat surfaces. If the wall is to have substance they have to be thickish slabs and not flimsy inch-thick slivers only useful as stepping stones. Taking all this into account, a stone wall even only circling a small raised bed makes such heavy demands on available resources that I felt it should only be two or three courses high. There just are not enough rocks the right shape and size at one time to be more generous. You might tell me to store rocks on a rock pile until there are enough for the job. But that requires storage space, an additional transportation job, and years of patience. You might advise me where to buy a load of rocks, even beautifully dressed, ready to build walls. But the common sense words of a local artisan ring in my mental ears: You would be an idiot to bring in *more* rocks to this place. You could advise searching the many abandoned foundations and stone fences for good rocks. We have done that already as many others have before us who needed hearthstones and doorsteps. There are a few treasures left in the woods but getting them home requires an effort out of proportion to their value.

I have also used our rocks in a desultory way to imitate rocky outcrops. I have never liked the results. An outcrop made of relatively small (but even one-hundred-pound) boulders bears the same relation to massive cliffs exposed on a mountain that a dish garden of cactus bears to a desert or an aquarium to an ocean. I don't think I have ever seen a rock garden of this type I really liked without reservation, except in so far as it provided a home for alpine plants. The reservation always has something to do with the artificiality of the rocky structure.

Well, I don't want to criticize rocks from that standpoint. I can easily live with the prevailing conventions of rock gardens and that includes all types and styles. There are some fine examples whose beauty is an internal beauty more to do with a recondite artform than a reproduction of nature, where the rules of the convention have overrun the rules of its source. But I have no hesitation about criticizing the rocks themselves in my own garden. When they are finally in place you forget their obstinate character, their refusal to be moved, their resistance to revealing the secret of which is their best position. In their own way they are as hostile as rose bushes. You visit a garden with its own enormous natural rocky outcrop, and come home dismayed by your own glacial boulders. They suddenly look insignificant and paltry in spite of their ponderous weight. The grandeur of a real outcrop has nothing to do with weight and the effort of moving and lifting. Even a two-man rock beside a half grown *Pinus strobus* is a speck of glacial dust. This discontent after such a disturbing visit vanishes within twenty-four hours but a lingering dissatisfaction remains that takes the form: Why am I moving this rock? What does this rock really represent?

Let us suppose now that divine discontent has been assuaged and that we have adjusted to our limited materials and flawed designs. Suppose we have grown to love our rocks and they have responded by growing mellow with mosses and lichens and are wreathed in alyssums or are nestled next to saxifrages and gentians. Suppose we have found niches for soldanellas and pockets for miniature bulbs. Dwarf conifers try to reassure us that the scale is right and therefore we dare to introduce a few flowering shrubs: a *Daphne cneorum* and a dwarf chaenomeles. Why then isn't the world perfect and the garden a giver of eternal joy?

Well, to begin with, your last introduction doomed it. That dwarf chaenomeles, though, is a real beauty. The early spring orange-red flowers glow in the background behind the blues of the gentians and the yellows of the alyssums. The rough textured fruit in late summer give a second welcome display of subtle color and gnarled fascinating shapes. Even the thorns make it look "authentic" as a mountain plant defending itself against marauding animals. It loves the rocks too. So much so, it sends out roots under the rocks and soon a new shrub is growing on the other side. After four or five years you realize you have made a mistake in putting this happy creature in your rock garden. At first a little subtle pruning seems to hold it in check, but soon a pair of loppers has to be brought to bear on the problem. Finally you decide it has to be tackled from below ground and a spade is needed. But of course the underground stem is already over an inch thick in diameter, the spade bounces back painfully and you mentally sign the death warrant of the whole shrub. The thorns are by this time showing their true value and your destructive work has to take them into account. But the main problem is the enormous rock you so carefully placed deep in the soil. By now it is engulfed in tough roots and thorny branches, and it is just as difficult to raise as it was the first time you moved it from deep below the surface of the earth.

And that is the crux of the problem with rocks. If you provide a home for rock plants by giving them large rocks to get their roots around and give them protection from winter cold and fluctuating temperatures, they love it. But *every* plant is a "rock" plant. Every weed in the garden loves the same conditions. Every horticultural monster you ever inadvertently introduced likes rocks. Every shrub, every dwarf conifer, every hundred-foot tree likes to twine its roots around a rock. And if they take over you eventually have to move the rock. I have now reached the conclusion that they always take over. I don't mean just dandelions, chickweed, sorrel, and oxalis. I mean inulas, ligularias, onopordons, verbascums, aquilegias, violas, asarums, lupins, arnicas, *Campanula punctata, Campanula latifolia, Campanula persicifolia, Phlox subulata, Rosa spinossisima, Kerria japonica, Echinops,* poppies of all descriptions, ferns in variety, cotoneasters, junipers, brooms of every kind, *Daphne mezereum,* and on and on.

So over a period of twenty years I have had to move and/or remove virtually every rock I have ever placed. This could be in the hundreds. A few monsters survive including half a dozen placed by bulldozer during a building spree when I had to find an instant home for some gigantic rocks extracted in digging foundations. There seems to be a critical size for a rock beyond which no root will attempt the underground passage to the other side. The conclusion that every rock placed must eventually be displaced is not so devastating and discouraging as would appear at first admission. I believe each bed of a garden must be destroyed and remade every seven, eight, or nine years. This follows not only because of soil exhaustion or the exhaustion of crucial elements in the soil, but because by the end of this period the multitude of plants you first crowded into the newly made bed have been reduced by elimination and death—even allowing for the necessary replacements—to a few happy species that take over large amounts of space either by self-sowing or by expansion. If you are satisfied with the result you tend to leave the bed in this climax state for as long as possible. But one day you eye it with some distaste and pronounce the successful plants weeds. Or the best loved plant succumbs to old age and leaves only the good old reliables. Whatever the reason you decide it is time to start again. When this happens pieces of each precious plant have to be potted up ready to be replanted or given away. Taprooted plants and plants too old or woody to be divided will yield cuttings, some of them with roots. Invariably you find little bits of unexpected treasure—plants you thought you had lost that are simply buried by the jungle of rampageous alyssums, geraniums, and campanulas. Pulling a bed apart is an adventure exciting in itself. The saddest part is finding buried in the mess labels of plants you forgot about that only lasted one or two seasons. Not quite so bad is rescuing a live piece of an obviously good plant without a label.

As I replenish the soil and remake the bed I sometimes use the rocks again, either because they are still handy as stepping stones or because the effort of transporting them to the nearest stone wall isn't worth it. Or could it be that having spent all that youthful energy twenty years ago in digging it up I want to get some more use out of it? There are several rocks I know intimately, not only because I dug them from two feet underground but because I have rolled them around and used them in three or four different positions. Many times in the last few years I have sworn not to dig up one more boulder, but "New England soil grows rocks" and the ring of steel against stone brings conflicting emotions—along with the sinking feeling is a challenge that stirs the blood. If you don't get that rock to the surface, it will thwart your plans some time in the next seven years. Should there be rocks in the rock garden? They may not be needed but I think if I didn't have any I would import a few.

∾ ∾

Plant Goals

⚘ ⚘ THIS MUST BE recorded before it all becomes a memory, growing in spurious importance like history or diminishing to ignominious irrelevance like stale News. Some people don't make growing specific plants an important aim in their gardening life and are willing to collect plants and plant experiences like tourists casually collecting countries because the exchange rate is good. But we all have vague desires of obtaining and growing some particular plant we have read about or seen a picture of. We may have invented our own mystique about a plant, allowing it to represent an ideal that seems in some way unattainable. What happens when these goals are actually reached? Before we can frame an answer to that question we have to ask what exactly constitutes reaching a goal?

Suppose we yearn to grow *Silene hookeri* and deliberately set out to do so. There are several routes that the odyssey could take and several stages in the journey.

We might get a plant from a nursery. This only needs the foresight to order it before it is sold out, getting it through the mail safely, and potting it up. Alternatively we could go to Oregon, find a plant with or without a local guide, take a cutting, get it safely home, root the cutting, and pot it up. Or we could visit a friend who grows it and by charm or guile proceed as before to the potting stage. Or we could order seed from a seedlist, sow it, grow it, and transplant it.

At this point we have a plant in a pot. Is our goal reached? I think not. Very few of us would be satisfied by merely owning a plant for a week or so. Most would agree on a minimum requirement—that it should *flower.* Some would have their eye on competition rules and want the flower only after the requisite three months have gone by making the plant eligible to be placed in a show. But most people would want to achieve more laudable results than merely to display a baby potted plant on a showbench.

Here are examples of alternative triumphs: The plant should live through a summer in the garden (and flower). It should overwinter in the garden. It should live a full year in the garden. It should live long enough to be propagated by cuttings or seed. It should live two or more years in the garden. It should selfsow in the garden. It should be a permanent denizen of the garden. Or it should live through several "pottings on" in the greenhouse, perhaps reaching the stage when it is too big to transplant. It should be the mother plant for a succession of alpine house and showbench offspring.

Alpine house aspirations are not on my agenda, but the pleasures of such goals are self-evident. As far as growing in the garden is concerned, for me *every* stage counts as a success. When Ulysses reached Circe's island he was nowhere near home, but it must have been a relief to stop rowing for a while and perhaps take time off to botanize the island. Later the urge to go on would reappear. Sublime gardening is also reached in stages; every stage yields contentment until a need to go further takes over.

Some goals are disposed of by going as far as you need to go in order to feel satisfied that you are doing the right thing by not going any further. You would want to halt asserting your mastery of *Dianthus deltoides* long before you filled your entire garden with its color forms. Perhaps not true of hemerocallis, but even there, there is probably a point where one says "Enough."

My goals have been in the same general direction for ten years or so, although they are constantly changing to accommodate the self-confidence of success and the wisdom born of failure. Let's state four early goals tentatively.

GOAL 1: To grow all the species and subspecies of androsace in the open garden.

GOAL 2: To find the right place for all species of primula.

GOAL 3: To recognize every species of penstemon (ditto delphinium, aconitum, paeonia).

GOAL 4: To grow the classic alpines *Eritrichium nanum, Physoplexis comosa, Draba mollissima, Jankaea heldreichii, Aquilegia jonesii.*

Well, these goals have been modified considerably as time passed. I no longer expect "the open garden" to be hospitable enough to please every plant and certainly not *all* the androsaces. Some plants will last a few years and that's okay; some will flourish in a container with winter protection, second best but still acceptable; some plants will have to wait until I have the facilities, time, and patience for year-round alpine house "treatment." This is not likely to happen.

GOAL 1 By now most of the androsaces fit into little mental boxes: open garden and raised bed (*sarmentosa, lanuginosa, chamaejasme, villosa, lactea, sempervivoides,* etc.); container (*mathildae, ciliata, carnea, hausmannii, taurica, barbulata, muscoidea,* etc.); container with alpine house or at least coldframe protection (*cylindrica, vandellii, pubescens, alpina, helvetica, hirtella,* etc.); easy with a little effort (I mean the biennial *A. albana,* which is very miserly with its seedlings and has to be sown afresh each year); easy with no trouble at all (annuals such as *lactiflora*); and not worth growing (the difference between this category and the previous depends on which form of *occidentalis, septentrionalis, elongata,* etc., you have sowing around). A few are unobtainable (e.g. *zambalensis*) or tantalizingly rare (*brevis, bulleyana,* etc.). There is one "kind" of androsace that is still not in any little box. My experience with large leaf kinds *(foliosa, strigillosa, rotundifolia, geraniifolia)* is inconclusive but I have decided not to care—they should probably be primulas anyway. Even if not, their effect on me is the same. The pleasure from growing androsaces has been maximal, and still is, making allowances for the fact that no repeat experience can compare with a first time success. Things may get better with repetition but there is no surprise after the first time. Repeating a success confirms our skill (feeding our self-satisfaction); failures are always temporary (we can always come up with an adequate explanation and a guarantee of success next time). I can now admire the 12" diameter mounds of *Androsace vandellii* on the show tables of England without envy, because on the whole Goal 1 has been eliminated, not by sailing downriver into port, but by finding the river opens out into a delta with some branches navigable, some boring, some forbidden.

GOAL 2 I have not been very successful at growing primulas. The vernales and the cortusoides sections are easy enough in the woodland. Farinosae (Aleuritica) and auricula (Auriculastrum) sections are still in an experimental stage (after twenty years of trying!), but I think I understand several species by now. Candelabras and nivales won't stay long without a stream or a well-made bog and that is still in an unlikely future, but *P. japonica* is easy enough in the woodland. I have grown many other species, always for brief periods of time, but long enough to see the varied profiles of this remarkable genus. The only fun has been the journey, the final destination is reserved for gardeners with the right growing conditions. I am reluctant to admit this but having seen primulas growing in splendor in gardens near running water, I realize that my attempts are objectively a sad failure. This is not a reason to regret the experience of trying to grow them. A poor plant in one's own garden can be a triumph—nobody else need see it. The optimistic conclusion is that the genus primula is big and varied enough for every gardener to grow a few of its members. For this be grateful. Many excellent gardeners are happy enough to succeed with vernales cultivars or forms of *P. sieboldii.* It seems pointless to be upset because one cannot grow *P. whitei.*

GOAL 3 At least penstemons are obtainable. The American Penstemon Society puts out a long list of available seeds every year; the North American Rock Garden Society always has thirty to fifty species in its seedlist, and the other clubs and societies a good number; every state in the West has penstemons growing in every kind of habitat. Also penstemons *are* growable. Nearly all of them will last through one New England winter and flower the following May, June, or July. Some of them need to make a summer rosette or a side shoot if they are going to last more than one year; in any case, if you know what to expect you won't be disappointed. Besides, you can collect seed and keep the ones you want going. Penstemons are fine as long-lived or short-lived perennials or even as biennials. They are beautiful, interesting, worthwhile plants. The problem is my goal. Shall I confess that I can't always see the difference between some of the scores of species? And even when I can see a difference I am unable to store and retrieve at will that much information when needed. Not enough for the *instant* identification needed when a visitor wants to know "which Penstemon is that?" So, while I have mastered several species, I no longer anguish over subtle and unmemorable differences. *Murrayanus, barbatus, alamosensis, kunthii, eatonii:* all scarlet, all beautiful—when I see you altogether I know you apart. Shall I know you next year? Would I know just one of you without the others to compare? Does it matter? Well, if it doesn't I have lost sight of my goal. If it does, I haven't arrived. Delphiniums and aconitums may be even harder than penstemons. My experience is still in the formative stage.

Perhaps the answer is to take species even more seriously and look at them botanically. Most of the time we look at a delphinium and see a plant for the border, piercing blue or subtle violet. Its leaves are all-purpose Ranunculaceae leaves that vary from species to species and not different in kind from anemones and trollius. We hope that by growing a dozen species of delphinium some magical picture will imprint itself on our memory with little arrows pointing out diagnostic differences between the species. Alas, magic is insufficient and we end up with homemade classifications: the red ones, the short ones, the annuals. I think it is impossible for ordinary gardeners to know all the penstemons and all the delphiniums, at least not all at the same time. Not for me. You could do it if you started at thirteen and made it your life's work. Or you could be satisfied with partial success, recognizing some of the species some of the time, never reaching the goal, forever learning and relearning, like some horticultural Sisyphus.

GOAL 4 The fourth goal is the excuse for this chapter. If and when it is printed my *Eritrichium nanum* may have perished; hence the urgency. Nobody really believes history. Even News taxes one's credulity. *Eritrichium nanum* has been the impossible dream, the ultimate criterion, the unfinished business of so many of us. With some trepidation I want to suggest that one of the reasons for the overall dismal failure to tame *E. nanum* is statistical. Not enough people have had enough seed to experiment on a broad enough scale. From the time we receive three seeds in an enormous envelope, or a pathetic seedling surreptitiously dug from the wild by a wicked friend, until the moment of truth when we are forced to admit "I lost it," we treat them as orphans and invalids. Our hands tremble as we sow the seed. We protect seedlings from dangers real and imagined. We fuss about whether to grow them indoors or out-doors, whether to fertilize, whether to water, whether to spray, whether to remove the soil before planting out, what the growing medium should be, etc. All legitimate fuss, but in this case there is no reliable guide to instruct us. One has heard of partial successes involving refrigeration and constant breeze across the plants, but these are two utilities most of us lack in the garden. So I shall out-line a little bit of history and throw in a little bit of method as back-ground for my own news and, as it turns out, photo opportunity.

Before 1981, I was too overawed by seedlists to think of order-ing anything really rare, believing that such seed should and would be reserved for Good Growers. But that year I threw scruples to the wind and ordered *E. nanum argenteum* from one of the exchanges. And got it. The names lumped under *Eritrichium nanum* are sub-species or varieties, I am not really sure which. They include *are-tioides, elongatum, jankae,* and *argenteum.* Sometimes seed is sent in simply as *E. nanum.* I got *argenteum* again in 1982 and in 1983 *are-tioides, argenteum,* and *jankae.* All these germinated but that is as far as I got. In 1984 I managed to get transplants of *elongatum* and *jankae* but these died in the open garden. All these seeds were sown in my usual mix of half-and-half coarse sand and commercial soil-less mix with a little slow-release fertilizer. They were left exposed to the weather from sowing time until germination and again left outside until ready to transplant. After transplanting they remained outside without any special attention (unless you count drooling). My aspirations almost petered out after raising plants yet I still be-lieved deep down that what everybody said was true—*E. nanum* cannot be tamed. But in 1985 I was again planting *argenteum* and *nanum,* this time in containers and the following year *jankae* in a raised bed. Many of these plants survived a winter but not the fol-lowing summer. In 1987 I raised plants of *E. nanum* from NARGS seed. One of these plants flowered and I collected seed. In 1988 I had two seedlings from my own plant grown in a raised bed. The mother plant died and so did the seedlings, but at least they had reached transplant size and died in their beds, not in the pots of infancy.

Meanwhile Vojtech Holubec had been to the Rockies in the summer of 1987 and collected seed of *E. aretioides* from Mount Evans (I believe). He shared his seed with me and I sowed it that fall. This germinated and one plant developed rapidly enough to plant out that summer. A black spot developed in the center late in the fall and I gave up hope for its survival. The summer had been hot and dry and I did two things I usually never do. I watered the crevice garden and I fertilized the eritrichium. This was before winter weather set in. The following spring the black spot was still there, but the plant was expanding and eventually the blemish was almost invisible and neither hurt the plant's well-being nor its looks. It flowered in May. The flowers were bright blue, on stalks that emerged horizontally from the base—unlike the plants of eritrichium I had seen on Independence Pass and elsewhere, where the flowers covered the top of the bun. Each stalk had several flowers and the flowering period was quite extended. There were plenty of opportunities for photographs and it turned out to be the most expensive plant I had ever grown. I was confident that I would be collecting seed and examined the spent bloom every day for weeks. I collected whatever the seed capsules contained. I didn't examine the chaff too carefully so as not to know if there was really no seed there. I shall sow it this winter with fearful hope. As for cultivation, the first plant to flower was on the summit of a small artificial hill with a good depth of sand over soilless sandy compost, over turfy compost. I'm pretty sure the roots never got below the sandy layer. The second plant to flower is still growing in the crevice garden made for me by Josef Halda. Originally the growing medium was pure, gritty sand, but before I planted the eritrichium I added some humus and slow-release fertilizer. By the end of the summer another dead patch had formed, this time covering half the plant. Unfortunately several good gardeners have been shown this plant and I fear that the gods that punish hubris will do a number on my er-itrichium. I don't want to single out any growing method—container, raised bed, or crevice garden—as the best way to do it. Everybody finds their own methods in their own garden.

As for *Aquilegia jonesii*, it is common knowledge that the problem is to make it flower. I had one flower once. It was encouragement enough to try it every year since. Jankaea is another story. I don't think I am entitled to try it until I have successfully grown ramondas and haberleas. That is also unfinished business. *Physoplexis comosa* needs another season or two and *Draba mollissima* has been written off as tender. There are many other "classic alpines" that are on my list but these are enough to illustrate my most pressing goals. Of course I have other goals than to grow individual plants, such as introducing running water into the garden with a waterfall and a Chinese bridge, making coldframes with lids that stay on in winter, building a pit house, a gazebo, and a fernery, but they seem secondary to my main goal. That is to grow every plant. Well, most of them.

∻ ∻

Why Did My Plant Die?

ᵔ ᵔ ONE SUMMER I planted five rather special pulsatillas all grown from the same packet of seed sent to me by a Czech plant friend. Next April all five flowered beautifully, but after flowering four of them died. Three of them were planted quite close to each other and one of these was the survivor. Why did the others die? I have to rule out possibilities such as annual, tender, bad location, wrong potting mix, and all the factors that all five shared. This kind of thing happens frequently enough to all of us. There ought to be somebody we could turn to who would perform an on-the-spot autopsy, and give us usable reasons for the losses.

Perhaps there really are three women sitting in the sky, spinning the life span of each plant and snipping the thread at the

moment of doom. Perhaps the plants were not satisfied with my attitude toward them when I planted them out. Maybe the plant that
survived is a Hero, defying pests and resisting disease. Possibly a
Mutant with strange new vigor. Or maybe a Saint that droughts,
cold blasts, and all things evil flee from. Or did the other four in-
herit genes for early death? Some species are so prodigal with seed
that in nature they cannot help but be distributed in a way that
makes competition with each other inevitable. Some of the seeds
are bound to be weaker than others. But when we pot up seedlings
we cannot always distinguish the weak from the strong. Is that true?
What mysteries we face. The real mystery of life may not be "Why
are we here?" but "How long have we got?"

When kings of ancient Greece had political or marital problems, they visited the Oracle at Delphi for advice and prophecy.
This was given in the form of bad enigmatic verse. Here is a snippy
oracular response to the eternal question: Why did my plant die?

> *You walked too close. You trod on it.*
> *You dropped a piece of sod on it.*
> *You hoed it down. You weeded it.*
> *You planted it the wrong way up.*
> *You grew it in a yoghurt cup*
> *But you forgot to make a hole;*
> *The soggy compost took its toll.*
> *September storm. November drought.*
> *It heaved in March, the roots popped out.*
> *You watered it with herbicide.*
> *You scattered bonemeal far and wide,*
> *Attracting local omnivores,*
> *Who ate your plant and stayed for more.*
> *You left it baking in the sun*
> *While you departed at a run*
> *To find a spade, perhaps a trowel,*
> *Meanwhile the plant threw in the towel.*

You planted it with crown too high;
The soil washed off, that explains why.
Too high pH. It hated lime.
Alas it needs a gentler clime.
You left the root ball wrapped in plastic.
You broke the roots. They're not elastic.
You walked too close. You trod on it.
You dropped a piece of sod on it.
You splashed the plant with mower oil.
You should do something to your soil.
Too rich. Too poor. Such wretched tilth.
Your soil is clay. Your soil is filth.
Your plant was eaten by a slug.
The growing point contained a bug.
These aphids are controlled by ants,
Who milk the juice, it kills the plants.
In early spring your garden's mud.
You walked around! That's not much good.
With heat and light you hurried it.
You worried it. You buried it.
The poor plant missed the mountain air:
No heat, no summer muggs up there.
You overfed it ten-ten-ten.
Forgot to water it again.
You hit it sharply with the hose.
You used a can without a rose.
Perhaps you sprinkled from above.
You should have talked to it with love.
The nursery mailed it without roots.
You killed it with those gardening boots.
You walked too close. You trod on it.
You dropped a piece of sod on it.

~ ~

Paths

⚜ ⚜ YOU START TO make a garden. The plot is roughly a rectangle. You are impatient to start planting and want immediate results even if only a few annuals or a dozen bulbs. You decide your garden will be made in sections, a little at a time. So you prepare a strip on the long side of the rectangle. It could be a rock garden, a scree, a perennial border, or just a "bed." Of course you love this bare patch of receptive ground and your imagination boils with the possibilities of the planting: What you will put in? What will it look like? (All the anticipatory joys that gardening is noted for.) As the plants start to grow and even before you have any notion that you are doing the right thing or that the picture you have in your mind will materialize, you want to enlarge the garden ready for the next phase.

Your strip is generously wide and you have a substantial garden going; as you walk around the strip you can just reach the center of it by raising your heels or by kneeling and stretching, or by standing on a rock placed in the middle. You can't make the bed any longer and don't want the bed to be any wider because of a phobia about treading on soil in sneakers or using funny muscles kneeling and stretching. So to get more garden the time has come to start a fresh piece. That is a separate strip or even a new shape. By doing this you have created a path—if we define a path as non-garden. Suppose your next effort is to be a strip parallel to the first one and the same width. Automatically there will be a path dividing the enlarged garden in two. You have only to make two decisions: How wide is the path to be? What is the path to be made of? The moment the second strip is started the first question is already answered.

Happy to be digging, you postpone decisions or rather refuse to worry about them and put your energies into making a third strip parallel to the other two. As you do this you are encouraged to see the plants in the first strip growing away and the second strip also doing well with its smaller plants settling in. As you get to the middle of the third strip you notice a dandelion insolently flowering in the middle of the first strip. What do you do? You could walk along the paths or you could cross the garden. It's your garden so you can tread on the soil—even on the plants if you slip. But do you want to and would you want your spouse/best friend/visitor to do the same? Absolutely not. You take the path and pull the dandelion and walk back.

It doesn't take long to realize that working in a garden in which paths frustrate your efforts to reach nearby points by compelling you to walk long distances is not fun. It is labor intensive and, though good for your health, not very good for your spirits, by the time your knees and thighs reach their extremes of endurance. There are many reasons for wanting to get to point A from point B besides the compulsion to pull a dandelion, which after all could wait an hour or so. You could have left your favorite claw or trowel there; you might need to carry a heavy bucket or a large shrub along this tiresome route. You can suffer an inconvenient design for months without complaining because: 1. You think you need the exercise; 2.You consider the design artistic, this makes it inviolate; 3. You can't admit making an error; 4. Someone you love or someone you paid designed it, and complaints spell trouble in either case; 5. Besides health, art, pride, and respect we have other absurd reasons for not changing the way we live. This obstinacy ensures that we shall put up with endless inconvenience to save face or whatever you call it when only one person is involved.

Rich people and patient people design their gardens before making them. They make little drawings on paper showing where the beds and the paths are going to be. This always seems to me to have an air of finality about it which is contrary to the spirit of a *developing* garden. It may work well if you garden on a grand scale and need cinder tracks for the horses, a generous driveway and parking lot for visiting dignitaries, and enough room in the garden for a horticultural seminar. It is also reasonable to see a design on paper from someone you pay and to expect it to materialize in due course. But if you do it yourself there needs to be latitude for a certain amount of whimsy with freedom to dream in winter knowing full well you will rethink the following spring. If you make a mistake and find yourself jumping over four feet of bed because you can't face going the whole way round one more time, then correct it. Make a short-cut path even if it means moving a few plants.

MATERIALS Every kind of path has good points and bad points and you have to decide what you can live with. Consider some of the choices.

    1. Grass. If you start a garden in a field or carve it out of a lawn the grass is already there. Grass is pretty. The color goes well with plants. Grass is living, organic, and you can shape it to any outline you like. Unless you live in desert country, grass is natural and the gardening tradition we belong to claims it looks right. But there are disadvantages: Grass grows vertically so you have to cut it. This takes time but also implies tools—scissors, shears, edgers, lawn-mowers. All of these bring problems of fatigue, noise, smell, and ecological guilt. Grass also grows horizontally and will invade the garden. You have to weed it out of the beds and at least once a year make the edges neat. Grass stays wet after rain, after evening dew has fallen, and before the dew has dried in the morning. I often wonder if Tennyson's Maud coming into the garden after the "black bat night had flown" got her feet wet on grass paths. Grass dies in drought and has to be watered unless you don't mind brown. Grass wears out with constant use like installed carpeting that cannot be moved around to hide the blemishes near the entrances. Grass harbors weeds so you will have to live with dandelions, sorrel, and chickweed unless you waste endless hours weeding or remember to apply the right poisons at the right time. Poorly drained grass can mean mud. Grass is a tyrant; if you leave the garden even for a week in summer the first thing you have to do when you return is get the grass paths looking tidy, otherwise nothing looks

right. Grass paths look marvelous at their best, tacky otherwise.

2. You could try organic paths. Woodchips, shredded bark, hay bales, shredded leaves, sawdust. Something of the sort is needed in the woodland garden since grass grows poorly and artificial materials look wrong. All of these cost money. All of them are subject to animal interference. It takes about two weeks for the worms to occupy a new path and a few more days before the surface is disturbed by a skunk or a raccoon looking for a meal. If you have laid newspaper or mathematics journals under the woodchips hoping to suppress the weeds you will be horrified to see discolored strips and sheets of paper all over your woodland one morning. If you used plastic sheets or bags the results are even more revolting as there is no way that the plastic can be coaxed back under the woodchips and you either have to wrench it out completely and discard it or live with black or white plastic triangles sticking out of the brown mulch. Because of its smooth almost oily texture, plastic has also the disadvantage of making a woodland stroll hazardous. Whatever you use it is fatal to be stingy with the material. Weeds will grow through eventually, but a skimpy layer to begin with encourages them to grow with gusto since the woodchips or whatever you use improves the soil for the weeds themselves. Be wary of hay, too. This may seem like a good beginning for a woodland path but it is only a temporary weed suppressant. Within a few weeks the seeds in the hay will sprout to give you a selection of meadow weeds quite alien to your woodland and just as pernicious as the weeds that belong there.

These organic paths can be used in the garden too. They need weeding or spraying to keep them clean. I prefer to weed because I like to leave violets, dianthus, helleborus, primulas, crocus, nigella, aquilegias, and so on in the paths. You can still walk but it sometimes needs a little care to pick your way along a crowded path without stepping on something nice even if it *is* expendable.

Individual surfaces have individual faults. Hay is especially bad because of the weed seeds and should only be thought of as temporary. Woodchips are coarse and need time to settle down to a walkable surface, they also can leave splinters in careless hands. Sawdust has a raw objectionable color for the first couple of months and packs into solid mat. This is good until a weed comes through as it will, but when you pull it large chunks of sawdust are disturbed. But these are all trivial criticisms, for once a path of organic material is established it looks great.

3. Then there are the earthlike materials—sand, gravel, cinders. These are hard to walk along until they are well used or perhaps rolled. Your feet slip and sink and knees feel as though you are climbing a mountain, especially when carrying a can of water. If you wheel a cart through sand or invite sixty people for a picnic, the disturbed surface looks untidy and you may have to rake. Pity the poor monks in Japan constantly raking the Universe back into the fragile sandscape. You have to do a little of that if you use sand. Also the color nearly always clashes with your own soil. Very few people live in a gravel pit so whatever you use that is introduced comes from a different geological environment and looks foreign. The weed situation is easier to manage though and since seeds germinate so readily in sand you will certainly get dianthus and viola selfsowing and you might get precious seedlings from androsaces, drabas, and so on. The coarser the stone the harder it is to retrieve these blessings.

4. Taking artificiality one step further you could make a path with pavement blocks of bluestone, slate, sandstone, bricks, cobblestones, ceramic. Sinking these in sand can be a fascinating game. If they are laid without much care they look untidy rather than informal and are a constant irritant to the mind's aesthetic eye. Crazy paving is meant to be informal but it has to be done with care to avoid looking badly made. Everything unnatural you introduce into a garden must be tidy as well as tasteful. You would think an urn lying casually around or a plaque hung on a wall or a stone fish sitting on a sawn-off tree would look romantic and picturesque but the eye stubbornly sees an object out of place, a piece of rubbish rather than a beautiful focal point as intended *unless* the site is cho-

sen well, the positioning is done with care, and the object is worth looking at. All these are difficult to achieve. So it is with paths that have the permanence of pavement especially if the arrangement is made final by the use of cement. The advantage of these materials is the comfort of walking on a smooth surface. Also artificiality implies formality and this may be exactly what you want to achieve.

5. Somewhere between these path types is the hybrid stepping stone kind of path that uses rocks or the equivalent to either economize on materials, provide an interesting pattern, or deliberately leave planting space between the blocks. One step beyond would be a rough, "natural" path where the rocks make no pretence at being flat and the idea is to imitate a mountain walk or a moraine. These routes through a garden are for the young and agile or for the gardener who knows all the bumps and hollows so well that walking without stumbling is second nature. But however beautiful your concept of nature is and however skillful your reconstruction, you should warn guests of the hazards and give them time to pick their way gracefully through what is essentially an obstacle race. Once large rocks are part of path-making, weeding also becomes an important chore. You may have to resort to weedkiller. Cobblestones have all the disadvantages of all paths. At university in England I had to cross a courtyard of cobbles to get to the nearest toilet and I have no love of this hazardous groundcovering.

6. Cobbles are also close to the ultimate in artificiality—concrete and asphalt. These are essential for public gardens and you may wish you had them in your own garden by the time you are old or infirm. But then we are talking about other gardens in other places at other times. Dirt too can make an excellent path for public gardens as well as private and intimate gardens. Whether it works for you is a function of your soil and drainage and how you manage weeds. But it is probably the most "natural" material for a path and should be your first thought. Every path requires use. It is pointless to bulldoze a path out of rough woodland if you are never going to use it. In two years you won't be able to find it. This also

applies to little used paths in a garden. Make them where you want
to go. Not where you think other people ought to go.

7. Finally there is the non-path. A route across a boulder-
strewn rock garden, through a water feature, or even through rough
woodland. It could include steep steps with precarious footing.
Such passageways are very uncomfortable places to walk. They are
made to please the gardener who worships Nature above Art and
Art above Comfort; they are not designed for the timid or aged. Visitors scarcely know where they are supposed to be, whether they are
walking on precious plants or spoiling lichened rocks. It isn't always
clear whether the next rock is safe or whether the next step will land
you in a bog up to your ankles. It goes without saying that every
rock used as a stepping stone must be firm and stable. But there are
also worries about slippery surfaces in wet weather, smooth,
rounded shapes that give no purchase, rocks too high to negotiate
as steps. Gardens for scrambling should have warnings preferably
on bronze signs and the owner should carry a lot of insurance.

In every garden there are paths that are meant only for the gardener. Paths at the back of a wide border, stepping stones that go
nowhere, deertracks, those slightly secret routes that reach otherwise inaccessible places. These should be recognized by visitors.
Never tread where your host wouldn't, but also be sensitive to those
places where your host would walk but where you may not. These
secondary paths, along with the main paths, divide the garden into
small planted areas—beds or sections of beds. This subdivision is
an excellent psychological aid to organizing work in the middle of
summer when weeds proliferate and the garden looks as though it
will never be tidy again. The paths themselves will have to be
weeded and as you crawl around a bed on your hands and knees removing unwanted aquilegias along with the sow thistle and jewel
weed, you can attend to the weeding, mulching, seed collecting,
cutting back, and rearranging of plants in the beds that is the
essence of dirt gardening. By the end of two or three hours you have
completed a whole section of the garden that won't need more than

a flick of the wrist for the rest of the season. Your fun will be spoiled though if you can't reach every inch of each subsection of your garden from the hands and knees position on the paths. Maybe you are a sitter or a croucher, or perhaps you only bend at the hips. The mechanics may vary but the principle remains the same—all parts of the garden must be reachable. If you have to stand on the garden to do a particularly difficult maneuver such as staking or digging up a large plant, then you will probably have to scratch the soil you trod on and neaten up the mess you made. But for ordinary weeding you don't really want to tread the soil too often and reachability is desirable. Every gardener has different techniques though and I have seen a large perennial border without mulch and with no access to plants by paths secret or otherwise walked on nonchalantly by the owner. There was a hard crust on the soil with weeds struggling through and the same patch needed almost weekly attention. But the border itself was magnificent so who is to judge our idiosyncracies?

~ ~

Keeping Records...

ॐ ॐ IT IS ONLY when you start to garden—probably after fifty—that you gradually realize that something important happens every day. Something you want to remember and think worth recording. Poetry is not the right medium for recording events and some kind of journal is indicated. At the very least you feel you need to know what the weather is usually like in April. How else can you plan your life? Even if you grow annuals or vegetables you have to work back from planting out time to determine seed sowing time. If you don't know the date at which it is safe to plant out cabbage, onions, and tomatoes, you could waste an entire season doing the wrong thing. It is useless listening to weather forecasts or reading other people's records. You need your own. New England is a jigsaw of microclimates and you are the only data collector for yours.

More than a single year is needed to give you enough information; even ten years is not enough. Ultimately to do it right you have to be a local weather expert. With numbers to back you up you are always right (in theory) and when you sow your peas you can overrule advice from the neighbor who lives in a frost pocket down the road or the one a hundred feet higher than you. There are side benefits too from keeping records: you can start a conversation with "this is the wettest March in three years"; you can start your own Book of Records; you can be legitimately surprised (or complacent or dismayed) by the weather and justify your emotion with solid statistics.

Next in importance to weather and related to it is the work you do in the garden each day. Work records are especially useful for vegetable growers. Thomas Jefferson's garden book is full of work and planting records and his triumphant "first dish of pease from earliest patch" sounds a refrain of justifiable pride among the lists of chores planned and completed. So here we have a second reason to keep records. It will not be every year that you succeed with *Gentiana verna,* and you want it on paper to remind you that you did it and even better how you did it. If your *Cypripedium pubescens* is growing happily, record the number of stalks each year. Record the diameter of your *Draba rigida,* the date of your first crocus, the number of *Kabschia saxifrages* in bloom at one time, the number of blossoms on the *Gentiana sino-ornata.* Next year these plants may be even bigger and better but on the other hand they may be dead. Record whether or not you fertilized. Did it do any good? Record the soil mixture used in different parts of the garden. This would mean constructing a plan of the garden and naming each section so that you can refer to it. Many gardeners, especially in what used to be Czechoslovakia, divide their garden into geographic regions (Alps, Pirin, North America, Japan, etc.). I wonder if they have limestone regions in each zone. Too much subdivision would be tiresome in a small garden.

In order to keep track of plants adequately you need to have acquisition lists. Suppose you grow plants from seeds: you need a list of seeds (in alphabetical order as well as order of arrival, so you may need a computer), and their origin (you need to build up a reliability index for people and societies who send seed whose names you can trust); when you received them (fresh seed obtained in September can then be compared with seed obtained from the exchanges in February); when you sowed the seed (does it matter whether you sow in December or in March? is April really too late?); how you sowed the seed (was it under lights indoors? in a greenhouse? in pots outside? in the open garden? did you use a special mix? did you try different watering methods?); when the seed germinated (and *if!*). You can also decide for yourself whether it pays to sow early, late, or just when convenient. You can test theories about the need for storage times and storage temperatures; when you transplanted (are you transplanting too soon? do all your campanulas and primulas die a month after you transplant? do you delay transplanting too long? are the roots of the lupins circling the pot and are all the draba roots too mixed up to handle?); how many transplants did you obtain (can you spare any to give away?); how many survived (can you still spare them?); what you did with them (did you actually give any away? who now owes you?); in which part of the garden did you plant out your seedlings (this will tell you where you can find the label next spring).

And now we are on treacherous ground. Record keeping has become top-heavy but some of the most important questions seem to be unanswerable. You are at a meeting talking to a pundit. Pundit: "Do you grow *Silene acaulis?*" You: "Excuse me. I left my records at home." That's pretty pathetic. You could say: "I think so" (very weak); or: "Yes" (an outright lie but you have your fingers crossed). If the pundit has arrived to see your garden you might want to say, "Please excuse me for half an hour while I check my records," but you know that a pundit should never be kept waiting. Even if your horticultural reputation is not at stake and you simply want to know the answer for your own information, you are in trouble. All your records tell you is when, how, and where you planted it. What you do not know for sure is whether you really have the plant. Plants die very readily. The test of a great record keeper is whether they record when their plants die.

Another quicksand. You plant one plant of *Dianthus subacaulis* in 1985, say. It dies. You know this is true because you find the label and no plant. You go back indoors and write in your book (or enter it in the computer) that *D. subacaulis* died in 1987. If it is March you could add "winterkill," if it is July you could write "drought." But suppose it does not die! Suppose instead it selfsows!! Are you going to record the number of seedlings? Can you actually count them? (some of them are snuggled next to mother). If you get six new self-sown plants you are perfectly happy, but are they the genuine species? Could they be hybrids with nearby *Dianthus gelidus?* Shall you give each one a label? (If you don't you will certainly forget what they are). Shall you collect seed for the next seed exchange from the offspring? Shall you label the envelope *Dianthus subacaulis?* If you think about aquilegias, which cross very readily with other aquilegias, the record keeping problem becomes a nightmare. So here is the crux of the problem: You *never* know how many plants you have or *exactly* what they are.

Keeping records of plants bought by mail or at a plant sale seems to be a little simpler. There is usually only one plant, one label, one entry in the record (where it came from, when, and where you planted it). But the problem of plant loss remains—do you go indoors to your records each time you find a label next to the blackened remnants of a plant that failed to establish? Or do you pocket the label and resolve to bring your records up-to-date that evening or the next rainy weekend? In spring after a hard winter this could be a serious problem as you tearfully tour the garden counting your losses. Labels themselves are a record and subject to error in reading them: What does it say? Is that denticulata or paniculata? What genus is .E..ANA ? And errors in location: Which plant is it next to? And how about labels scattered and shattered by frost or stepped on by animals? You collect the remnants, match up the broken pieces, find a nearby plant that *could* be the one on the label, and insert the bits. If you are clever you have in your pocket replacement labels and a pencil. You kneel on the wet soil to form a human writing desk on the other thigh, and do your best to write legibly on your quivering leg. Normally though you will not have a new label or your pencil's point is broken and the three bits of broken plastic will be left to mark the plant for the rest of the season.

The ultimate record keeper would seem to be the photographer. In theory a photographic record gives you all the information you ever need about a plant: first and foremost that you *have* it, its height, color, foliage, habit, time of flowering, location in the garden, its artistic effect next to its immediate neighbors, and how this particular species differs from all the others in the genus. But in practice the record is far from perfect. Usually the photo itself is taken just before the flower opened fully (at the time you took it you wanted to be sure of at least one picture, and you never got back to take the really good shot). So this feeble leafy picture has to stand in for a proper record. Even if the picture is good none of its elements are really satisfactory; the color is slightly off, the height is indeterminate, the foliage is either hidden by flowers or mixed up with a nearby plant. You can't have a fully descriptive close-up and a plant association in the same shot. You can't have a picture of a plant flowering that also describes the foliage. The species is never unequivocally distinguished by a photograph. Of course you could probably distinguish *Lewisia cotyledon* from *L. tweedyi* even if the pictures are indifferent. But think about trying to tell the cushion dianthus apart if they are in full bloom, or medium-sized penstemons or any of the drabas. If you had to choose which one of only two possibilities you are looking at, the problem is relatively easy, but to get the species right from one picture with a multitude of possibilities is a gamble. Even in books a photograph never substitutes for a good botanical drawing or a key. In the end foolproof records have to include both words and pictures.

So why keep records that are less than perfect? Because even a little information is useful and whenever you refer to your records you wish you had written down a bit more and taken a few more photographs. This cumulative information, however imperfect, adds up to more than a series of individual items. It becomes part of one's own past because it is part of the garden's past. As you reread the soil-stained pages, the garden as it used to be springs to life again. You relive the phases that led to its present shape and design, the plants you used to grow and the ones that failed; those that were your pride and joy if only for a couple of years and the ones you only dreamed about. And while a journal never adds up to anything approaching scientific truth, the generalizations and the knowledge you can deduce from your own experience become a reality to share with other gardeners. Many gardeners are happy enough to use their brain as their only information file and processor but those of us who have tried, however casually, to keep a garden journal know that record keeping doubles one's pleasure.

❧ ❧

...and in Particular, Keeping Lists

❧ ❧ A FRIEND ONCE said rather petulantly, "I never keep lists." At the time I had no particular feeling about list keeping in general and was at a loss to understand how keeping lists could generate such passion. After twenty years of gardening I know that lists, however tiresome, are an indispensable part of gardening. Even the lists you don't keep are an expression of a point of view. If we go defiantly to the supermarket without a list we return overloaded with impulse buys plus the vexation of forgetting several vital items. Inventiveness and large cupboards will enable the true list-hater to manage without forgotten items and make room for things that wouldn't have been on the list if there had been one. Very laid back. If you carry this attitude over into gardening you would be ordering plants by mail in January without reference to what you already have in the garden, unconcerned with duplicates and happy to buy compulsively from the catalogs. Obviously you have to be rich or spendthrift, or you don't order enough of anything for it to matter. An ideal session ordering plants requires a long list of lists.

You first look through the catalog and list all the plants that attract you by reading their glowing descriptions. Then you look at last year's list of plants ordered from this nursery and eliminate any plants that arrived and survived. This last criterion has you searching for the list of plants you planted out last year according to location in the garden. You look sadly at this list and try to visualize exactly which plants really and truly died and which just might have gone dormant early. Was the label pulled? Did you keep it? Did you make a list of all the dead labels? After this gloomy requiem you brighten up by noting that a dead plant means a free space. This encourages you to indulge yourself with this year's order.

Next you compare this possible order with your want list. This is usually a vain activity. There are so many plants in existence, so few in this catalog, and your want list seems so short and arbitrary that there is no reason to expect any wanted plants to appear in any catalog. Still the exercise of finding the want list and reading through its entries brings back memories of garden visits, descriptions, and illustrations from books and journals, conversations at meetings, and all those other sources of inspiration and yearning that generated the want list in the first place. You end up ordering the closest thing in the catalog to whatever it was you really wanted. Perhaps it was a color, a leaf form, a degree of difficulty, or an unusual habitat. Anything can trigger a burning desire and catalogs brazenly fan the flames. The final step in making your order list is to eliminate on the basis of cost. This is plant triage, a gloomy necessity, but it sharpens one's desires from a vague "I would like that" to a more intense "I must have that" and sometimes to an uncontrollable "I shall order three of that. Surely at least one will survive!" Then you make the list that even non-listmakers must make and send it to the nursery with your check. The list of plants you just ordered now joins another list already started on the computer of all the plants so far ordered. A computer of course is just a typewriter that makes lists.

When the plants start arriving in April and May, this list has to be revised or a new one started that shows the plants that actually arrived. These will include substitutes and bonus plants and will also include plants that dribble in in ones and twos from friends and plant sales.

The same procedure has to be used for seeds but this needs completely separate lists. Old lists must be referred to constantly to check whether you have tried the seed before, whether it germinated, if you transplanted it, and how many transplants you got. If these plants ever achieved adulthood you want to know where they went in the garden. This means a separate list for each bed in the garden. The plants from your plants-by-mail list are also transferred to these lists after the mandatory recuperation time in cold frames.

As the garden blooms and burgeons through the spring, two things happen that are not actually gardening. Friends arrive to give you plants, which then go on one list, and request, subtly or otherwise, pieces of plants they would like themselves. If you can dig up a piece without spoiling the plant or ruining the garden you are glad to comply. If the plant is only a small one or something very precious you promise to give them a piece or collect seed at a later time. So you start a list of people and their plant needs. This is a list with a shelf life of about two years. After that time one or both of you will forget and the promise will reduce to a slight grudge on one side or a minor guilt feeling on the other. The other non-gardening activity is photography. You would expect this occupation to be pleasurably carefree in contrast to the anxieties of gardening, and so it is if you only take pictures of people in the garden or whole beds ablaze with color, or poetic shots of mist after the rain and icicles on eavestroughs or instructive steps in the making of a new bed. But as soon as you start taking pictures of plants you must record the names of each plant. Otherwise you cannot remember and if you cannot remember you will forfeit any pleasure you might have felt when the slides come back. Even familiar plants such as *Alyssum saxatile* or *Silene acaulis* lose something of their personality when reduced to two dimensions and are not impossible to misidentify. White plants become virtually interchangeable. The sad truth is that the more floriferous the plant the harder it is to be sure of its identity. Plants out of flower are just as troublesome. But if you know what the plant is, a photograph has real meaning and your mind assents to the name in a straightforward way. Of course this means making a list. Every picture of a plant or group of plants must have names recorded. Once the names are on the slide mounts you can discard the dirty scraps of paper covered with illegible scrawl that has such tremendous significance.

Other temporary lists crop up as you tour the garden photographing or showing a friend around or just walking around for pleasure (if that is ever an option). These lists are directives that may or may not be implemented but seem vital to commit to paper (Divide phlox in Bed 4! Move *Rhododendron carolinianum!* Mulch needed! Prune forsythia! Take cuttings of heathers!). This potpourri of orders can be distilled into another list: the list of things to do that day that you may want to write down before you step out into the garden. The act of writing down a necessary chore as part of a list burns it into my memory and I rarely have to refer to the list again to check it off. In fact making the list has a peculiar negative effect. As soon as I leave the house and step foot in the garden to do the first job on my list I instantly start doing something different. For instance, say my first job is to mulch a bed with buckwheat hulls; I get out the cart, load up the bag of hulls, a bucket, a pair of scissors to open the bag and head for the targeted bed. On my right I pass a large plant of *Ligularia hodgsonii* that has gone to seed. The day is breezy and if nothing is done at once there will be a thousand seedlings of *Ligularia* to pull up next spring. No list will stop me cutting down the threatening monster. So back to the greenhouse

for clippers and a container to collect the seed; the cart is left standing and may stand there the rest of the day if more urgent work reveals itself, and the mulching has to wait a day.

Late in the summer you may be tempted to leave the garden
and go to the mountains. Naturally you will make a list of things to
take with you: clothes, toothbrush, seed envelopes, and film. Also
on the list will be a notebook to make lists in: a list of plants found,
seed obtained, and plants photographed. But first you do a tremendous amount of research into which plants you expect to find in
Arizona or Switzerland or wherever, and then you make a list of all
the information you can glean from NARGS and AGS journals,
travel books written for gardeners, floras of the locality, and the advice of other travelers. You will return after your ten days to a
changed garden—new flowers in bloom, old friends departed. You
race around the garden listing them, because of course you keep an
annual record of blooming times so that you can plan plant associations rationally; also so that you can reminisce in winter and so that
you can follow the history of important individual plants.

There are other lists to compile as gardening aids. How about
a list of lime lovers? A list of plants together with their geographic
provenance so that you can section off the garden into little enclaves
of plants of common origin? Make a list of conifers and shrubs too.
These are long lived plants and inevitably their labels will disappear.
A list may help you disentangle the names and help you get fresh labels to the right places. And there are purely intellectual lists to
make mostly in the winter months when the only sounds are freezing rain against the windows and the roar of the furnace fan. This
is a good time to sort out the penstemons by botanical section and
discover whether making a list helps you make any sense out of
them. Or try the primulas or the saxifrages.

I have never made a list of plants to avoid. These could only be
discovered by bitter experience and once you have had it out with
a troublesome or uncomfortable plant you rarely need to have your
memory jogged by lists. I have sometimes changed my mind about

what is troublesome and made room for beautiful weeds and interesting but hostile plants. But their faults are too glaring to warrant putting them on a list.

I suppose I should end with a list of lists assigning a grade to each list for its usefulness, interest, and difficulty of upkeep. But lists are very personal and what I think is worthwhile you may dismiss as a trivial waste of time. If you despise them all, just think of your favorite garden book—does it have a list of plants? Isn't *Hortus III* just a list? Isn't every dictionary and encyclopedia a list? Our own lists are just a summary of thoughts about something precious to us.

Sometimes I find a list of plants with no date and no title, nothing to identify it. Shall I keep it in case its significance comes back to me? Shall I discard it knowing that life will go on exactly as it was before I found it? Since it is no longer useful I should probably destroy it. But instead I shall file it. It seems a pity to destroy information even if you are not certain what the information means.

A modern fanatical listmaker would keep a list of lists in its own subdirectory on the computer, but before computers there were only slips of paper.

> *He kept a list of lists:*
> *Of all the plants he wants to grow,*
> *Of all the plants that now exist*
> *In every bed. And he insists*
> *On making lists of plants to show*
> *And lists of plants that died last year,*
> *And if it lived—another list*
> *And was it grown in scree and schist?*
> *And all the plants he holds most dear*
> *Are on a list, and this list listed.*
> *No other master list existed.*
>
> *He listed penstemon by sections;*

Blooming times of every Gentian
Verna and a lot you'd never mention.
There was a list of hybrid plant confections
Rhodo crossings with their ratings
And cultivars of subulata phlox.
He listed plants that grow on rocks
Saxifrage and primrose matings.
And there were lists of plants by height
And several different lists by color
Which blues bright and which were duller.
Those seeds that germinate in light
Were listed too, and which to freeze.
He had a hundred lists of seeds
And then a list of which were weeds,
Which flowers had odor, which attracted bees.
At first he listed seeds by source
Combined them in a list alph'betical
Followed by a list the'retical
For making six new lists of course.

But now he keeps two lists of lists:
Those lists to keep and those to burn.
Of all the lists that now exist
Will ever one of them be missed?
Or will it yet become the turn
Of each sad list to face the fires
Change truth to ash as it expires?
But still continue to exist
An entry on the list of lists.

✌ ✌

Patience

❧ ❧ IF YOU GROW plants from seed you are very much aware

of the great differences in the time it takes for different species to produce a flower. Annuals bloom the year they are sown, biennials form a rosette the first year and bloom the second year after sowing. Perennials, too, usually bloom the second year but may take much longer. Fritillarias and trilliums are notoriously slow to become mature plants. If you try to explain this to a non-gardener they will usually accuse you of patience. The implication is: I wouldn't waste my time waiting three years for *that*. Gardeners themselves know they are the most impatient people alive. Throughout winter impatience is almost a disease that becomes seriously aggravated whenever gardeners congregate and infect each other with their own particular virus. Even after the season has started and the steady parade of flower debuts begins we are constantly waiting for the next species to open. We are never satisfied with the current display. We dart from bed to bed looking for new growth, bud formation, and the expansion and coloring of the buds. By the time the flower actually opens we are sated with expectation and longing; we satisfy ourselves that the first flower really is what we expected, that more flowers are on the way, and then we move over to the next plant to start the anticipation process over again. By the time the whole plant is covered with flowers and we have taken a final photograph, that plant fades into the overall garden picture and another plant engages our attention. It usually needs a visitor with a fresh eye to rekindle our own happiness at being partially responsible for this exquisite object.

The non-gardener who believes we have waited two or three years for this triumph to unfold is sadly mistaken. I think it is true to say we are never waiting for one particular thing to happen. If that were true, gardening would be a state of perpetual disappointment as each year that one thing we were waiting for failed to come up to the ideal or even failed to come up at all. Of course there are plenty of disappointments but they are easily outnumbered or at least outmatched by the successes. The truth is our expectations are numerous but individually low-key. We keep the number high so that at least a few will be fulfilled. We expect little of each one because we are wise/humble/superstitious/indifferent/realistic.

We don't however tell the non-gardener we are *not* patient. Patience is nearly always regarded as a virtue, and there are many situations where we should try to practice patience. We should *wait* for instance, until seedlings are large enough to be transplanted. There are several ways of handling seedlings: some people insist on transplanting while they are small—with only one pair of true leaves and very little root. If you do this I think your pots should be fairly small. Single little seedlings don't like oceans of compost to live in. Maybe you should also feed them (weak solution of fertilizer) and grow them under lights to keep them growing quickly. This means too that you have to have somewhere to put them when their headroom runs out, so the timing is crucial if you want to avoid frozen plants when you put them outside too soon. This is not my style. I like seedlings to live their whole life outside or at best in a coldframe. I transplant mostly when the second pair of leaves emerges and the roots reach the bottom of the seedpot. Timing is not all that scientific and like everybody else I go by feel and common sense for what is the right time. But I know I have to be patient and not try to do it too soon. This is especially true of the first few seedpots and even more so of the slow growers: primulas, meconopsis, saxifraga, gentiana. If you can't control yourself and start work on a pot of too small seedlings, at least pot up a few clumps and don't try to separate every unhappy little orphan to die alone in a sea of compost.

Wait too for weedkiller to take effect before you walk or pull. If you use Roundup or whatever (and of course you try not to; don't trust professionals who tell you that there is no danger of damage to you or your plants) then it is pointless to try to pull half-dead weeds and dangerous to walk on the sprayed area too soon. In any case the idea is to kill off the weeds totally without ever touching them. You can then plant over their corpses.

Wait until seed is ripe before you gather it. In the wild you may have to take a green stalk and allow the seed to dry and mature at home. In the garden you are more or less in control and you waste your own time and that of the people who are going to try to grow the seed if it is not collected at the right time. Collecting seed is an "art." The kind of art that is part common sense and part experience tells you when the seed is ready. You will lose a lot of seed (like lewisias and violas) because they are smooth and spherical and roll off into the dirt before you realize you have lost most of them. You will lose a lot because they pop out before you are ready with your seed packet (like phlox and geraniums). You will spoil some by collecting too late, (brown instead of just past the green stage is too late for adonis for example) or too early (you have to wait for brown for most seeds, campanulas for instance), and in any case the seeds should not stick to the capsule (beware pulsatilla, dryas). If you want seed don't be impatient to dead-head. Tidiness can be an enjoyable vice but collecting seed may be more important. *Never* dead-head just to please your visitors. You will constantly make errors of judgment. If you feel you have to excuse your negligence (and that is never needed), say you want the seed for an important seed exchange. You can acquire a taste for seed heads that allows you to see beauty where you might previously have seen only a dead flower.

In New England *wait* until spring to divide and move nearly anything. Beautiful hefty plants carved up in September usually rot and fade away before spring. You can move and divide the early flowering plants such as primroses just after they flower, i.e., in late spring. I usually pot the pieces so they can be kept watered and shaded in a frame near the house through the summer. Expect the worst to happen if you don't take care of them—a rapid demise in a drought. Don't try to transplant tiny divisions in the open garden. Better to pot them and put them in hospital. Moving a large plant can be done any time provided you take a large enough root ball *and* you don't damage the roots, *and* the soil is moist enough both in the root ball and in the planting hole, *and* you don't lose soil in

transit, *and* you don't have an accident. Some or all of these conditions may be lacking and the plant may survive but don't count
on it.

Wait until a plant is big enough before you plant it in the garden. This means common sense and judgment again, but after you
have killed a few tender adolescents you will know what I mean. If
it isn't big enough in May you may have to wait until late August
before you can plant it—if there is the usual dry spell in June or July.
The small root ball from a 3" or 4" pot will lose its moisture to the
surrounding dry soil very quickly. Even watering the surrounding
ground well can't prevent the moisture dispersing by evaporation
and by absorption into the infinite earth. Anyone with only a few
plants to accommodate and plenty of time to stand with a hose can
ignore this advice.

One of the worst waits of all is for plants to start growing in
spring. I assume it is useless to implore you not to poke around
where you know a plant should be, not to pull at apparently dead
rosettes, not to weed too vigorously or plant a new plant next to a
suspected winter casualty. But at least try to remember that nothing is deemed dead until late April unless you have already flicked
off the brown bun with your finger and can actually see the neck is
rotten. Even then you could give the roots a chance to regenerate
(but at this point it is usually hopeless).

Are there any occasions when patience is downright wrong? I
think I can name a few:

1. Don't wait if you find an animal burrowing in your garden.
A quick response may discourage him right away. (Try an oily rag
down the hole. Try something that is offensive to one of its senses:
radio, chicken wire, Ropel, smoke bombs). No animal is cute if it
sets up home in a flower bed. Like bats in the living room or spiders
in the bathtub, normal life has to stop until they go away.

2. On a par with animals are plagues of insects. You accept just
about every kind of ant, bug, beetle, caterpillar, millipede, or whatever as an integral part of the ecology of a garden. But every so often

an army of ants burrows under an *Arctostaphylos uva-ursi* or digs up enough sand to bury a dianthus planted in scree; bag worms make disgusting webs on a cherry branch overhanging a primrose patch and casually drop into the inviting pasture; Japanese beetles decide to strip a favorite crab apple; aphids mutilate the lupin spikes. Some of these situations require prompt action. You have to decide whether you can tolerate the damage but if not don't wait until the only available action left is one of revenge. I don't have a list of situation-specific strategies for each of these skirmishes. Victory is never a sure thing whether you use mustard, sprays, hand picking, broomsticks, diatomaceous earth, a dab of alcohol, or a jet of water.

3. If weeds are in fruit don't wait for them to blow or jump around and colonize the rest of your garden. This also applies to the prolific plants you introduced yourself: *Siberian iris, Lychnis viscaria, Dianthus deltoides,* and many other members of the Caryophyllaceae. Most large campanulas and adenophoras, and every composite are under suspicion. This advice runs counter to the patience required for wanted seed to ripen. It also explains why visitors may deplore your lack of tidiness. In their minds most plants in seed are potential goldenrod and dandelion.

4. Cut back in haste any branch of a dwarf conifer that reverts. Break off the candles of pines you want to keep short before they lose their brittle quality. Obviously neither of these operations can be described as urgent, but unless you carry pruning shears wherever you go you will forget which branch is misbehaving and forget the candles completely until they accuse you of neglect in winter.

5. Don't waste a second if you see a seedling in a pot wilting. Rush to get water. To a lesser extent take care of wilting plants in the garden but remember that many big leaved plants such as ligularias and primulas can wilt day after day and revive every evening after the sun has left them. Some people hate to see this and hurry to irrigate lavishly. In my case, carrying pails of water long distances is out of the question. I either harden my heart or work in another part of the garden. I can't remember a case when an established

healthy plant died because I didn't water (but it is possible that some were weakened). Small gardens are easier to maintain and for appearance's sake need more maintenance. A large plant of *Ligularia* 'Desdemona' in a small garden with leaves drooping sulkily in the sun could be a tearjerker demanding instant action. Going a step further with seedlings, I would recommend watering them long before they wilt. You can usually gauge the best time by the weight of the pot. Even if rain is predicted it is better to water when you think they are ready. Too often promised rain is too little or too late. Wilted seedlings may forgive you once but not often twice. There is nothing like real rain to water plants properly. It may be too heavy and knock down a few, especially ones that grew without enough light, but it never seems to be too long. Plants are perfectly happy sitting in a puddle until it drains off so you don't need to rush to their rescue. But don't leave them in a kitty litter tray or any other non-draining situation for more than a couple of days. If the plant is a hairy, woolly, precious bun such as *Draba mollissima* I know you will take better care than this implies, but one is always surprised at the resilience of actively growing young plants.

6. If you order bulbs for fall planting don't wait until they arrive to decide where you are going to put them or to prepare the ground. They could arrive after the ground is frozen. Bulb sellers are either not in full control of their merchandise or they are insensitive to the vagaries of northern climates. Or maybe they are just too busy. You should dig holes with plenty of depth for hefty narcissus bulbs (probably a foot) but also covering a much larger area than you think possible for each group. Planting a lot of single bulbs in frosty weather is a great nuisance so don't plan this method if the delivery might be late. Dig large areas and cover the mounded soil with trash to prevent premature freezing. The bulbs you can't delay planting are the fall flowering colchicums and crocuses. The flower shoots start to grow and will break off very easily. Also you want the flowers in the garden—a colchicum flowering on a windowsill looks faintly ridiculous.

Patience and haste can be rewarding virtues or fatal errors depending on the situation. Common sense is usually a good guide.

ᴥ ᴥ

Seven Gardens in Search of a Gardener

ᴥ ᴥ ONE WINTER'S DAY I daydream about seven gardens. None of them is exactly my own, but each one looks familiar and is uncomfortably close to being a caricature of what I remember my garden to be. The first garden in this daydream has been influenced by Chinese philosophers, Gothic novels, Japanese religions, great explorers, medieval monks and witches, Victorian villas, French chateaux, Florists' Feasts, and Reginald Farrer. It is not a historical garden yet embraces all History. The rocks were placed with reverence and respect. They were chosen with care from special places and each rock has an imagined special meaning dictated by its shape and origin. Fanciful relationships between the rocks could be described using the language of philosophy, religion, and mysticism. The words are occult and abstruse and are like an exchange between a Zen Buddhist and a Jesuit, empty of meaning except to the speakers. The plants seem to be secondary, an afterthought—*Cerastium tomentosum* ramps among the rocks chasing an unkempt thyme. A tree, originally a dwarf conifer, threatens to upstage a rock symbolizing the life force. An incongruous selfsown sapling wedged between two important boulders cannot be removed without leaving a stump or destroying the configuration of rocks. The garden was finished long ago and the gardener has moved on to yet another religion.

The second garden is small and utilitarian. The paths are four feet wide allowing two people to walk abreast easily as they talk about irrigation devices. A computer hanging from a spigot is programmed to release water to a sprinkler system three times a day for seventeen minutes on Tuesdays and Fridays. A bright yellow hose leads into a jumble of couplings and shut-offs, continuing on in three directions. One of these disappears underground to form the drip system for a moraine. Another trickles into a bog. The third services a vegetable garden a hose-length away. Rocks in this garden are used for stepping stones; they lead across the rock garden almost randomly, their placement is designed simply to avoid plants. A large rock, evidently in place before the garden was made around it, has pockets of soil on all its aspects to simulate a north-facing slope. The other rocks were collected from the roadside and none of them would be large enough to seriously damage a small car or its driver when he transported them to the garden. A few rectangular concrete slabs are scattered among the more natural looking rocks waiting to be replaced by a lucky find. A large mat of *Androsace sarmentosa* grows next to a four-foot Spuria iris. A compost heap of high visibility has been recently turned to reveal rich healthy material for the next project. The rock garden is almost an afterthought to a vegetable garden, coldframes, and a mixed border.

The third garden is "straight from the mountains." All the rocks are from one quarry and laid in perfect simulation of uptilted stratified rock with uniform bedding plane. Small rocks have been grouped together to give the impression of single, larger rocks. The mountain scene sits on a horizontal lawn, so that it is only when the eye and the mind are firmly fixed on the rocks themselves that the illusion of being in the mountains is maintained. To the left of the mountain is a garage and to the right a neat alpine house. The plants in the garden are buns and mats none taller than 4". They include *Saxifraga oppositifolia, Lewisia rediviva,* and thirty or forty of the "ten best" alpines. No trash. A few dwarf conifers adorn the rocks but, after only five years, already look like Gulliver in Lilliput.

The fourth garden is a collector's garden. The first impression is an exuberant tangle of greenery broken by scattered bursts of color. The garden has no visible structure. Bare patches here and there are covered with labels, many broken, most illegible. Little piles of labels sit at the edge of a bed waiting for the moment when an unlabeled plant is recognized and can be matched up with a name on one of the labels or until the gardener is reconciled to the probability of the plant's demise. The living plants are so closely planted that the resemblance to an alpine meadow is convincing even if not intended. Many of the plants are exquisite rarities that are well grown except for the intense competition from their neighbors. Others are less garden worthy and are being grown as though on probation. Several dingy salvias with yellowish and bluish flowers, tall hostile echinops with grays and blues hardly distinguishable from each other, silenes richly endowed with ripe seed pods threatening to shower their neighbors with fertile seed, thistles and knapweeds clamoring for space, and endless variations of Queen Anne's lace. If you lift the gigantic leaf of an *Inula magnifica* you will find the remains of a rare androsace and labels of six others that took three years to grow and two weeks to kill. The gardener will not know he has lost these plants until late October when the inula leaf shrivels to reveal their deathbed. Happily the gardener has passed the "androsace stage" and is concentrating on a group of edraianthus far enough away from the inulas to be safe from competition. Each edraianthus has a label with a different name though many look alike. The best plant has no label at all, so it is simultaneously a source of pride and embarrassment to the gardener. The part of the garden called "New Zealand" is quite bare except for the local oxalis.

Garden number five is a carefree garden—well, the gardener is carefree. At one time the rocks were positioned with care and intelligence, but the significance of the placement is now forgotten and their chief function is to assert that this is a rock garden and not any other kind. In May, *Phlox subulata* billows over the rocks; in June, *Dianthus deltoides* asserts its presence. These healthy plants need no labels. The other plants are timid infants with names in many hands on labels of many shapes and colors. This gardener does not raise plants from seed nor order boxes of expensive plants by mail each spring. The plants are gifts from friends or plants from the chapter seedling sale bought at the end of the sale at reduced prices. Although the garden is well loved, it is left for weeks at a time without a qualm of conscience. Weeds accumulate during these absences but the garden can always be pulled back into shape in a couple of days. Tucked away among the obnoxious *Veronica filiformis* and the *Draba sibirica* are a few precious plants—a large patch of *Dryas octopetala, Linnaea borealis* running around, and could that be diapensia? This gardener succeeds where more caring gardeners fail.

Before garden number six was begun the gardener read numerous books and attended numerous meetings and conferences. The garden reflects the accumulation of knowledge dealt out by the pundits whose dictates the gardener follows with enthusiasm and respect. It is like an examination paper with every question attempted but with incomplete or slightly wrong answers some of the time. The rock work represents a rocky pasture; a stream that seems to rise at the cellar window disappears where the rock garden borders a woodland garden. A bog garden had been planned at the point where the stream vanishes but the balance between recirculation of the running water, input of fresh water, loss of water to the bog, and evaporation has not been solved and the bog is usually dry. A moraine has been constructed using drip hose a few inches underground, but the plants on it could have been grown just as easily in less specialized conditions. A raised bed filled with sand grows acantholimons and physarias, but nothing much else has taken. A pit house stands empty, still recovering from the floods of spring that filled the house up to the benches. There are coldframes with shattered lids, one of them was meant for bulbs but mice cleaned it out over the winter. The greenhouse has windows that automatically open when the temperature reaches sixty degrees. Unfortunately they fail to close when the temperature goes down, so the mechanism has been disconnected. The garden is a success in spite of all the effort to do the right thing. Each experiment seems to have some redeeming feature and a residual bonus even where the original intent failed to materialize.

The seventh garden contains objects as well as plants. There are four half-dressed concrete babies representing the seasons; a series of hollow logs planted with saxifrages; a raised bed, too short and too narrow to house more than three plants, affectionately called "The Tomb"; a piece of driftwood; five ornate Italian terra-cotta planters; a drift of dead-white water-smoothed pebbles; a lead toad; a yard square wooden planter originally a depository for cigarette butts in a New York theater; a wooden plaque with a short verse in poker work. The rock work is profuse and unrelated to geology. A grotto with a perpetual drip is home for ferns and moss while *Spiranthes cernua* and a carpet of primulas adorns the outflow. There is a bird bath, a sundial, a water butt, a small plastic pool, a concrete flight of steps, a niche for a saint, a rustic bench supporting a *Clematis tangutica,* a trellis arch with a climbing rose, and lights along the walkways and spotlights directed at focal points in the garden for nighttime strolling.

These seven gardens are all more or less components of my own and the gardeners are all aspects of me. Like you, I am the cultural descendant of an army of gardening ghosts. If my efforts seem trivial and inconsequential my participation is not. There would be no fraternity of gardeners if gardening were reserved for the elite, the rich, and the professional. Even more than music, gardening is an activity of amateurs and small scale practitioners. The show gardens need such lovers of gardens from which to draw their audience of connoisseurs.

And for various reasons, I work for myself so I am obliged to be pragmatic in the sense that I do things the easiest way in order to conserve my finite amount of energy. I endure the barbarisms because it is better to have tried an activity with incomplete and imperfect results than not to have tried at all for reasons of age or lack of resources or some such nonreason. I want the mountains in my yard because I love them, I overlook the incongruities of scale and location in order to have the constant presence of wild flowers and alpines.

Nor can I help being a collector of plants and things. The discipline of rejecting a plant on account of its being in some way unsuitable is misplaced. There is no compelling morality that requires me to restrict my activities to growing daylilies for instance or alpines, plants under 6" tall, or plants from the Engadine or Peru. If and when I specialize, it will be because the time is right for me.

If part of my garden is uninteresting this year I shall certainly leave it to its own devices giving it just enough attention to prevent it from becoming completely overrun. It has already given me a large amount of pleasure and now I need to think about its next phase without guilt. Leaving it horticulturally fallow may be the best I can do for the time being and the best in the long run. If the whole garden needs rethinking, being away from it may produce a masterpiece later. Looking at other people's gardens and at gardens in nature may trigger the ideas. I accept the fact that some of my adaptations are amateurish and even ludicrous, but nobody understands a problem unless they have tried to solve it. Reading a pat textbook solution to a problem is only a first step.

The objects in my garden will stay. They fulfill the function of all possessions: souvenirs of people and experiences, gratification of a longing for beauty, ostentatious display of wealth, furtive admission of greed, assertion of my taste and defiance of yours.

I think I recognize my own motivations in every garden I have seen and you may see your own aspirations, faults, and virtues in mine. Some we share, some are yours alone and don't apply to me at all.

↲ ↳

Gardening in Old Age

☙ ☙ WHEN WE TOOK our house guest to Lincoln Foster's garden, we were given the usual comprehensive tour. Linc was his usual informative, enthusiastic self and the garden looked pretty much as I always expected it would—relatively tidy, expanding at the boundaries, nibbled by the deer, and full of familiar plants. Also rare plants that one had seen time and time again in Linc's garden and therefore thought of them as familiar. It came as quite a surprise as we were driving off when the visitor said out of the blue: "It is an old man's garden." I didn't agree or disagree, I wanted more time to think about his estimate before asking for an explanation or an amplification. Did he think *my* garden was an old man's garden? Was it judgmental or descriptive? What exactly is an old man's garden? Is it something one has by default because one isn't forty anymore? Or is it something to aim for, something I should be doing? Am I doing it and don't know?

Thoughts of age are irrelevant to the young. They hardly ever think about it seriously; like death, old age only happens to grandparents and other peoples' great uncles, one's own parents are never old in that ultimate sense. Usually old age is equated with sickness and disability, especially the visible defects of skin, hair, muscle, and bone, and the unmentionable effects age has on sex and food processing. It may never occur to the young and healthy that inside every slightly worn body is another like spirit, possibly hiding behind a veneer of pompousness and privilege. Similarities are there nevertheless; learning never stops even though memory becomes more selective; unsureness and insecurity are never far away unless they have been obliterated or obscured by habitual faith. By now I am long past my seventieth year so I easily qualify for Old Man status. Isn't it time my garden began to look like an old man's garden? So far it has been just a middle-aged man's garden growing a little more portly year by year. Isn't it time to settle down? To decide exactly what kind of garden I want?

I confessed to Ellie Spingarn, a gardening friend, that I was cutting back on seed sowing this year. Well under the two thousand packets I sowed last year, it will be more like seventeen hundred when all the orders are in. The fact is I still keep trying species that I know will not do well for me. This isn't a fault so much as a strategy. You are not wasting time when you grow slightly tender plants,

plants that you end up not liking and plants that you end up getting rid of for one reason or another, or plants that you are already
growing but want to see a different form of or verify a name. There
are many valid reasons for growing plants that will not be permanent residents of your garden. The process is interesting whether or
not we learn anything new. There is pleasure in repetition. So what
shall I do if I sow fewer seeds? Well, it will give me more time to
propagate plants from cuttings, more time to move plants around
in the garden, time to try for artistry instead of rarity, to make containers, to make a bog that works, time to start a bulb frame. Stop!
Isn't the idea to do less, not just to do something different? Absolutely not. I only want to do less if I have to. As Ellie said of Linc,
he had the right idea. He cut down on sowing seeds by being selective; he stopped growing revolving door alpines—those he had
grown many times for all too brief periods. Instead he moved over
to hybridizing rhododendrons. Presumably the aim was to grow a
collection of *long-lived* plants that would take care of themselves
without too much attention. Except for his extraordinary deer
problem this worked.

I don't think rhododendrons are for me though, so I can't follow Linc's path to an old man's garden. I can admire the results of
this obviously engrossing hobby only with many reservations. I
concede that in the doing of it grows the love of it—plenty of first
rate intelligent gardeners have been captivated by the genus. Surely
it was this aspect of Linc's garden that revealed it as an old man's garden—the reduction of one activity to almost zero and the prolifer-
ation of another that in theory would lead to a permanent but still
developing garden. I wonder if the visitor had fully understood the
process; perhaps he saw only the dearth of Aretian androsaces,
alpine dianthus, and Western drylanders.

It doesn't matter what he was looking at, the fact is, the alternatives to not eventually having an old man's garden are two, neither of which are very attractive. Either you give up your garden or
you die. I can think of five or six gardeners in their eighties and

scores in their seventies who are still gardening. Only a few chose to leave their house and garden to live in a retirement home without a garden. The big question is whether to retreat gradually, purposefully and rationally, or whether to hold on to every activity, every inch of cultivated ground, every pot and plant until a muscle pops, a joint freezes, or a final catastrophe strikes one down.

I hope that when visitors leave my old man's garden they understand this very real problem and do not drive away exchanging glib observations: "He took on too much" (I was already doing that when I was your age), "It's a bit overgrown" (try to use the word "mature"), "What a mess" (this has *nothing* to do with age—I know at least one middle-aged man's garden which is worse), "Too many plants to absorb" (next visit plan to stay longer), etc., etc. Actually doesn't everybody face the same problem? We all try to do slightly more than we have time for, we try to grow unsuitable plants, we are overwhelmed by the garden for at least one week every year.

So here are few resolutions I made on my seventieth birthday: 1. Give up one bed each year from now on. 2. Sow at least two hundred fewer pots of seed each year. 3. Stop trying to grow *Dianthus alpinus, Eritrichium nanum, Physoplexis comosa.* 4. Hire a landscape architect for an hour a year. Just for weeding. 5. Stop photographing every penstemon as it flowers. 6. Sit on a bench once a week. 7. Stop buying dwarf conifers and rhododendrons.

So if my friend comes around again he will say: "There's another old man's garden."

POSTSCRIPT: That year I made eight new beds. For the next three years I sowed even more packets of seed. I am moving away from dwarf conifers into more flowering shrubs on the theory that spring is more fun than winter. In 1993 I constructed four more crevice gardens, mostly to accommodate the unusually large number of seedlings I ended up with this year. In 1994, I sowed over 2,100 packets of seed. Oh, well.

~ ~

Part Three

❧

GROWING PLANTS

A Plant List: The First Hundred

க்க WHEN YOU FINALLY decide on rock gardening there seems to be an overwhelming number of plants to choose from. Do more expensive plants give more pleasure? Is it better to go for the inexpensive ones and get more plants for the same money? Shall I start with a color scheme in mind? Shall I collect a single genus? Shall I grow exactly what X or Y is growing? (The answer to all these questions is *no*.) I started out by wanting a beautiful rocky outcrop with colorful mats flowing over the rocks and delightful buns tucked into pockets of soil between the rocks, with a few taller plants for variety. My ideal would start flowering in early April and continue nonstop through September at least. Maybe this is your aim too. How to do it? Without some experience, growing plants from seed is a lottery and hardly a viable way of filling a garden as quickly as an eager beginner would like. Then there are plant sales at the chapter meetings. You can get excellent bargains and excellent plants too, but it is not a swift and reliable way to fill a garden. You can't expect to find at a sale the particular plant you have just seen or read about and have set your mind on growing. There is no point in taking your want list to a sale. The chance is too remote that anyone else knows what you want or could supply it if they did. The best way to get something you want is from a reliable mail-order nursery, but you still may have to adjust your want list to what is available. Of course you must visit local nurseries too, to find out what is available there. The plants you buy there will probably establish better than plants that have been subjected to the indignities of air travel. But once you open a mail-order catalog you realize that the world of plants is far bigger than your local nursery can handle.

Here follows a list of plants that are "easy." That is they will probably prosper if you give them reasonable care; they are also easy in the sense that they are obtainable. This is not a comprehensive

plant list for beginners; I am recommending plants that I would recommend to a friend who was just starting out and wanted advice to
follow or ignore. Their virtue is that they were available recently and
will probably be available for several years as they all have durable
value. I ransacked all the catalogs that arrived in January and February to look for the plants that everybody should grow. Sometimes
I give the description offered by the nursery and sometimes my own
experience. There are many other plants other than rock garden
plants offered but I have included only plants suitable for a "rockery" that has relatively good drainage, plenty of sun, and is free from
the competition of shrub and tree roots and large perennials with
big leaves. Some plants are woodlanders and will be described as
shade plants. You can decide whether to have a special woodland
area or whether to try them in the shadier spots in your rock garden. In any case the soil for them would need to contain more
humus and not drain as rapidly as for alpines.

Most of the plants we grow from seed are species; that is they
are plants you would expect to find in the wild. If an observant gardener finds a plant with some unusual quality such as larger than
normal flowers, double flowers, or variegated leaves, he or she wants
to spread it around. Plants grown from seed nearly always vary from
each other and from their parents so the only reliable way to propagate a special plant is vegetatively—by cuttings or division. Such
a set of plants is called a clone. The best distributers of such clones
are nurseries. They have the skills and equipment needed to produce the hundreds of plants of each good form or hybrid that will
satisfy the nation's gardeners. Most forms and hybrids are given
fancy names that designate them as having a special quality that
most wild plants don't have. Not only beginners but more experienced gardeners are always on the lookout for new and good forms.
I like to try out every new plant I can find and afford, to evaluate it
against my own idea of beauty and interest and to see whether it
likes the conditions in my garden.

I shall not recommend many clones explicitly because to appreciate an unusual form you ought first to know what the standard wild form looks like. But don't be deterred from getting a named form—that may be all that is available. Besides visitors who know only the standard species will be fascinated to see an unusual color form or a dwarf form growing in your garden. There is one caveat: if every plant in your garden is a large flowered form, a double flowered form, or has variegated leaves, the garden will not look very alpine. It will lose its innocence and appear "artificial." This may be the effect you want and that is fine. But if what you really want is a natural mountaintop effect, sooner or later you will have to grow the species plants and that probably means growing some plants from seed. Nurseries also propagate many alpines from seed and the absence of a fancy name implies that even though the plant may have been propagated from cuttings it is a true species and not a man-made hybrid.

In the following descriptions of the plants I have quoted excerpts from some of the fine descriptions by the nurseries themselves. A quote from a particular nursery doesn't mean that the plant is only available there. Some nurseries don't write descriptions at all; there are certainly several other good nurseries selling these plants, but the ones listed have the best descriptions.

A list of mail-order nurseries follows this listing, and you might want to do some comparison shopping, though there is no way of comparing quality and size without seeing the plants. There are also many good nurseries that I have never used. More important there are hundreds of plants a beginner could grow and this list is meant to lead you on rather than limit your vision.

The authors of these affectionate puffs are unknown, although I have included a letter designating the name of the nursery. But I imagine Baldasarre, Betty Ann, Nancy, Evie, Dick, Rene, Eleanor, Marty, and all the other nursery operators will give credit to their writers. It is fascinating how different eyes notice different aspects of the same plant.

S= Siskiyou; R= Rice Creek; M= Montrose; C=Cricklewood;

W=WeDu; Rk.= Rocknoll; WR= Woodland Rockery; CA= Colorado Alpines; NG=Nature's Garden

Note that any remark not in quotes is my own opinion.

Achillea ageratifolia: "A permanent mat of little silvery lance-shaped leaves and numerous white-petalled flowers with off-white centers. The white-on-white effect is most appealing." [S] "A cheerful plant." [WR] There are a number of useful yarrows. This one is as large a plant as you would want in a small rock garden and you could even use it at the front of a border. This has better flowers than most. This *Achillea* is often called *Anthemis aizoon.*

Actinea herbacea: "Large yellow daisies on a dwarf plant makes a bright accent in the spring garden." [R] This plant is described as a form of *Hymenoxys acaulis* (see entry) that is essentially a high mountain cushion, but is actually a plains plant about 6" high and takes up as much space as *Aster alpinus.* Could even be used as a front of the border plant.

Aethionema 'Warley Rose': "Dwarf shrub for hot, dry positions. Tiny colorful blue-green leaves smothered in rose-pink. Daphne-like blossoms in May and June." [S] "Evergreen bushlets with Daphne-pink rosebuds." [Rk] This plant is probably a form of *A. armena.* Other *Aethionemas* such as *A. pulchellum* are just as good but you may have to start them from seed. They may then self-sow attractively in cracks and crannies. 'Warley Rose' is a good color but never produces seedlings for me.

Aethionema grandiflorum: "The steel-blue, needlelike foliage is lovely all winter, and in spring heads of delicate pale pink flowers are produced. Give it sun." [M]

Ajuga: Don't plant ajugas in your rock garden. The only exception might be a form of *Ajuga* usually called 'Metallica Crispa'. "Curly bronze leaves. Non-spreading. Looks like red dwarf spinach." [R] "Speckled silver and purple curled and shiny leaves." [Rk] "A foxy specimen plant for a partially shady area. It's composed of congested crinkled leaves with a purplish sheen that emit short racemes of deep-blue flowers." [WR] There is also a form with redder leaves.

Alchemilla alpina: "Dark green foliage with silver edge and reverse." [C] This is primarily a foliage plant. The flowers are greeny yellow. It is at its most attractive after rain when drops of water sit in the upturned umbrellas. The leaves are quite large for a small rock garden. *A. mollis* is more often seen but it is far too large and weedy for a rock garden. Both species merit space only if you are very fond of leafy landscapes.

Alyssum saxatile: See *Aurinia saxatilis.*

Anacyclus depressus: "Wheel-like patterns of lacy, grayish-green foliage develop white, red backed, daisylike blooms at their tips." [Rk] There is a good reason to get this from a nursery; the seed you get from exchanges is very rarely viable. This beautiful daisy comes from North Africa and southern Spain so you wouldn't expect it to be hardy in Massachusetts. It survives and selfsows.

Androsace lanuginosa: "A vigorous, easy plant from the Himalayas with silvery trailing stems ending in clusters of lavender pink, white-eyed flowers. Valued for long summer bloom. Zone 4." [S] "Easy Himalayan." [CA] This is one of the few *Androsaces* that are perfectly happy outside. It is not a bun and not really a mat but it needs a foot of room to sprawl around. The stems don't seem to root down.

Androsace sarmentosa: "Hardy Himalayan species with hairy, silver foliage rosettes that spread by stolons densely covered with light pink verbena-like blossoms in April and May. Zone 3." [S] This is the first *Androsace* to plant and a never ending source of delight. You can move bits of it around when it roots down. There are a number of forms equally good. *A. primuloides* is the same or a very similar plant. "Makes a patch of furry buttons that sends up quantities of pink flowers in May. Even out of bloom the silvery rosettes are attractive." [R] *A. sempervivoides* is neater but not so reliable.

Anemone X lesseri: "Bright red flowers. Will grow to 12" in maturity. Likes a moist soil in sun or part shade." [R] It does not actually need moisture. The color is unusual since most rock garden anemones are white.

Anemone multifida: "Full sun, good drainage. Elegant, finely divided foliage; cream, red, or yellow flowers on long stalks in late spring. Native to the Rockies." [W]

Anemone nemorosa: "An endearing early spring blooming wildflower that carpets woods and shady hillsides of northern Europe to northwest Asia. The species has lovely white flowers, light pink reverse. Plant the woody rhizomes horizontally, 2" deep." [S] There are several color forms from white to deep blue and red, also some doubles. A broad sheet of them in a woodland would be great but the pretty forms look good singly in a shady part of the rock garden.

Anemonella thalictroides: "This native perennial is happy in a woodland setting or in a shaded rock garden. The blue-green foliage provides a collar for the delicate white to pink flowers. It grows from a tuberous root and occasionally reblooms in the fall; however it disappears during the summer. To 9" but usually much shorter. Zones 3-10." [M] "Extremely delicate in appearance, but tough and long-lived in the garden. White or pinkish anemonelike flowers in earliest spring; often bloom sporadically through the season." [W]

Antennaria dioica: "Dwarf carpeting, mountain plants, easy in full sun and well-drained soil." [S] "Flat silvery-white mats." [Rk] Pussy-toes is a spreader but easy to control. The flowers of some of the forms are worth having, the usual species flower is a little dingy. It adds a gray patch to the green mats of summer.

Aquilegia bertolonii: "One of the smallest and finest. Large, rich blue upturned flowers." [S] There are a number of miniature aquilegias for a beginner. Taller ones also are at home in the rock garden but there is a good deal of crossing that goes on and the subsequent selfsowing will give you a mixed bag of sometimes uncontrollable seedlings. Some people want this effect but once you have it, it is hard to change.

Aquilegia flabellata: Is probably more permanent than *A.*

bertolonii. "A wonderful Japanese native well suited to our climate. It grows to about 15" and blooms with blue-and-white flowers in early spring. The lovely, blue-green foliage is more resistant than most to leaf miner. Semi-shade. Zones 3–10." [M] "Fleshy fringed foliage produces 3–4" stems of long-lasting, deep blue-and-white flowers with recurved spurs. Blooms early summer. Prefers a cool position." [CA] "Prefers a mostly sunny site." [WR] Note the differences between advice from North Carolina, Vail, Colorado, and Michigan. In Massachusetts it doesn't mind sun. There are dwarf forms, some all white.

Arabis ferdinandi-coburgii variegata: "A valuable foliage arabis forming a mound of neat rosettes of 1". creamy-white leaves, each with a narrow center zone of green. White flowers on 5" stems." [S] Another arabis you can get from any local nursery is *A. caucasica.* This is not to be despised but must be kept tidy by shearing and not allowing to ramp unchecked. There is a variegated form of this too but *Arabis ferdinandi-coburgii* is neater though the flowers are not as good. Another name for *A. caucasica* is *A. albida* and there is a double form "which blooms all spring and makes an effect like popcorn. An old-fashioned plant that has become rare." [R]

Arenaria montana: "Clouds of large, pure white flowers smother the plant in early summer. Attractive dark green foliage year round. Alps. Zone 5, but grown in Zone 4 with winter mulch." [S] "Myriads of white cup-shaped flowers. Foliage is deep green needlelike in mats. Classic rock plant." [R] This is one of the best sandworts for flowers. I have found it impermanent without protection in the Berkshires but I have seen it growing very happily in Hartford a little bit south of here. Arenarias on the whole are easy but this one is worth a little extra trouble.

Armeria juniperifolia (= *A. caespitosa*): "Minute hummocks of leaves. Long lasting white flowers nestle right on the foliage. 2". [R] "Dense buns sprout short stems topped with papery, rose-pink flower heads. This little fellow prefers a mostly sunny area with a well-drained soil." [WR] "Spherical pink flowers rise just above the foliage." [CA] White and pink forms are first-rate plants. Perhaps the best of the thrifts. When it begins to look shabby after a few years you can easily propagate it by pressing tufts of foliage into sand.

Armeria maritima: This is a plant of wide distribution on both sides of the Atlantic. It has white, cherry-red, and pink forms. "Foliage makes a fine-textured grassy mat." [R] "The fine, evergreen leaves will form a tight bun, and you will be rewarded with heads of mauve-pink flowers in spring." [M]

Asarum hartwegii: "The cyclamen-leafed ginger is doubtless one of our best native plants. Green leaves with conspicuous silver veining. Requires extra gritty, woodland soil. Succeeds even in Zone 4 though usually rated Zone 6." [S] Indeed it is hardy for us. This is a woodlander with large glossy leaves but it might be happy in a shady, moist spot at the foot of a cliff.

Asperula gussonii: "Compact cushion of short, needlelike leaves that become covered with small, fragrant pink flowers." [CA] "A mini-mat of dark green leaves nearly hidden by the abundance of small, tubular, flesh-pink blossoms in late spring." [WR]

Asperula sintenisii (= *A. nitida puberula*): "Makes a light green cushion smothered in a sheet of pink, tubular star flowers in spring. Zone 6." [S] Actually both these asperulas seem to be okay in Zone 4–5 if they are planted in fast draining scree. Keep trying until you get one of them established. I have heard it said that hairy-leaved *A. suberosa* would also survive with proper care but I have only been successful with this in the alpine house.

Aster alpinus: "Daisies in spring above clustered leaves." [R] Color forms vary from deep mauve, pink, and white. At least one color should be found in everybody's garden. Note that most other asters bloom in the fall and this distinguishes them from *Erigeron*.

Astilbe chinensis pumila: "A nearly flat mat of heavily dissected foliage and 10"–12" spikes of fuzzy, shocking-pink blossoms. A dependable summer bloomer for a partially shady rock garden." [WR] Or you can put it in a woodland setting where it is vigorous enough to fend for itself. Most of the *Astilbe* cultivars only look right in a border or a very formal woodland garden; this one has a natural look but gives lots of color at a low point in the year for woodland.

Aubrieta deltoidea: "Classic rock plants." [S] The forms of this species are legion and splendid. Plant several to find out whether you like the reds or the lilacs and near blues. The one with variegated foliage was easier to establish for me than many of the hybrids from England. They are easy enough from seed but you will get some of the less clear colors. If you succeed with growing this species from seed, go on to other species of aubrieta that are less flashy but very good plants.

Aurinia saxatilis: 'Basket of Gold' is obtainable at any local nursery. There are some color forms, pale yellow, and even a buff color. Also double and compact forms. "Pale moonlight-gold flowers. Soft gray-green foliage." [Rk]

Bolax glebaria: "Glossy green leaf rosettes make an intriguing armorlike pad. Little yellow flowers." [S] "Tough, plasticlike, glossy green foliage produces a low, spreading mat." [CA] True for both the normal size plant and the tiny leaf variety. In shade the "pad" is more lax but is a refined ground cover like an out-of-flower mossy saxifrage.

Callirhoe involucrata: "Full sun; good drainage. Midwestern native. Procumbent plant with long trailing stems, forming a loose mat. Beautiful, silky wine-colored flowers over a long period in midsummer." [W] Winecups is the common name. It sprawls around the rock garden without doing much harm to its neighbors.

Campanula barbata: "Flat foliage rosette, pale-blue, fussy bell flowers." [C] This is a short-lived perennial and may be biennial in your garden, but it seeds around sensibly.

Campanula carpatica: A very dependable campanula, a little on the large side but well within acceptable size for a rock garden or a wall garden. It will selfsow quite readily and forms extensive colonies but also will sow itself charmingly in crevices that are otherwise unplantable. "It blooms all summer just like an annual." [R].

"Compact tufts of heart-shaped leaves." [Rk] The white form is pretty too.

Campanula cochlearifolia: "Fairy children of dusky blue on 2" stems. Spreads into a nice patch." [R] "Profuse, dainty, bell-shaped, light-blue flowers. Needs well-drained soil." [CA] In my experience it runs around at random invading but rarely harming other plants. It may die out so let it go where it thinks best. Some forms are difficult to establish.

Campanula kemulariae: "An easy, valuable groundcover and wall plant for shade, under shrubs, even in dryish soil. From a creeping rootstock rise tufts of shiny leaves and foot-long pendulous stems carrying many big, open blue bells in June." [S] "Showers of deep lavender bells just above attractive glossy leaves." [R] "Toothed leaves and decumbent 10"-12" stems of good-sized bluish-mauve bells. It is best grown in a sunny wall, or where it can cascade over rocks." [WR] I have it growing and mingling with *Geranium dalmaticum* and both survive their close relationship. The blue is good and goes well with the pink of the *Geranium;* the color may depend on soil and exposure. In another raised bed it flows poetically over the sunny side but also tries to creep backwards into the drabas and other small fry. It has to be periodically restrained.

Chrysanthemum weyrichii: "Large pink daisies hug the shiny deep-green carpeting foliage in late summer." [R] "Year-round a neat spreading plant of cut shining green leaves and in summer 3"–wide pink daisies on 4" stems. Ideal running through crevices of a sunny wall." [S] "Darling pink daisies." [Rk] "Leathery, glossy green foliage." [CA] "A spattering of pink, daisylike blossoms in late summer." [WR] It always takes me by surprise in mid-July. It hugs a large rock next to a path and runs along the base in a long line not trying to invade the path. The flowers are summery pink but the size of fall chrysanthemums and it looks like a rock plant, not a bedding chrysanthemum.

Chrysogonum virginianum: "Yellow daisies above bright, green foliage mats." [R] "This is a splendid, long-blooming native plant that is happy in sun or shade. It produces bright yellow flowers from early spring through fall and is nearly evergreen with leaves disappearing only after extreme cold." [M] "6" quarter-sized gold buttons. April to frost." [Rk] "Lavish clumps of hairy green leaves and bright-yellow flowers. Well-drained soil that leans towards the acid end of the scale. It should do fairly well in a mostly sunny garden if it is not allowed to go bone-dry during the summer." [WR] A composite with lots of character and a useful carpet-former at the edge of a wood. The low form is superior and more commonly found.

Claytonia virginica: "A delicate native plant, less than a foot high that thrives in shade or sun. Growing from a corm, it makes a brief appearance from winter into very early spring. The flowers, which are pink or white with pink stripes, are produced in racemes." [M]

Cotoneaster apiculata: A good small shrub for a small garden. Plant it next to a rock and watch it mold itself to cover the rock. 'Tom Thumb' is a good dwarf form: "An elfin form of the 'Cranberry Cotoneaster' with dainty near-oval leaves. Quite slow growing, but will root where its little branches touch the ground and form a small mat after a few years." [WR]

Cyclamen hederifolium: "Makes colonies of marbled leaves." [R] "This is one of the hardiest species. The beautiful leaves are infinitely variable even on a single plant and the white or pink flowers are produced occasionally during the summer and in abundance throughout the fall." [M] You may have trouble with cyclamen if animals discover the corms. The wrong combination of cold and wet may decimate them, but grown in the right place there is nothing to compare with a sweep of *C. hederifolium,* or in a warmer spot, *C. coum.*

Cytisus decumbens: "Low shrub, 6"-10" tall by 3"-4" wide. Bright yellow flowers." [CA] There are a number of good rock garden brooms. Some will provide medium-sized shrubs for large accent. Some are spiny. A good hybrid that some catalogs have sometimes is *C. 'Kewensis'.* Grow something near brooms that self-sows a little, such as *Erinus alpinus* or *Chaenorrhinum oregani-folium,* so that when the shrub expands you won't need to rescue anything precious.

Daphne cneorum: A lovely sweet-scented, low shrub. After *D. mezereum* this is the most often seen daphne in gardens and therefore has less rarity value than the cult species that can be trouble-some to grow and hard to find. But it is probably the best of them all. *D. mezereum* is one of the first plants to flower in the whole garden and therefore worth keeping in spite of its slightly weedy habit. *D. cneorum* never misbehaves except to die off in patches without adequate explanation. "Covered with masses of intensely fragrant pink flowers." [CA]

Delosperma nubigenum: "Full sun, good drainage. Very low-spreading, succulent, yellowish foliage, bright yellow-orange flow-ers in June." [W] "This succulent-leaved plant makes a fine ground cover in a sunny location. It is drought tolerant and noninvasive, producing bright yellow flowers in spring. The vivid green foliage turns red in the winter sun. It is 1" high and hardy enough to grow in the Denver Botanic Garden." [M] Yes it is hardy for us too. Other delospermas, which are South African natives, are not hardy here but are worth trying a little further south. Try for instance *D. cooperi.* "Hardy in Denver but not in Vail." [CA]

Dianthus: Grow several of the alpine species, for instance *D. freynii* ("stiff, gray-green leaves" [CA]); *D. gratianopolitanus* ("tight cushions, fragrant" [CA]), *D. microlepis* ("tight carpet, nearly stem-less" [R], "green, curved, needle like leaves" [CA]); *D. nitidus* ("bright green rosettes...shiny pink flowers...dark calyx" [CA]); *D. petraeus noeanus* ("spiny buns...reminiscent of shimmering fire-works" [WR] "white fringed flowers" [R]); D. simulans ("tufts like pincushions" [R]); *D. subacaulis* ("gray-green...nice pink" [CA]). If you don't mind losing a plant soon after it blooms with only a sport-ing chance of having it a second year, grow *D. alpinus.* Also grow a few of the many dwarf hybrids such as 'Little Joe', 'Mars', 'Tiny Rubies' ("tiny double rosy carnations" [R]) but not the larger hybrids unless you can find a place in the border for them. Anything that looks like a carnation looks wrong near rock plants. *D. deltoides* has some good color forms but can become a nuisance when it produces endless seedlings of indifferent colors.

Dicentra cuccularia: "Dutchman's Breeches. Snowy flowers like little pantaloons hung out to dry in the April woods." [R] "Racemes of nodding, two-spurred white flowers." [W] What you get are tiny rhizomes. Plant these, watch the leaves disappear and understand that you will have to wait until next April to see them. Meanwhile they sit for most of the year just underground so mark the spot and don't disturb or slice them inadvertently.

Dodecatheon meadia: "Delightful cyclamenlike white or pale pink flowers on a tall spike in May; basal rosette of narrow leaves." [W] "Robust Eastern species that retains the firm green leaves well into summer." [S] You will need a location that retains some moisture for this. Everybody should grow some representative of the emblematic genus of NARGS and this is one of the easier species in the East. *D. pulchellum* is okay too.

Douglasia vitaliana: See *Vitaliana primulifolia.*

Draba dedeana: "Pure white flowers on 2" stems. Small, wide, bristle-tipped leaves. Spain and the Pyrenees. One of the best species. Zone 4." [S] Most of the white drabas are rather dull plants and the good drabas are nearly all yellow, so this has two advantages.

Draba lasiocarpa: "Forms a small hummock of most unique foliage. Stiff, green, pine needle leaves. Racemes of pale yellow. Eastern Europe mountains. Zone 5." [S] Zone 4 is okay too. *Draba oligosperma:* "Small, rigid, gray-green leaves form tight rosettes that huddle together in a hard cushion." [CA] These are just two of many species of *Draba* blooming before the crocus and into May. Get several species to compare the tight foliage of the buns and mats. If you succumb to drabamania you will graduate to growing them from seed. Some need protection from winter wet but most are hardy through the worst weather.

Draba sibirica: "Is one of the easiest species to grow in a mostly sunny site." [WR] And therefore needs a special mention because it makes quite extensive mats and not just tiny buns.

Dryas octopetala: "Easy and beautiful. Large white flowers and silky seed heads. Most attractive dark, mottled foliage makes a neat ground cover." [S] "Evergreen creeper with large white flowers like single roses. Leaves like miniature oak leaves." [R] Probably best in a sandy scree in our climate. Some gardeners grow enormous mats of dryas but mine gets damaged each winter and takes time to revive in spring.

Edraianthus graminifolius: "A stunning crevice plant featuring especially thin grassy green foliage. The violet-blue flowers are abundant on prostrate stems." [S] There are many subspecies of *E. graminifolius* from different geographic locations with small differences. All the kinds I have grown have been excellent and the abundant selfsowing they do is welcome. *E. pumilio* is even prettier but not so amenable. "Beautiful violet-purple trumpets in late spring." [CA]

Erica carnea: There are so many varieties of heathers that some nurseries specialize in *Calluna* and *Erica,* and devotees form societies to exchange cultivars and cultural information. Plant a few specimen plants at first to test your site for soil (it should be peaty and never dry out totally) and climate (some member of the family will grow in most parts of the United States and Canada). Collecting forms can be addictive.

Erigeron compositus: "Bright lavender flowers on dwarf downy foliaged plant an inch high." [R] You can expect to get a plant of *E. compositus* at most plant sales. Since it is variable, a plant from a mail-order nursery is probably going to be a good form. In any case you should plant several forms of this Western daisy.

Erigeron scopulinus: "Rock crevices. Small white daisies. Excellent for troughs." [S] The small leaves make a tight mat and the daisies are not very numerous but look just right.

Erinus alpinus: "Rose-purple flowers." [Rk] Will selfsow into cracks and crannies but it is small enough to be harmless to most of its neighbors. There are white and pink forms.

Eriogonum umbellatum: "An attractive mat of green, silver-backed leaves and tall stems of cream flowers in July." [S] "Can form mats or sub-shrubs." [CA] It is very variable with forms of differing size, color, and habit. But it is one of the easier buckwheats.

Erysimum kotschyanum: "This excellent plant soon forms carpets of yellow over tight foliage. An easy and valuable plant for any sunny position." [S] Most erysimums are short-lived, even biennial. This one is "permanent" and divides easily to spread around. I have never found seedlings though. Its disadvantage is that it resembles a draba and one would like different genera to look different.

Eunomia oppositifolia: "One of the tiniest woody shrubs known. A delightful plant that creates a flat, even mat of gray, fleshy, round leaves less than 1" high. Short stems carry heads of pale lavender flowers in very early spring. A hardy plant from the mountains of Lebanon." [S] It has lived for me through the harshest of winters without protection. The leaf-flower color combination is ravishing and it blooms with the earliest drabas. It may be listed as *Aethionema oppositifolia.*

Genista delphinensis: "Short, flattened stems make an interesting effect. Yellow broom flowers. Zone 4." [S] This plant makes a mat that is impossible to weed. If weeds get out of hand you will have to dig up pieces and replant them. But it is well worth having for its winged stems and cheerful color. Another good easy broom is *G. dalmatica.* The leaves are spiny, but not ferocious, complicating weeding.

Gentiana acaulis: "Gorgeous deep-blue trumpets in late spring. Creeping evergreen mats of rosette foliage." [S] "Royal-blue trumpet flowers in early spring." [CA] Several subspecies of *G. acaulis* exist with different-sized leaves, usually from different locations in the Alps. Some people have had difficulty in finding the right place in the garden to produce the trumpets.

Gentiana scabra: "Usually producing procumbent stems with many large, brilliant blue flowers in September and October. Wonderful draped over a rock." [W] "An exquisite fall blooming gentian from Japan. Very late season, deep-blue flowers clustered at the stem tips making a striking scene set against fallen autumn leaves." [S] "A fine October-blooming gentian with a somewhat candelabralike pattern of growth. It should be allowed more than one season's growth to produce its lovely upturned flowers of blue." [WR] All true but in the Berkshires three factors must be reckoned with: falling leaves may cover the flowers, early frosts may damage them, deer are poised at the edge of the garden in search of *G. scabra.*

Gentiana septemfida: "Dark-blue, late summer flowers in big clusters." [S] "Narrow, bell-shaped, dark-blue flowers form in terminal clusters." [CA] There are gentians for all seasons and this is about the best of the summer bloomers.

Geranium dalmaticum: "Mounds of shining green, aromatic leaves, tinted crimson in autumn, are smothered in clear-pink flowers in summer." [S] "Plant this in a mostly sunny area with other mid-sized possessions." [WR] There is also a white form. Give it plenty of space to make a carpet a yard across. Geraniums on the whole are overbearing in a rock garden but this one is well behaved and lovely.

Geranium sanguineum is not to be let loose in a small garden but there is a form "Lancastriense" that is nearly allowable. "Pale pink flowers, 6" mat." [C] "Light pink with darker veins." [WR]

Gypsophila cerastioides: "Low mounds of rounded velvety leaves. In summer large, white cup-shaped flowers striped pink. Best in rich scree or trough." [S]

Gypsophila repens: "Creeping Baby's Breath has multitudes of quarter-inch flowers and blooms for weeks in late spring." [R] "Dainty pink flowers." [Rk] Normally white, good forms are pink but not often a very strong color. "Low haze of pink...effective in a cascading position." [WR]

Helianthemum nummularium: "Delightful flowers display in

A terrace rock garden built on the foundation of an old barn.

ABOVE. A woodland garden in May.
BELOW. A scree bed.

ABOVE. A crevice garden.
BELOW. Young plants in a covered coldframe for the winter.

ABOVE. *Iberis sempervirens* colonizing the wall of a raised bed.
BELOW. Seedlings in a sand bed need watering during droughts.

ABOVE. Kabschia saxifrages growing in a hollow log.
BELOW. A raised bed.

ABOVE LEFT. Saxifrage 'White Pixie' is an easy, mossy saxifrage.

ABOVE RIGHT. Kabschia saxifrage 'Queen Mother' growing in a container.

BELOW LEFT. *Arnebia echioides*, the prophet flower.

BELOW RIGHT. *Draba rigida* forms a hard, tight mound.

ABOVE LEFT. *Lewisia cotyledon* is native to the U.S. Northwest.

ABOVE RIGHT. *Phacelia sericea* is widespread in western U.S.

BELOW LEFT. *Erigeron chrysopsidis brevifolius* is one
of the great yellow daisies.

BELOW RIGHT. *Talinum okanoganense* is a permanent,
slow growing mat.

ABOVE. A variegated hybrid daphne, 'Carol Mackie'.
BELOW. *Silene acaulis* growing in a crevice.

ABOVE. *Phlox subulata* selfsowing in the grass.
BELOW. Pavement garden with raised beds.

ABOVE. *Houstonia caerulea,* also known as Quaker Ladies
or bluets, at home in a crevice.

BELOW LEFT. *Asclepias tuberosa* is a magnet for the monarch butterfly.

BELOW RIGHT. *Cypripedium calceolus,* one of the many forms
of yellow lady slipper.

ABOVE LEFT. A low thrift, *Armeria juniperifolia.*

ABOVE RIGHT. *Jasione amethystina,* a tiny member of Campanulaceae from southern Spain.

BELOW LEFT. *Edraianthus pumilio,* or wheel-bell, is nonweedy and precious.

BELOW RIGHT. *Iberis candolleana* is endemic to the French Alps.

ABOVE. A raised bed in spring.
BELOW. Conifers and deciduous shrubs in June.

ABOVE. A perennial border in early summer.
BELOW. Heathers in August.

ABOVE. Grasses in October.
BELOW. A weeping larch in fall.

ABOVE. Conifers in winter.
BELOW. The author transplanting in his greenhouse.

ABOVE LEFT. *Dianthus alpinus* is perhaps the most recalcitrant of the alpine pinks.

ABOVE RIGHT. One of the many forms of *Gentiana acaulis*.

BELOW LEFT. *Erigeron scopulinus* is a small, compact plant from Arizona.

BELOW RIGHT. *Townsendia eximia* is short lived but worth growing.

sunny colors." [S] Most of the species helianthemums are yellow. This species is very variable and scores of color forms are available. The leaves too can vary from green to gray. They also vary in hardiness and you may want to take cuttings of the ones you are fond of. In any case a given plant is unlikely to last more than two seasons but they are so colorful that it is worth trying to keep them. Allow at least one to two feet across for final size.

Hepatica: "Some of the most beautiful and earliest of spring flowering plants for rich leaf mold soil in the woodland garden. Good drainage is a must." [S] "Very early in spring the blue or white blossoms emerge and open in the sun." [R] There are two North American species—*H. americana* ("leaves with rounded lobes often mottled" [W]) and *H. acutiloba* ("evergreen leaves with three sharply pointed lobes." [W])—that seem to differ only in leaf shape. There are many variations in form. *H. nobilis* is the European species; it has bigger flowers and more varieties. Rarer is *H. transylvanica* and its hybrid *H. X. ballardii.* Any one of them could be tried in a shady rock garden even though a woodland setting is more like home.

Heuchera hallii: "A petite alpine from Pikes Peak in Colorado. Slender stems of tiny white bells above little 1" leaves." [S] The border coral bells look wrong in a rock garden and the larger species are better at the edge of a woodland garden, but there are a few suitable alpine species. It doesn't mind sun.

Hippocrepis comosa: "Heads of yellow pea-like blooms are generously produced on a flat mat of green pinnate foliage." [WR]

Houstonia caerulea: "Sun or part shade; good soil. Tiny tufts of evergreen leaves; solitary, rather large, pale to medium blue flowers on long stalks; blooms primarily in April or May, but at least in the South, sporadically all year." [W] For us it grows wild in full sun, grass meadow, poor soil. Bluets, or Quaker Ladies, is delightful. If you move a good color form into the garden it fades away seeming to prefer the crowded meadow.

Hylomecon japonicum: "Early spring yellow poppies. Elegant pinnate leaves. A beautiful herbaceous perennial native to Japanese woodlands." [S] It resembles *Chelidonium majus,* the weedy celandine poppy, but is shorter, prettier, has fewer flowers, and is not weedy.

Hymenoxys acaulis: "Rocky Mountain native with dense tufts of silky, woolly leaves." [CA] This lovely yellow composite is not always a "beginner's plant," there are so many forms from high alpine to tubby Great Plains kinds. If it lives and blooms through its first summer collect seed and sow it next winter.

Hypoxis hirsuta: "Yellow Star Grass. Sun or part shade, ordinary loam." [W] An iris relative like a small yellow Sisyrinchium.

Iberis saxatilis: "Dense mat 2"-3" tall." [CA] I like all the iberis I have ever grown.

Iberis sempervirens: "Mounds of white in spring and deep green masses the rest of the year are indispensable in the rock garden." [R] Candytuft white is bright and clean, making this a very useful foil for too busy or too drab color schemes.

Iris cristata: "A woodland dwarf from eastern America. Running habit in loose humusy soil. Deciduous." [S] "Sky-blue flowers on 4" stems." [R] "Give it a little sun and well-drained soil." [M] "Should form nice little drifts in a hurry." [WR] Usually blue. Many color forms have been selected, including a vigorous white. It will tolerate a rock garden but wants to run around and prefers the edge of the woodland. If it has good roots, plant it with the rhizome top showing above ground. If the root system is weak plant it slightly covered to keep it stable. The rhizome has to be horizontal.

Lavandula angustifolia: Lavenders are good shrub substitutes in a small rock garden, especially in their miniature forms. In time they grow too bulky, so keep them trimmed back and neat-looking during the spring clean-up.

Leontopodium alpinum: "Gray-green foliage covered with woolly hair bears thick, white woolly bracts on 10" stems. A European classic." [CA] Everybody has to grow edelweiss at least once in order to impress one's nongardening friends. If you like it go on to the more refined *L. nivale* and many other species.

Lewisia cotyledon: "Our glorious native is considered one of the best. Striking fleshy leaves often crinkled or notched. Numerous spring flowers in a rainbow of possible seedling colors (pink, white, orange, salmon) often candy-striped. Needs perfect drainage, grit around the crown. Afternoon shade of rocks." [S] "Grow in humus and grit. Likes part shade and acid soil." [R] "Likes well-drained soil or scree. Avoid winter wet." [CA] You must try out many places in your garden if at first you are unsuccessful. When you find the right spot expect an unimagined burst of pride and pleasure.

Lilium pumilum: "The coral lily is a delightful, small plant suitable for a rock garden. It blooms in late spring with small, scarlet Turk's Cap flowers and does well in sun or part shade. One and a half feet tall." [M] This is one of the few lilies that look well in a rock garden but you have to remember that even a small lily is a large plant compared with the mats and buns that predominate. Place it with this in mind.

Linum flavum: "Sunny, yellow flowers and lush, broad-leaved foliage make this a notable plant in late spring." [R] The other good yellow flax is *L. capitatum.*

Linum capitatum: "A robust and free-flowering species from the mountains of Bulgaria. Dense heads of sizable, rich yellow flowers." [S]

Lithodora oleifolia: "A splendid wanderer from the Pyrenees with tufts of hairy gray-green leaves spreading by underground stolons. Pink buds open to large opalescent blue flowers. Quite hardy in loose, rich, neutral to lime soil. Zone 5." [S] When you first see *L. diffusa* 'Grace Ward' you will certainly want to grow it for its rich blue flowers. It is tender in my climate but occasionally worth a one-year stand. *L. oleifolia* is a more faithful companion.

Mentha requieni: "Purple, moss-like, aromatic. Moist soil or part-shade, half-hardy." [NG]. This is a tiny mint from Corsica with the most delicious smell when you crush the leaves or walk on it. It nearly always comes back each spring, even though it is not really hardy, either by selfsowing or by stoloniferous roots that survive.

Mitchella repens: "This beautiful native plant is a wonderful ground cover in shaded rock gardens or woodland areas. It blooms in spring with pairs of small, white flowers followed by red berries. The dark-green leaves are a delight throughout the year. Zones 3-8." [M] "Small leatherlike dark green leaves with a paler mid-vein; charming paired white flowers densely pubescent inside." [W] "Partridge-berry is a wee creeper that slowly forms a flat-as-a-pancake patch in a woodsy, shady, slightly acid site." [WR] Wild in our woods so we don't need to plant it.

Orostachys aggregatum: "Succulent rosettes somewhere between pea and jade green." [WR]

Orostachys iwarenge: "Bouquet of gray roses sitting flat on the ground." [Rk]

Orostachys furusei: "Spreading blue rosettes that send up smokestacks of dusty rose flowers in October. It doesn't look hardy but it is. From Japan." [R] *Ohwi (Flora of Japan)* says these plants are different and should be called sedums. Perhaps they look more like sempervivums. They get a lot of attention in flower though you could hardly call them flamboyant.

Orostachys spinosum: "Intricately scaled, heavily spined globes, up to 2" across." [R] The spines are not very frightening and the flower stem is phallic. Unlike *O. furusei* this doesn't spread by stolons. The rosette that flowers will die but usually there are offsets that grow to make a larger plant next season.

Papaver miyabeanum: "Japanese. Related to the Iceland Poppy but more heat tolerant. Gray-green basal leaves, beautiful delicate white flowers." [W] "Lemon-yellow flowers over interesting compact foliage." [CA] This poppy is in the nudicaule group, usually a low-growing plant.

Penstemon davidsonii: "Creeping evergreen mats. Small round leaves. Lavender to purple from the California Sierras." [S] The most permanent of the penstemons are the "shrubby" group. The stems are woody and the leaves try to stay green all winter but often lose the battle to cold winds. Don't cut off the damaged stems until after flowering. The plants usually recover their good looks exactly at flowering time. A handkerchief of spun polyester spread over a plant and held down with stones helps with the winter-kill problem.

Penstemon fruticosus: "Miniature evergreen shrublet." [R] "6"–12" tall with blue to lavender flowers." [CA] Another shrubby penstemon with many forms. Some of them can be bushes two feet across. On the whole, easier than most members of this group.

Penstemon hirsutus pygmaeus: "Rosettes of summer green and winter bronze foliage as well as violet flowers in spring." [M] "A little guy with smokey-mauve blossoms on compact 5"–6" stems." [WR] This is one of the eastern penstemons (nonwoody). Seedlings are likely to appear and may yield plants that look like the tall form of *P. hirsutus.*

Phlox amoena: "This native phlox produces vivid, deep-pink flowers in mid-spring. The decumbent stems are lined with somewhat hairy, slender leaves that turn a lovely purple red in winter. Sun or part shade. 6"." [M]

Phlox bifida: "Dainty, starry flowers of palest blue. Native Midwestern species is enchanting." [R] "A dome covered in early summer by large lavender-blue flowers with deep-cut petals like perfect snowflakes. Zone 4." [S] "8"–10" mound of spiny foliage." [CA] "A fantastic species." [WR] This makes a mound or mat as big as *P. subulata* and can be treated in much the same way.

Phlox divaricata: "The eastern American woodland phlox. Branchlets spread and root to form colonies." [S] "Woodland phlox makes running clumps of blue in streamside woods. Sweetly fragrant flowers in clusters for weeks in spring. Grow in rich soil in shade or sun." [R] "Indispensable in the spring garden." [M] You could have this in a rock garden but only for a short time. It needs the full run of a woodland to seed and spread. Many color forms but the ordinary blue is probably the best.

Phlox stolonifera: "The creeping woodland phlox from the East Coast." [S] "Abundant clusters of long-tubed blossoms adorning 6"–8" stems." [WR] Again best where it can spread in a woodland clearing. Choose one of the good color selections, the species has a more dull color.

Phlox subulata: "Prostrate mats smothered in late April to May with showy flowers." [Rk] My favorite species amongst the "common" phloxes. Go to town selecting good colors and leaf forms. The word subulata means prickly (actually awl-shaped). Allow seedlings to flourish in the lawn and gain a convincing wild look to that stretch of garden—this stands a certain amount of mowing and foot traffic. If you have a very tidy mind you may not want the garden to spill over in this way. We have it with thymes too, much nicer than weedy grass and by now beyond control. Nurseries use the name *P. douglasii* to cover many hybrids of unknown origin, but *P. subulata* is frequently in their heritage.

Potentilla verna nana: "Sun, rockery. Tight buns of lustrous bright-green evergreen foliage. Bright yellow flowers in early spring." [W]

Primula acaulis: "Flowers borne singly on 3" stems, keep succeeding one another for weeks." [R] This is *the* primrose. Not as easy to keep as the showy polyanthas but much more elegant. Its correct name is now *P. vulgaris.*

Primula denticulata: "The drumstick primrose. The early appearance of flower buds means that occasionally the very first ones are caught by late frosts. Put it in a protected position in shade in either a very wet or average garden soil." [M] "Spherical heads of crowded purple flowers on stout 12" stems." [CA] There are some strong violet-reds and pale lilac-blues and a good white. The first buds nestle low down among the leaves and gradually grow to as much as a foot high as the flowers open.

Primula japonica: "This is a beautiful, late spring-flowering species that has flower stalks to two and a half feet. It requires considerable moisture to bloom well with one to six superimposed, many-flowered umbels." [M] You can use it in the woodland but it likes to be near water. It is the easiest of the candelabra primroses. If your plants selfsow they will produce all colors from red on the blue side to white. If they don't, they are probably not happy enough to stay very long at all.

Primula X juliana (correct name is *P. X pruhoniciana*): The julianas are hybrids of *P. juliae* and should display its stoloniferous habit. "Relatively small plants with dark green crinkly foliage and good-sized flowers." [CA] The crosses can be with *P. vulgaris* in which case there would be only one flower on a stem, or with *P. elatior* or *P. veris* (or *P. polyantha*) in which case there would be multiple heads. Give them a shady place rather than the rough and tumble of a woodland to get them established. Later you can move chunks to the woods. In any case division after two or three years is needed to keep the plants flowering well. Primulas respond to fresh ground and feeding.

Primula vulgaris: "The English primrose. Pale yellow, fragrant, early." [C]

Ptilotrichum spinosum: "A shrubby alyssum relative. Densely branched and spiny shrub covered in a haze of rosy flowers in early summer." [S] "Shrubby domes of wiry silver stems, just 2" or 3" high. Rosy pink flowers in summer." [R] The word shrub needn't scare you, this is just a low mound only a foot across. The color you get from seed is off-white and it pays to get a "roseum" form if you want a brighter color.

Pulsatilla vulgaris: "Pasque flowers usher in spring. Their huge purple goblets are furry on the outside and close at night. On bright April days, before the leaves are on the trees, their blossoms will amaze you with their determined insistence that spring is here!" [R] "These anemone relatives emerge in late winter as furry buds that open to big satiny goblets with golden stamens. Then the leaves unfold and the flowers become long-lasting, fluffy, seed heads that are quite showy." [S] "Exquisite, chalice-shaped purple flowers. Decorative fluffy seed heads." [W] All the rhapsodies about pulsatillas are warranted.

Sanguinaria canadensis: "Pure white, single flowers in the spring. Woodland." [C] "Ethereal 2"–4" flowers, white with yellow centers; attractive broad-lobed leaves last all summer." [W] "An early spring delight as the striking white blossoms appear on stems that are clasped in the unfurled leaf." [WR] The lovely bloodroot only lasts a few days but it is so exquisite it should be in every garden. Besides, the leaves are elegant masterpieces.

Saponaria ocymoides: "Pink spreading flowers late May–June. Easy. Bright." [Rk] Good mat-forming and easy going.

Saponaria X olivana: "A crisp clump of bright green leaves, about 2"-3" high, with showy bright pink flowers that lay out flat on the ground, tightly around the exterior of the plant." [WR] Another reliable soapwort.

Saxifraga X apiculata: "Closely packed cushion made up of 1/2" rosettes. Yellow clustered flowers on three-inch stems. The easiest kabschia saxifrage to grow in the garden." [R] "Crisp foliage and an inflorescence of primrose yellow flowers on compact 2" stems." [WR] Most of the Porophylla section of *Saxifraga* (kabschias) flower too early, grow too slowly, or display too much temperament to grow in the open garden. Give them container conditions with coldframe protection. This one is quite reliable outside.

Saxifraga: Mossy section. These plants are common enough in England but many gardeners in the Northeast find them troublesome. I feel they are worth trying and if and when they produce the brown patches that disfigure the mats after blooming and after winter you can root cuttings in a sandy mix quite easily. Some people step on them to get the stems in contact with the soil and claim they will root in place, but I have had no such experience. "Peter Pan" is a good one. "Vivid crimson flowers in spring." [S]

Saxifraga paniculata: The silver saxifrages are the easiest and most satisfying for permanence. This species covers many forms and subspecies. All of them are suitable for any rock garden but are better if you can avoid full sun all day. "Clumping mounds of silvery green foliage with white to pale cream flowers." [CA]

Sedum cauticola: "It has rounded, succulent leaves, wants part-shade and produces rosy-pink flowers several weeks before those of its cousin, *S. sieboldii.*" [M] "Ascending stems with broad gray-green leaves, erect inflorescences of rose-purple flowers in early autumn." [W] "Picturesque rock plants with deep grayish-blue leaves and near ruby-red flowers." [WR]

Sedum pluricaule: A well behaved and handsome sedum.

Sedum kamschaticum: "Semi-evergreen mat forming species from northeast Asia; lax stems with rather thin, spatulate bright-green leaves; large yellow flowers in midsummer." [W]

Sedum spathulifolium: Some forms of this West Coast native are a bit tender for me and they all get damaged by very cold exposed conditions. It is probably okay in southern Connecticut though and all forms are very beautiful.

Sempervivum arachnoideum: "Heavily webbed white in spring." [Rk] "Compact buttonlike rosettes with a white web. The more sun you give them the stronger the webbing will be." [WR] "Threadlike hairs from leaf to leaf." [CA]

Silene schafta: "Long blooming from May to September." [Rk] This plant has the same "value" as *Saponaria ocymoides* and is a standard in everybody's garden. It may selfsow and need a little discipline.

Silene virginica: "Sun or light shade; good drainage. Spectacular plant; rosettes of evergreen leaves; branched stems bearing 1 1/2" to 2" flowers with brilliant scarlet bi-lobed petals; blooms for long period in spring." [W]

Thymus lanuginosus: Introduce thymes into your rock garden with great circumspection. This one is woolly and slower than most. If you love them, try to clear a sunny bank just for their benefit and find companion plants that can compete.

Tiarella wherryi: "Pink flowered foamflower that stays in a

clump. Has more pointed, palmate leaves than *T. cordifolia.*" [R]
Whether or not you lump these two species you may still want this
form. Grow it in woodland or a very shady place.

Trillium grandiflorum: "Queen of the spring woodland all over
the East. Large snowy flowers produced in abundance on a mature
plant are breathtaking." [R]

Veronica armena: "Small charming plant only 2" tall, with ra-
diating stems. Produces small loose sprays of gentian-blue flowers
in mid-summer." [CA] "Deeply divided leaves and bright blue
blooms." [WR] Some veronicas are a bit weedy but this is quite
well-behaved.

Veronica prostrata: "Makes a deep green carpet that bursts forth
with cobalt blue flowers in early summer." [S] "Beautiful patch of
long lasting color in June." [R] There are white, pink, and blue
forms of this mat-forming plant.

Viola labradorica: "This native violet has beautiful dark-purple
leaves throughout most of the year and small violet flowers for
much of the summer. It is compact and not invasive." [M] It is difficult to recommend any easy violets because they are all more or less
invasive. This one produces such small plants that they are not too
destructive and you can pull them out if they are in the way. The
only violets not to fear are the impossible to grow ones from the
Rockies and the Alps.

Viola pedata: "About the showiest violet and one of the
showiest wildflowers, flattish inch-wide (or larger) blue-purple
flowers, dissected leaves." [W] Some people find this spreads
around. We have found it a good violet.

Vitaliana primuliflora (=*Douglasia vitaliana*): Lovely mat of
hard silver-green foliage with yellow flowers just after the drabas
have gone over. "Clear yellow flowers on a carpet of gray-green
leaves." [R]

Though they are not the only sources for the plants, these nurseries
can be a convenient way to get started. I want to thank the nurseries

mentioned for allowing me to quote from their catalogs.

Siskiyou Rare Plant Nursery, Dept 1, 2825 Cummings Road, Medford, OR 97501
Cricklewood Nursery, 11907 Nevers Road, Snohomish, WA 98290
We-Du Nurseries, Route 5, Box 724, Marion, NC 28752-9338
Woodland Rockery, 6210 Klam Road., Otter Lake, MI 48464
Colorado Alpines, Inc., P.O. Box 2708, Avon, CO 81620
Nature's Garden, 40611 Highway 226, Scio, Oregon 97374

As of summer 1994, Montrose has closed, Rocknoll has been sold, and Rice Creek and Colorado Alpines no longer sell mail-order.

∾ ∾

Postscript: Aftercare

৯ ৯ WHAT DO YOU do when the plants you have ordered by mail arrive? Here are a few suggestions. There are no fixed rules to follow because there are too many variables: the nursery of origin, the size of the plant, its state of health, and most of all your own facilities. However you must assume that the plant that has traveled by air has all the potential ills that you might have on your first flight; it could be dehydrated, hungry, travel sick, jet lagged, and just plain tired. It also could be very young and possibly ill. If you have nowhere to put it except in the garden then do something like what I will now describe.

Bare root plants, (shrubs and trees): Half fill a bucket with water and sit the roots in water for several hours. For a small plant use a vase or a cup. Put the container outside in a shady spot if the weather is warm; if it is really cold try a porch or somewhere cool indoors. It must not freeze or boil or bake—common sense obviously, but you would be surprised how easy it is to forget the sun moves, nights get cold, furnaces kick on, etc., etc. Overnight is not too long for a shrub or a wilted plant to sit in water and since UPS arrives in the afternoon, overnight is a good idea for most plants.

Bare root plants (alpines and small perennials): Treat these as you would a transplant of your own seedlings. Have prepared a container of compost and several clean pots of different sizes. The compost should be a mix of "what works best for you." I would use fifty-percent soilless peat-based compost and fifty-percent coarse sand with a good helping of slow-release fertilizer. There would be nothing wrong with adding soil or leaf mold and varying the proportions. You must remember that the aim is to get the plant actively growing again, so the mix should be airy, moist but not soggy, and contain nutrients. Also the plant will be planted out in the garden before long, and this means the compost must be compatible with your soil. There is no point in coaxing a plant to start regrowth in a mixture heavily laced with perlite if you are then going to plant it out in a garden of heavy clay. Nor should you overdo the sand if the ultimate planting out place is a leafy woodland.

Plants already in compost: Many plants arrive with something clinging to their roots that will be wrapped in foil, plastic, newspaper, or some other material holding it all together. You should shake off the loose material and find out whether the roots are actually growing in it or whether the material is merely for protection. Protective material, usually peat, may hide the fact that the roots are folded over or bunched up in an unnatural way and need to be spread out before planting. Don't incorporate the dry peat with your own compost, it may throw the texture out of balance and decrease wetability. If the roots are in fact growing in the medium it is more than likely they were taken from a rootbound pot and are bunched up. Straighten out the root endings, trim off the broken pieces, use judgment about how much growing medium to retain, and place in an adequately large pot—one big enough to hold the roots comfortably spread out, but not so large that the plant "drowns" in soil. "Almost potbound" is about right. You may have to trim off an unusually long root, but this requires great discretion and even greater courage.

Plants still in their containers: You could knock it out and discard loose compost from the rootball and replant it in a slightly larger pot if needed. If the plant looks perfectly happy in its pot, then leave it there (I mean not hopelessly potbound or loosely planted).

When the plants are repotted, stand them in an inch of water and leave them overnight. Next day take them outside into a shady place for a week or so before you plant them in the garden. If you have to delay planting out they should be fine for weeks but may need more sun and water. I think it is a waste of time to plant out real invalids or plants that are too small, so find a protected home for these orphans. What is "big enough" and "healthy enough" to plant out is a matter of judgment accumulated over years of failures and successes. Don't expect a hundred-percent success rate with any shipment.

If you have nowhere to put plants except in the garden (you may not have a holding place or even a work place; the roots of a bare root plant may be larger than you can accommodate in any of your store of used pots) it is imperative to cover them with an upturned pot or bucket to protect them from sun and harsh weather. Since these will be left in place until the plant shows signs of new life or dies, the pots will need a stone to hold them in place. By the end of the shipping season you will be thoroughly tired of looking at a garden full of upturned plant pots.

In general, discard as much imported soil or compost as is compatible with the health of the plant. It will be a different compost from the one you use and may carry pests, slug eggs, diseases (not likely but it has happened), and weed seeds, moss, liverwort, or other weeds (this very often happens). This advice is even more important if you are going to keep the plant in an alpine house as the whole house could become infected. Be ruthless in destroying liverwort. Many gardens have been disfigured by this pest being inadvertently or carelessly introduced from a nursery. Remember that during their busiest season a nursery may not be able to weed every plant before shipping so you have to be prepared for Good and Evil to arrive together by UPS and take necessary precautions.

⌁ ⌁

Succulents

⅋ ⅋ WE USUALLY THINK of succulents as greenhouse plants, those sensuously touchable plants with bloated leaves that ooze unpleasantly when wounded and attract nibbling rodents. The mesembryanthemum family, the euphorbia family, and the crassula family come to mind. Perhaps most of the euphorbias should be lumped with cactus as succulents that are mostly hostile to casual touching, brushing, and feeling. There are many succulents that are hardy and not only behave well in the rock garden but look well. They have a presence that some people find exotic but which in fact is a fairly commonplace look in nature and one that can be used to provide contrasts with other textures such as the mounds of dianthus, the buns of androsace, the mats of campanula, the shrubby quality of helianthemum, and the leafyness of geum and potentilla. Unfortunately many happy succulents seem to need a lot of space and grow rather quickly, so care is needed in placing them. A better way of putting it is that care is needed in choosing neighbors that will resist being overrun. But there are plenty of succulents that not only make well-behaved neighbors but which are "choice" themselves and difficult plants to keep.

The genus that everybody grows willingly or not is *Sedum*. This is a satisfying genus to collect because usually the only reason for failure would be cold and wet. The leaves often change color in the fall and are retained for a long time even when not strictly evergreen. Most of them are only too eager to show their accommodating ways. I would divide them into a half dozen types and relatives. If you don't want to collect species for fun and only want to grow a few representative species, you might still want to take into account that two sedums with similar qualities can have enough decorative differences so that placing two or three of them together can provide a subtle carpet of color and texture that only thymes can rival. The flowers too cannot be dismissed but to get any effect from them you need a large patch, not a one-inch cutting, or better still several adjacent patches of contrasting color or texture. The flowers are starry, like saxifrages but perhaps individually not as handsome. The whites are not as clear, the pinks are brownish, and the yellows greenish—but en masse the effect is completely satisfying. One important item to note is that small pieces of sedum root very easily. Do *not* drop little bits of sedum anywhere. If you transplant, move a neat plug discarding any trailing pieces carefully on to a compost heap. Deep in the heap is best. If you drop a dianthus leaf it dies; if you drop a sedum leaf you get a sedum plant.

The following are horticultural, not botanical, types to help find the best place in the garden for a given species.

Type 1. Really weedy, even if handsome, sedums have a place in the garden but you have to understand and be prepared for their wicked ways: *S. acre, S. album, S. lydium, S. hispanicum, S. brevifolium, S. dasyphyllum.*

Type 2. Sedums with larger leaves that, although they grow outwards, remain more or less large mats: *S. spurium* and *S. kamtschaticum, S. ewersii, S. pluricaule, S. cauticola.* Since they lose a lot of stem and leaf over the winter the biggest danger here is that you plant small new plants too close to them in the spring. Try to remember their summer diameter and keep other plants outside this circle.

Type 3. Sedums that grow longish stems with handsome leaves that may be variegated either naturally or have special forms: *S. cauticola* is naturally multi-colored; *S. spurium* 'Variegatum'; *S. sieboldii* 'Medio-variegata'. These striking plants may not look comfortable with innocent alpines and perhaps may find better companions with hybrid dianthus or medium-sized composites such as *Aster alpinus*.

TYPE 4. Tall sedums that belong in a border or as accent plants in a large rock garden: *S. spectabile, S. telephioides, S. purpureum*. Some of these have variegated forms and can be used effectively even though the combination of succulence and variegated foliage may seem bizarre.

TYPE 5. Annuals. *S. coeruleum* is a haze of pale-blue stars among a pale film of succulent green. It never selfsows for me. *S. pilosum* makes tubby salt shakers of closely packed leaves with a bright pink (for a sedum) flower cluster. Save the seeds for this one too. It is strictly speaking a biennial.

TYPE 6. These would be plants worth growing as companion plants of alpine buns. It would really depend on where you lived what the list would consist of. They would be handsome, low, and non-invasive. The last qualification means not quite hardy to ensure that their inability to colonize is guaranteed and that cuttings would have to be carried over in the coldframe or alpine house. For me that would include *S. spathulifolium* in its various forms, *S. moranii, S. laxum,* and hybrids like 'Silvermoon'.

Rhodiolas are close to sedums and sometimes called sedums. *R. rosea* is typical. It has a thick root. The plant dies down for the winter leaving a circular medallion of buds showing on top of the stem. The exposed stem looks vulnerable but is quite hardy. There are other rhodiolas: *R. kirilowii, R. rhodantha*. Their arching stems can be very attractive when planted at the edge of a raised bed.

The genus rivaling *Sedum* in importance is *Sempervivum*. These form rosettes that look like miniature cabbages and that vary quite a lot in size. This has to do not only with the species but with the culture and age of the rosette. There are some with rosettes that stay small. The mat effect can be very beautiful. You might also like the non-homogeneous effect of a plant whose mature rosettes are two or three inches across while the immature rosettes remain small. Flowers of sempervivums are also of importance, sometimes quite beautiful as phallic columns are sent up from the center of each mature rosette and gradually form graceful croziers before they bloom, or flower looking vertically upwards with a flat bouquet that barely exceeds the width of the top of the column. Some people hate them or say they do. Like sedums, the colors are not vivid—creamy browns, brick reds, greeny yellows—but the individual florets are larger than sedums. The rosette dies after flowering and when you ultimately pull off the dead stalk, be gentle; try not to pull away too many adjacent rosettes. The hole you leave will be filled in quickly enough but there will be a ragged look to the mat and you are sure to spill earth over the mat that will stay there until the next heavy rain. Sempervivums have been hybridized extensively for color and size of mature rosette. The variations are particularly noticeable in spring but are lost amid the glorious garish colors of many other alpines. So if you want subtlety, grow them with silver saxifrages and other non-assertive plants. My own advice is to allow the flowers to mature and propagate the ones with interesting form and colors. This would not be the advice of most semp lovers who value most their enchanting early spring metallic grays and chestnut reds shining through the buttoned up dullness of the winter rosettes.

If I had to classify sempervivums, I think it would be how they reproduce themselves vegetatively. Type 1. The new rosette forms around the old one. Type 2. New rosettes form on the mound and roll off the mother plant. These tend to be "weedy." Type 3. New rosettes form on stolons. These are sometimes a strong, reddish color and affect the "look" of the plant. The stolons are above ground and easy to keep in check if needed. Type 4. The rosette splits, forming interestingly congested, hard shiny leaves.

Another way of classifying would be to distinguish the species from the hybrids and forms. The vast number are probably forms of *S. tectorum.* I assume everybody collects these forms at one time or another. The extravagant names and the ease of culture makes it a very attractive hobby. They can be used in containers of every description from seashells, logs, ceramic bowls of all sizes and shapes to discarded tires and chipped kitchen ware. They adorn and dignify the humblest *objet trouvé* and exist or subsist in the shallowest soil. Even a crack in a lump of discarded concrete has been the home of a semp. One utilitarian aspect of this willingness to grow is to use sempervivums as erosion controllers in the cracks of raised beds and dry walls.

Similar to *Sempervivum* in having rosettes but closer to *Sedum* is the genus *Rosularia.* The leaves are not as leathery as *Sempervivum* and they are not reliably hardy on the whole. According to the late Ronald Evans, the great authority on *Sedum*: They have five petals, sepals, carpels, and ten stamens; sempervivums have six to twelve petals and sepals and twice the number of stamens; in both cases the petals are separate. In *Rosularia* the flower is like a campanula with petals joined in a tube.

Orostachys is botanically like *Sedum* and can be lumped with it if you want. As far as the garden is concerned some of them look quite different from sedums. *O. spinosum* forms rosettes that are not only hard like a sempervivum but each leaf has a terminal spine. The rosette dies after flowering but often an offset forms to carry on the life of the plant. This is a specially desirable plant and far from weedy. *O. iwarenge* and *O. aggregata* are more sedumlike in the way they spread but the rosettes look like soft sempervivums and the colors are pale green and pinky gray.

In some warmer areas, *Crassula* and *Echeveria* and even *Dudleya* could be tried. In Massachusetts these would have to be taken indoors for the winter and therefore would "look wrong" in a rock garden. However in California these would certainly be considered rock plants.

Another family of plants that provides the rock garden with some worthwhile and some first rate plants is Portulacaceae. The genus *Portulaca* itself reminds us of two species. One is the annual weed (*P. oleracea*) that haunts the garden in summer. It grows by leaps and bounds, sprawling on the ground, from a tiny blob to an octopus with barnacles in a matter of a week. Its color isn't unattractive, a glaucous green, and its flowers are insignificant. But, it is intolerable, especially in good soil. It arrives in my garden at the same time as a pernicious mat-forming euphorbia weed and both have hundreds of seed in every inch of soil waiting to be stirred up close enough to the light to be reactivated. Fortunately both can be pulled out easily but not before they have grown big enough to make it worthwhile. In the meantime their presence defines a dirty garden. The other portulaca is the pretty annual with bright colors that selfsows even in cold climates. It doesn't look very good with alpines in general but you might want another kind of rock garden that includes a few.

Talinums are less flamboyant than the annual portulaca but are still too neon for some tastes. They have fleshy, linear leaves and like portulacas tend to open only in full sun. The flowers are characteristically cup shaped and tend to shiny magenta. This describes *T. grandiflorum* (6", tender), *T. calycinum* (6"), *T. spinosum* (low cushion, rose). The gem is *Talinum okanoganense,* a tight bun of crisscrossed stems with white flowers. *T. paniculatum* ('Jewels of Ophar') is a tallish leafy perennial grown as an annual but not colorful enough to give space to, except once in a while for fun.

Claytonias are also succulents. The eastern woodlander *C. virginica* has fleshy, linear leaves and makes corms. The white to pink flowers on weak stems look delicate but it is a fairly easy plant to establish. It seems to be happy in the woodland where it blooms with the spring ephemerals or in sun. *C. caroliniana* is similar but the leaves are broader. The genus *Montia* has a number of species nobody can tell apart. The general look is like the claytonias with broader leaves still, but they are later to flower and weedier. They are very good for covering a shady area quickly and giving summer flowers. *C. megarhiza* is a beautiful plant from the Rockies. It forms a rosette of thick, fleshy leaves with a reddish tinge at the edges. The flowers emerge at the rim of the circle mostly and scattered ones sit on top of the mound. The variety *nivalis* is found in the Wenatchee Mountains in Washington, and is a deep pink. Not many people grow this well and it is more rare, more beautiful, and more difficult than the rare, beautiful, and difficult *Claytonia megarhiza*. Actually if one is honest these three adjectives are not independent attributes. Nobody would deny that rarity induces beauty, difficulty induces rarity, and to grow a plant to full beauty in cultivation implies difficulty.

Some of the lewisias are a bit like talinums, for instance *L. rupicola,* and some are like *Claytonia megarhiza,* for instance *L. tweedyi.* But all the lewisias are like themselves, elegantly showy and without coarseness. Even weedy *L. pygmaea,* which selfsows too thickly for the plants to spread out and flower, and *L. cotyledon,* which has suffered the hybridizers' disease with its symptoms of high color and bloating, still retain a desirable quality that every rock gardener recognizes. *L. tweedyi* and *L. rediviva* go a step beyond and are perhaps the best succulents in the repertory. I love *L. cotyledon* in all its manifestations—the cool white with pink stripes that they say is the norm for the species is my favorite, but the gaudy oranges, magentas, yellows, and reds that have been selected and sometimes hybridized are fantastic plants that plead to be segregated in drifts or walls of their own. That is if you can grow them at all. In spite of their popularity and availability, not everyone has found the right place in their garden for these wonders to grow, let alone look right. Bringing them through the winter is problematic and one frequently sees close neighbors, one flourishing, the other with shrivelled crown and squashy neck. Don't bother to look too hard for the varieties called *howellii* and *heckneri,* they intergrade with everything else and the forms themselves have no special interest. But they are no worse either and are more likely to produce the simple, white, striped pink flowers.

Lewisia tweedyi is never out of place in company with any plant in the rock garden, but it does grow fairly large if happy—certainly allow a foot across. All the colors, white, peach, pink are good. One year you may get a plant with a dozen blooms. If you do, rush for your camera. Next year it may produce one flower each month for three months. *L. rediviva* is a lovely plant but has to be thought of as ephemeral. It never has a presence except in bloom, at which time it commands all of your attention. Remember where it is planted in the long periods when little or nothing is showing and leave a 4" diameter circle in case it produces three or four of its exquisite goblets. The white form is almost as lovely as the pink.

There are a few hardy euphorbias too. *E. myrsinites* is successful especially in a wall where it can droop or on a pavement where it can sprawl. The beauty is in the gray-green leaves that clothe the long fleshy stems. There is a fair amount of selfsowing but some of it is in cracks that you couldn't handle otherwise so you can't complain. Anyway I have never found it obnoxious since it is easy to see and pull before it gets lethal. *E. polychroma (epithymoides)* is reliably hardy for the border. I have had a plant called *E. wallichii* for ten years. *E. griffithii* may be hardy in slightly warmer climates than mine. All of them have the colors of sedums, greenish yellows and brownish reds and oranges.

The huge family of mesembryanthemums (Aizoacceae), which includes *Lithops,* the imitators of stones and other fascinating plants grown in greenhouses, also produces a few hardy species: *Delosperma nubigena* and possibly *D. sutherlandii* and *D. cooperi.* Many more could be tried outside to test for winter hardiness. These plants have the colors of *Portulaca grandiflora* and the covering power of sedums so careful placement is necessary. Many of them can be grown by taking cuttings and keeping them cool and dry over the winter. They never seem to belong. You put them out fat and clean from their winter quarters so they look like intruders from the start. Later when they bloom they have the look of annuals, which seems to reduce their value. They are rock plants as surely as lewisias, but they need their own special bed and should not be used as fillers among larger plants such as penstemons. It is always a matter of personal judgment whether something looks right, and if room is in short supply you will put things wherever you want and like the result. Never submit to sneers of taste-makers in your own garden.

At this point one should talk about cactus. After years of growing hardy cactus I think the only way to grow *Opuntias* is in a special bed. Even if you have only one plant, giving it its own bed and treating it as a specimen plant will save a lot of acute physical pain and uncomfortable decisions about suitable neighbors. A few *Coryphantha vivipara, Echinocereus triglochiatus,* or *E. viridiflorus* could be used with other rock plants since these are small, ball cactus. Even then the danger of forgetting the spines is so great that it makes close association with other plants questionable. So a special corner for these beautiful plants is warranted.

Presumably plants are succulent because they have to live in arid conditions for part of the year and fat leaves are their way of storing water. This would indicate that scree conditions are the right way to go, or raised beds with a large component of sand. This is a good way to bring them through a winter where winter is wet. On the other hand, in nutrient-rich soil, even with humus, *Opuntias* grow better (authority John Spain) and *Lewisias* can stand any amount of feeding (*L. cotyledon* surely and *L. tweedyi* probably). So you will have to strike a balance between soil rich enough to produce good flowering and growth that allows you to propagate vegetatively if you want, and soil with enough drainage to ensure that the crowns don't rot in winter. I believe that most gardeners are not too confident about their ability to do this balancing act and always have new plants coming on from seed, which is relatively easy, or through the mail, which is even easier.

Succulents can take a beating in the winter and still revive in the spring. Shriveling, shrinking, and losing leaves is not all that bad. If the crown turns to mush you must say your last farewells. I try to keep lewisias coming from seed because their mortality is unpredictable. In a few places in the world, lewisias are considered easy—if you can believe your informants. These places seem to be very localized north of Toronto, north of Edinburgh, and a few places in the northwestern United States. You hear of many success stories in alpine houses, and in fact they got their easy reputation there. If you want to grow them, don't despair over a few losses. You could be successful for a time anywhere from North Carolina to Maine and coast to coast.

~ ~

Gentians

❧ ❧ THERE ARE SOME genera in which many of the species are considered good alpine plants. *Androsace* is such a genus, although we tend to dismiss the species that are not up to the highest standard as not worth growing. For instance *A. lactiflora* or *A. albana*. It is a mistake to make such odious comparisons of species within a genus. Instead we should look at a plant for its own sake, assess its properties and beauty, and ask whether or not we can use it in our garden. A genus with a great variety of species is *Gentiana*—it contains a wide range of architectural form, color, intensity, and garden usefulness. Think of *Gentiana tibetica:* every reference describes it as ugly, rubbish, not worth growing, and other epithets too numerous to list. Think of *Gentiana verna:* everybody sighs at the intensely blue darling of early spring. Poor *G. tibetica* doesn't get a chance when compared with *G. verna* because there *is* no comparison and none should be made. *Gentiana verna* is a difficult, capricious plant that is totally unreliable from one year to the next. It wins prizes in shows and accolades from visitors. It is one of the hallmarks of a good grower if a large patch can be produced and maintained year after year, but the despair of most of us who have only occasionally seen a few small plants in our own gardens and then not always with the astonishing color we associate with the species. So try comparing *G. tibetica* with, for instance, *Trillium luteum.* It still may not win this beauty competition either but there is a fairer comparison to be observed. Both have that faded, yellow old paper look and both depend on leaves for their garden effect. They fill just about the same niche in a slightly shaded area—that is if you start with a nice clump of the trillium. A small garden would probably prefer *Trillium grandiflorum* and *Gentiana scabra* but an imaginative gardener with enough space can easily accommodate the other two.

So if you read Wilkie or Clay or Farrer or Bartlett on gentians, put what they have to say in context and grow a plant yourself before you make your mind up about its beauty and its usefulness. You may still end up calling *G. tibetica* rubbish or at least not allowing it in your own garden, but one day you may see it planted where whatever beauty it has is revealed and you could end up conceding that you misjudged.

Gentians have been classified by botanists into sections of related species, but I think that grouping them according to garden use might also be of some value. So I am going ahead with my own classification. You can dig this out for yourself by reading the above authors and of course the Harkness seedlist. You could also make your own classification and if you want to pull mine apart by realigning a few species here and there you can have a lot of fun on a rainy day. I won't stick to species I have tried to grow myself, and my authorities may not have grown these species either, but their descriptions are fairly convincing and you can judge for yourself after reading them.

The flower of a gentian is essentially a trumpet, a tube that flares out dividing into the petals. Looking down on the flower you see five petals most often (fours and sixes are possible) and between the petals there may be connecting "petals" called *plicae*. These may consist of one tiny point, a double point, a whole fringe of points, or be nonexistent. If this feature is prominent it adds richness of form and texture. There are stripings and spottings in some species that are also interesting close-up. At a distance too much artwork tends to diminish the impact. The calyx can also be sculpted with ridges and divisions but this is not a feature you would grow a plant for. Sometimes the trumpet does not flare but closes at the end giving an effect like a balloon. Comparing this with a platycodon in its early stages we expect this to "open," but in the case of the bottle gentians the flower remains with only a tiny opening for pollinators. Some gentians have petals fringed at the margins.

THE BEST
My first group is the *best* group. I mean the difficult, beautiful plants that would probably not last many years outside. These need alpine house treatment to grow well and if not you have to find exactly the right spot in the garden. Try growing them from seed. You need a lot of plants to achieve even moderate success with a few. Buying plants is frustrating—to begin with they are not easy to find.

The *verna* types flower in April to May: *Gentiana verna* has many geographic forms that are sometimes given specific names. The best *G. verna* has very fine blue flowers about half the dimensions of the familiar *G. acaulis* and perhaps not so intense a color even at its best. There are less good blues too but none are to be rejected. It forms a ground hugging mat that can be pulled apart after flowering when it gets sufficiently large (the second year maybe). The pieces will have enough root to pot up and ought to be large enough to plant out by September. I have tried it in a very peaty compost in a plastic pot and it did quite well. In the same mix outside it was less successful. In sandy soil it flowered too but sulked and failed to increase. Mary Bartlett insists that it is a lime lover and I have given it additional lime or grown it on tufa so you may want to experiment in that direction. The flower shape is a longish tube in a green, ribbed calyx with five petals opening to a star with a white center. Some geographical subspecies are *balcanica* (a brilliant greenish blue outside, endemic to the Balkan mountains); *pontica* (wider, dark green leaves, large flowers); and *sibirica* (tiny).

G. angulosa or *G. verna v. angulosa* (= *G. tergestina* or *G. verna ssp tergestina,* dark blue) is a bit larger and taller with lighter blue flowers and longer leaves and wings along the calyx tube.

G. *oschtenica* is a yellow species close to *verna* from the Pirin Mountains of Bulgaria. We saw this in Czechoslovakia grown by a few experts and it is a real prize winner.

Other species of the aristocratic group of gentians worth growing in a container and needing extreme care are: G. *bavarica* (with deep blue trumpets and tiny rosettes of light green, spatulate leaves, grows in wet areas in nature) has a subspecies *subacaulis;* the dwarf Bavarian Gentian, a compact form with circular leaves; *brachyphylla,* a 2" tight cushion with dumpy leathery leaves; *favratii,* a subspecies of *brachyphylla,* from Turkey (=G. *orbicularis*) with large, deep-blue flowers with rounded petals and tiny oval spathulate leaves; *pumila,* a smaller *verna* with narrow lance-shaped leaves and deep blue trumpets; *pumila delphinensis* has blunt petal lobes and a different calyx; *rostanii,* sky blue with narrow bright green leaves. It doesn't form rosettes; and *boissieri,* a dwarf *septemfida,* 2" tall and bright blue, from Turkey.

Still in the most precious group but flowering later are G. *pyrenaica,* whose range goes as far east as the Balkans, a violet beauty with pleated corolla looking as though it had ten petals and narrow lanceolate leaves, in May-June; G. *djimilensis,* possibly the eastern form of *pyrenaica,* is from Armenia and violet, 1" tall; G. *olgae,* from Tadjikistan, 6" bluish violet; G. *terglouensis,* a miniature version of *verna* with finer leaves than *bavarica* forming dense tufts of tiny rosettes. It wants lime and blooms in July. Its subspecies *schleicheri* forms dense tufts and may be the tiniest of the verna group. G. *froelichii,* the Karawanken gentian, sky blue in August, is an "aristocratic blue *frigida*" without the streaks. It is also from the Julian Alps.

GENTIANA ACAULIS AND ITS RELATIVES

These are the gentians you think of when you think of gentian blue. Only slightly less beautiful than the *verna* group (or slightly more?)

they are bigger plants with enormous trumpets and therefore less alpine looking but more showy. These are also spring gentians, but in my garden they flower a little later. My success is intermittent so I will content myself with negative advice. Not deep shade, not hot scree, not bog, not too lean a soil. Try the edge of a border with rich soil or the shady side of a rock. If you get heaving and rotting, improve the drainage. There is a lot of speculation about the acidity of the soil. This may be important if you live in a region with alkaline soil but in our slightly acid soil I think almost anything grows. You should try *G. acaulis* even if you live in a limestone pocket. Sometimes the plant flourishes but doesn't flower. Divide it by pulling the rosettes apart, pot up, and try several locations after the divisions have started growing again. Healthy plants can be divided as often as every year.

The name *acaulis* is used to cover a number of species, subspecies, or varieties, all with large trumpets and from different geographical locations. Look for *alpina,* the southern gentian (i.e., southwest Europe), which is small with one flower on a stem, but also stemless; *angustifolia,* rounded petals of deep to sky blue, narrow strap-shaped leaves, supposed to need lime; *clusii,* large skyblue or gentian blue flowers, with deep green rosettes of stiff leathery leaves, has varieties *clusii* with narrow pointed leaves and dark blue flowers and *rosea,* which is violet rose; *dinarica,* no spotting, big flowers, later than *acaulis,* from Yugoslavia, it is one of the species most likely to bloom well; *kochiana,* the "standard *acaulis,*" deep blue with green spots inside the trumpet, acid soil, low plant; *ligustica,* green spots and petals ending in a fine point needs lime; *occidentalis,* with pointed petals and no spotting; *rochellii,* a variety of *clusii* with gray narrow leaves and bigger, dark blue flowers; *undulatifolia,* wavy leaves. These all vary in leaf shape, size, and color and in flower size and color but all form rosettes that make clumpy mats. The foliage is interesting at close quarters but not very distinguished out of flower from a distance. It is understandable why nonflowering is so frustrating. I visited a nursery in Ireland and watched in horror as a large black dog first walked on and then stretched out on a large patch of *G. acaulis*. The owner was not only undisturbed but walked on the patch herself claiming that the pressure improved flowering. Ellie Spingarn has a large patch twenty years old that flowers without being trodden on.

SUMMER GENTIANS

First is a group of species that forms a tight mat of leaves or a single rosette with thick, long leafy stems sprawling up to a foot or more in all directions to present an octopus of green tentacles. The flowers are in ones, twos, or bunches at the ends of the stems. The colors are nowhere near as good as the spring gentians, being deep blues both rich and dull, on the purplish side, sometimes striped or strawy yellows and greenish yellows (but I shall group the yellows later). They are useful because of their later blooms and they look good at the edge of woodlands or add interest to a border. They overwhelm their immediate neighbors so you have to allow plenty of sprawl room. These are the gentians that Bartlett omits from her delightful book, presumably because she doesn't consider them worth growing in a rock garden. But many of them are quietly beautiful and worth trying. Some names in this group are *decumbens* (dark blue, one to three terminal flowers, 10" stems from rosettes); *olivieri* (blue terminal umbels, 9"–12" stems from rosettes); *gracilipes* (10" stems from rosettes, single flowers in axils, poor color outside, good blue inside); *cruciata* (greenish outside and not a strong blue inside, clusters in axils and terminal, up to 16" stems from dark green rosettes); *phlogifolia* (subspecies of *cruciata,* smaller flowers); *dahurica* (8"–12" stems, single, dark blue funnels in axils, pale spotted throat); *lhassica* (close to *dahurica,* flowers solitary); *macrophylla* (12", pale blue, late summer); *tianshanica* (about a foot high, terminal and axial clusters, purplish blue); *fetisowii* (24" erect stems from rosette, deep blue flowers in clusters a bit like *decumbens*); *kesselringii* (like a whitish *decumbens* with a split calyx); *waltonii* (larger *decumbens*); *cephalantha* (18", light blue);

rigescens (similar); *microdonta* (slenderer, with better color).

Much better but in the same league are *cachemirica* and *loderi* with better blues and better behavior. These are about 8" high from low rosettes with up to three terminal flowers of clear, light blue striped attractively. *G. grossheimii* is a low, pretty plant from the Caucasus. *G. altaica* has funnel shaped, deep blue flowers in early summer. *G. septemfida* is a well-known, frequently grown plant with stems about a foot long, deep blue, spotted flowers in terminal clusters and the plicae so cut up that at a casual glance it looks as though there are hairs growing between the petals. The name comes from this seven times slashed fringy effect and has nothing to do with the date of flowering, which is August. Garden forms of *septemfida* are 'Doeringiana', 'Hascombensis', f.*olivana,* var. *cordifolia,* ssp.*latifolia.*

Related to *G. septemfida,* and also summer growers that form good mounds of flowers in clumps: *freyniana* (like *septemfida* but no fringes and flowers usually solitary); *lagodechiana* (a botanical variety of *septemfida,* no rosettes, prostrate 15" stems, flowers are solitary, i.e., not in clusters, no fringes, deep blue); *fischeri* (similar to *septemfida* with dark blue flowers with green spots). *G. pneumonanthe,* the Marsh Gentian, has funnel-shaped flowers both terminal and axial, about twelve inches, deep-blue with green striping outside; *G. siphonantha* from China has flower clusters of purple-blue, 12"; *kaufmanniana,* 6"–8", is from Asia minor; *paradoxa* is a beautiful Caucasian endemic blooming in late summer from a spiral of ground-hugging leaves. *G. wutaiensis* from China is described variously as 8" or 20".

There are two taller gentians for damp places or woodland edges. *G. asclepiadea* is 24" with arching stems and deep blue flowers. The white form is just as good. The common name, Willow Gentian, comes from the shape of the leaves. *G. trichotoma,* 24", China, blooms in June to July with good flowers, deep blue outside and spotted inside.

NORTH AMERICAN GENTIANS

North American Gentians with similar garden value include *affinis,* which is about one foot tall with clusters of blue to streaky clusters of flowers in the axils and terminal, looking like a bunch at the end of the stem, grows near wet ground. Similar to *affinis* are: *oregana* (broader corolla); *bigelovii* (purplish stems, this integrates with *affinis* in New Mexico and is sometimes lumped with it); *parryi* (succulent leaves, can be a compact plant); *G. calycosa,* the blue Pleated Gentian of Logan Pass, but widespread, is caespitose with 12" stems, and has solitary dark blue terminal flowers. *Bisetea* is similar. *G. bracteosa,* from the Midwest, has 12" stems, no rosettes, purple blue funnels. *G. platypetala* from Alaska has thick tall stems and brilliant blue flowers. *G. puberulenta* is 24" tall with flowers in terminal clusters. The petals are only blue at the ends and flare out. It comes from the Plains states. More choice than any of these is *G. newberryi* from California, Nevada, and Oregon. This I have never succeeded in keeping over the winter. It forms 2"–4" mats of blue striped flowers, white inside. From the New Jersey Pine Barrens comes *G. autumnalis* (20" with indigo flowers) and its form *porphyrio* with brown spots inside. The former has been grown by Jerry Colley in an artificial bog with heavy feeding. *G. sceptrum* grows in wet places and reaches up to 48" tall. It has been called one of the best American gentians but it needs the right location. *G. menziesii* and *G. orfordii* are either the same or similar. *G. adsurgens* is a Mexican alpine gentian, seed collected by Sally Walker. *G. setigera* (previously confused with *G. plurisetosa*) is said to grow in a tight peaty bog and to have the appearance of a robust *G. newberryi* but with black-blue coloring of the flowers. It is a Californian, probably tender in the Northeast.

JAPANESE AND EAST ASIAN GENTIANS

Later than these and blooming into the fall are Japanese gentians. *G. scabra* has no basal rosette, the deep blue flowers are on racemes at the end of 12" stems, and bloom in September, deer permitting.

Variety *buergeri* is Japanese. Variety *saxatilis* is a shorter plant. *G. sikokiana* is like *scabra* with a different calyx. Others Japanese are *jamesii* (red stems, purplish blue flowers from July on); *nipponica* (like *jamesii* but smaller and a good blue); *yakushimensis* (10", solitary blue flowers in August). *Suendermannii* is a late blooming hybrid like a *septemfida*.

Also from Japan and East Asia is *G. triflora*. Over 24" tall, the dark blue flowers are small clusters at the top of the stems. The corollas have five or six parts and the foliage is attractively glaucous. This has a number of forms: *f. montana, f. horomuiensis, v. japonica* or *axillariflora* may claim *montana* as a form. *G. thunbergii* is an annual or biennial, 6" blue from rosettes.

NON-BLUE GENTIANS (i.e., yellow, white, greenish, and slatey) I realize that color is neither of botanical nor horticultural significance, but some people's reaction to non-blue gentians is very strong, so here they are in one group. The word yellow must be understood to be any color from creamy or lemony or strawy to almost white but never a good strong yellow.

Gentiana lutea is very tall, up to 60", has yellow flowers in several whorls around the stem, each whorl supported by a couple of leaves. The Asian equivalent of *lutea* is *G. stylophora,* sometimes put into the genus *Megacodon. G. gelida,* lemon yellow to white, 12", is related to *septemfida* with dwarf forms as low as 3". Also in this group are: *grombczewskii* (16", yellow funnels), *alba* (dirty white with green veins, nearly closed flowers), *punctata* (24", yellow, purple spotted with flowers in whorls down the stem), *flavida* (yellowish, may be the same as alba); *G. frigida* (the Styrian gentian, 4", yellowish white flowers with blue stripes and streaks, needs a cool place); *G. algida* (from both Asia and North America, pale yellow to white with blue spots and stripes, blooming at the end of summer, a low plant for a rock garden, may be a subspecies of *frigida*); *G. walujewii* (dirty white, spotted); *G. makinoi* (slatey blue with spots, good blues are reported, so this could belong with Japanese blues); *G. glauca* (greeny blue, white interior); *G. przewalskii* (bluish white, streaked); *G. purpurea* (purplish red with dark purple spots, yellowish throat); and the related *G. burseri* (brown-spotted greenish or creamy yellow flowers in showy bundles; *G. villarsii* is a subspecies of *burseri* with bright yellow flowers); *G. pannonica* (brownish purple, i.e., soft maroon, flowers, heavily spotted, in substantial clusters); *G. dendrologii* (whitish, 14"); *G. straminea* (Asian, yellow with three to five flowers on a stalk); *G. crassicaulis* (greenish white).

And then there are the purer white gentians of New Zealand. These are not hardy in New England but could be tried in an alpine house. The names one is likely to meet in lists are *G. saxosa, G. bellidifolia, G. divisa, G. patula,* and *G. serotina. G. corymbifera* is probably too tall for the alpine house (18").

BOTTLE GENTIANS

These are North American gentians without the flaring petals that we normally associate with the genus. At first you might wonder when the flower is going to open, but then you realize that its charm is the balloonlike flower head. Some can be extraordinarily beautiful, especially our local *G. andrewsii,* given a rich soil and plenty of light.

G. andrewsii is about 24" with blue bottles aging to purplish blue, borne at and near the ends of the stems. The ends of the *plicae* are fringy, which distinguishes it from *G. clausa,* which has pleats divided two or three times only. There is also a magnificent white form of *G. andrewsii. G. austromontana* is said to be even better with deep violet flowers. *G. linearis* has very thin leaves and is 24" tall with blue terminal clusters. *G. saponaria* has leaves like Bouncing Bette with purplish, club-shaped flowers that are mostly closed. *G. villosa* or *ochroleuca* is from the Southeast and is also whitish and probably blooms too late for New England. *G. rubricaulis* is 24" with pale violet tubular flowers.

FRINGED GENTIANS

These are annual or biennial. They belong to the genus *Gentianopsis* but sometimes appear as *Gentiana*. The corolla is in four sections. The fringe is on the lobes of the corolla and there are no *plicae* between the lobes as there are in *Gentiana*. *G. crinita* is our local fringed gentian. It is a graceful plant up to 36" tall, an annual, the lobes fringed all the way around. *G. procera* is fringed along the sides only. *G. detonsa* is 24" and variable blue; it has a variety *elegans*. *G. barbata* is similar and taller. *G. barbellata* is perennial and fragrant. *Gentianopsis thermalis,* of North America, is a deep blue annual with streaks, probably the same as *detonsa*. The European *Gentianopsis ciliata* is the only other fringed gentian you are likely to find in seedlists. The fringed gentians are not easy to grow and harder to keep but charming plants if you can succeed.

OTHER ANNUAL GENTIANS

These are seldom grown, apparently because they are difficult to keep going. *Gentiana aquatica* (Asia, 4"); *concinna* (New Zealand, white); *nivalis* (widespread in Europe, the Arctic, and North America, slender, 2"–6", and bright blue flowers, but untamed); *G. utriculosa* (with a baggy calyx like a silene), widespread, hard to keep; *G. pseudoaquatica; G. prostrata* (Swiss, small spoon-shaped leaves). There are many other annuals that never appear in seedlists, probably for good reason.

OTHER BIENNIALS

Gentianella differs from *Gentianopsis* because the lobes are in fives rather than fours. The members don't have *plicae* as true gentians do. *Gentianella germanica* is a beautiful red like a *Centaurium* and grows in Switzerland. Others are similar: *G. austriaca* and *G. bulgarica. G. moorcroftiana* is a biennial from Kashmir. *G. amarella* (*=plebeia*) is blue or reddish violet. These have hairy throats and grow from basal rosettes. Another *Gentianella,* brought back from Tadjikistan by Josef Halda, is *G. turkestanorum* and is blue.

G. campestris is a dull violet; *G. columnae* from the Apennines has clusters of large purplish flowers; *G. diemensis* is from Australia.

HIMALAYAN GENTIANS

These are some of the most desirable plants in the genus. There are many crosses but very few can be obtained in the United States. Seed is not often available either, so you have to be on the lookout and try it whenever you can. Perhaps the most startling color is the turquoise blue of *G. farreri*. This forms rosettes from which prostrate stems emerge like a Medusa head. The leaves are in pairs and very slender, which distinguishes it from other species. However, there are so many offspring of hybrids around it is not always certain you have the true species. Close imitations are still very beautiful. The flowers are solitary and terminal with a striped exterior. *G. hexaphylla* is also recognizable by the leaves in whorls of six and the corolla in six parts. It doesn't form a rosette and the flowers on 6" stems are blue spotted with green. *G. sino-ornata* makes mats and loose rosettes with 7" stems and deep blue, tubular flowers. *G. ornata* is rarer and the flowers are tubby and pale blue with dark spots. *G. veitchiorum* has royal blue funnels with yellow stripes. The flowers are on 5" stems that sprawl then turn up. I have never seen seed of this offered, nor of *G. gilvostriata* (beautiful sea-blue); *G. prolata* (blue-striped purple) and *G. lawrencei* (like a weaker *farreri*); *G. depressa* (mat-forming, rare, late, fat bells on short stems). There are many other superb Himalayian gentians not yet in cultivation and not all the ones listed are reliably so, but all should be tried if they ever appear in seedlists.

G. kurroo forms rosettes and the flowers bloom at the ends of 10" stems. They are blue spotted with green. There are many plants misnamed *kurroo,* so if you don't find yours very pretty it is probably not genuine. *G. sikkimensis* forms mats. The leaves are in pairs and the flowers in clusters, blue with a white throat at the end of 6" stems. *G. stragulata* is larger, purple outside and blue inside.

There are many hybrids of these Asiatic gentians that are occasionally available. Seed from one of these hybrids will not give the same plant as its parent but it should be worth growing. If you do this, abandon the name (e.g., 'Macauleyi', 'Susan Jane', 'Inverleith', etc.) and use an imprecise name such as "Asiatic Hybrids." Otherwise, the original names will cease to have much meaning.

~ ~

Which Gentians Should I Grow?

❧ ❧ NATURALLY THIS DEPENDS upon what kind of person you are, what your tastes are, and what kind of garden and facilities you have.

Gardener 1. You are a "good" gardener; i.e., you like plants and take care of them, but you are not interested in specializing and can't really be bothered to remember the names of too many plants that look alike. Try *verna* in various spots until you hit the right one. Keep it going by collecting seed and by division. *G. acaulis*—try to get hold of a clone or species that blooms. If it doesn't, try another location in the garden. Finally try another clone. Also indispensable are *septemfida, scabra, asclepiadaea,* and some species such as *parryi* or *fischeri,* ending the season with *farreri* or a Himalayan hybrid.

Gardener 2. You are a beginner branching out. You want something available, something new, something easy, something blue. Try *dinarica, cachemirica, septemfida,* and *scabra.* The same nurseries don't have the same plants every year but try Appalachian Wildflowers, Nature's Garden, Colorado Alpines, and Siskiyou Rare Plant Nursery.

Gardener 3. You only allow the very best in your smallish garden but you have an alpine house too and you are willing to grow species from seed. Grow any and all of the *verna* group, the *acaulis* group, the Himalayans, and the New Zealanders.

Gardener 4. You want to win prizes at shows. Grow *oschtenica, pyrenaica, froelichii, bavarica,* and look for names not on this list of Southern Hemisphere gentians as well as the rare Himalayans.

Just seeing the name on the label makes judges swoon.

Gardener 5. You have a perennial border and a woodland garden. You want tasteful, good-looking, reliable plants that provide useful foliage and are not temperamental. Color is important but only as part of your scheme and it must be unifying, not assertive. Grow *lutea* for architecture, *asclepidaea* for the edge of a woodland, *andrewsii* a little deeper in the woods, *septemfida* for the late summer border, *scabra* for the fall border, and find a place for *triflora* and *purpurea.* For a spectacular ground cover blooming late grow a massed planting of *G. farreri.*

Gardener 6. You want the unusual whether or not it is truly decorative. You have seen the attractive gentianellas in the European Alps; these are something to look for (if you can't find them, Centaurium is quite a good substitute). You like the vapid creams and yellowishnesses of *tibetica* and *lutea* but don't want all that leafage. Try growing another gentian relative: *Swertia* and its cousin *Frasera.* Also grow the bottle gentians for their perverse refusal to open. You can spend hours watching the bees struggle to get inside. Grow white forms of *acaulis, verna,* and *andrewsii.* These are truly beautiful plants but most people can't forgive them for not being blue.

⊰ ⊱

To Feel It Is to Want It

⊰ ⊱ MOST OF THE time we grow plants for the flowers, less often for the leaves—i.e., the way the flowers and leaves look. A few people grow plants for their fragrance; vegetable and herb gardeners for their taste and food value. It is very rare to grow plants for their sound—even plants with very noisy seedpods, such as *Baptisia australis,* would have few devotees without an attempt at attractive flowers. We expect the wind to make natural music in the trees and grasses without having to pick and choose plants especially for their aural delights.

The exercise of the fifth sense—touch—is usually associated in the garden with its unpleasant aspects of cold, wet hands, abrasions, bites, and wounds; it comes as a revelation that we can experience pleasure from touching plants and that the feel of some plants can make us want to grow them. We usually grow the mounds in a bunnery for their visual effect; one of the surprises is just how different one mound feels from another. The nicest buns are the hard ones. The texture of these varies from velvet through velcro to pincushion, but if a bun is firm and solid you get a sensation that runs from your fingers through your entire body and piques your mind and imagination.

The best and most unobtainable must be *Raoulia eximia,* the vegetable sheep that dot the mountainside of Mount Hutt in New Zealand. These ancient plants form mounds up to two feet across and defy tactile belief with their rock-hard embroidered texture. *Kelseya uniflora* in the Bighorn Mountains is almost equally pleasurable. In the garden we cannot grow either one to any age approaching maturity. In fact I have found it impossible to get them past the tiny seedling stage. But there are other plants to compensate. *Arenaria tetraquetra* is a wonderful substitute. It is not usually very lavish with its white flowers that sit on the flat mat. After the flowers have gone, the seedpods slightly spoil both the look and the feel of the hard textured mat. *Raoulia australis* has the same general effect but you can only keep this alive outside in Massachusetts over mild winters.

For a smoother sensation, perhaps *Draba rigida* is the most satisfactory, growing hard mounds a foot across in a dozen years. Its pincushion of yellow flowers in early spring matures into a forest of flimsy stems when the seeds are ripe and they can be removed gently without scissors. *Silene acaulis* always disappoints us with its sparse ragged flowers, but the mat itself comes up to our expectations when we touch it. *Gypsophila aretioides* grows painfully slowly and never flowers for me but the tiny mat is fine-grained and hard. *Vitaliana primuliflora* has several subspecies of more or less firm texture; so have the mat *Asperulas—gussonii* and *pontica.* Most of the porophyllum saxifrages form hard mounds and some of them fall into the next category of touch experience.

Do you enjoy touching prickly? Go up to *Dianthus erinaceous* and gently lay the palm of your hand over the mound. What a surprise the sharp hard mound has in store. It doesn't look at all prickly—more like an ordinary dianthus with short gray leaves, but each of them ends in a point. There are not many flowers on this plant and they are only a wishy-washy pink but it is well worth growing for the hard mound and astonishing texture. Some porophyllum saxifrages have a similar but less pronounced effect. *Orostachys spinosa* has visible spines at the leaf ends but invites careful stroking and palming. For true masochists or the willfully foolhardy there are the openly hostile prickles of *Erinacea pungens*—a mass of spikes with rich violet flowers. It is probably better not to touch this or *Genista horrida* too cavalierly and best not to touch *Carlina acaulis* at all. Still we can enjoy them for the tactile fantasies they induce.

More directly tangible are the plants with leathery leaves. The rock plant that comes to mind is *Carduncellus rhaponticoides,* with its stemless, purple thistle flowers sitting on smooth blue-gray leather. Collectors of rhododendrons must be attracted by the leathery leaves of most of them. But there are a number of plants in the *Erica* family that give us this texture. Ledums, vacciniums, and gaultherias can have tough small leaves with shining upper surfaces sometimes grooved and wrinkled. Trailing arbutus is a great plant to touch as well as to smell. Have you tried fondling *Dryas octopetala* or better still *Salix reticulata* for the same sensation? Asarums are often smooth-leathery and if you don't mind your leather cut up into strips, try *Saxifraga longifolia* or some of the other encrusteds.

Perhaps the most sensuous touch-type is the felty. I believe rhododendron growers get more of a kick from the backs of *R. yakushimanum* varieties than from their glossy upper surfaces. Indumentum is a rare pleasure for the thrill seeker. But in the garden itself are many felty-leaved plants. *Salvia argentea* is a good example. The tall off-white flowers add nothing to the near white leaves and can be cut off to keep the plant alive longer. There are many hieraciums with soft gray leaves, but don't expect attractive hair on all members of this weedy genus. *Leontopodium nivale* is the best edelweiss for near white color and soft touch and the grayer ones are almost better to touch than see. The three difficult gems of rock gardening that you would love to touch are *Veronica bombycina, Jankaea heldreichii,* and *Centaurea achterovii.* We are never allowed to touch them in someone else's garden and we are quite incapable of growing them ourselves so touching these three must remain a fantasy.

Looking leathery but easily marked by careless finger nails are succulent plants. Perhaps we should never touch them at all—*Claytonia megarhiza, Lewisia tweedyi,* and even sedums *(S. moranii, S. spathulifolium). Primula auricula* and *P. marginata* fall into this forbidden area. Their leathery-looking leaves are easily spoiled by touching the farina, which enhances the leather. And as with *Lewisia tweedyi* you can knock off a leaf very easily by a quick careless movement.

In the late forties young men began to have their hair cut first in crew-cut style, then in a brush that was more exaggerated. They were the boys who missed the war and possibly felt they had to do something macho to compensate. The feel of this cluster of vertical hair was very much like running your hand down the drooping needles of *Pinus wallichiana.* That soft, hairy feeling is duplicated in *Larix decidua pendula* especially at two times in the year. In the early spring when the leaves first emerge the fresh softness is irresistible. In late October when the maple leaves have fallen the larch leaves turn orange and the softness returns. I don't know any alpines with this quality.

Maybe growing plants for the way they feel is a little crazy, except that if you have a blind member of your family I am sure they would be very appreciative. But the sense of touch is a real bonus in the garden. We are so used to rough skin, broken nails, and callouses that touching a plant makes us a little more complete.

❦ ❧

Composites

❧ ❧ THE COMPOSITAE (or Asteraceae)—the Daisy family—
is sometimes called the sunflower family or the thistle family. This
is an enormous family that has, depending on your source, as many
as eight hundred genera and between ten and twenty thousand
species. Hieracium alone has fifteen sections, several with subsec-
tions containing as many as twenty species. Even allowing for a bit
of splitting this is rather daunting. How can one select garden worthy plants from such a huge array? One needs to know something
more than family membership to get a picture of the plant, so let's
break down the family into smaller groups and stay on the lookout
for plants worth growing. The family contains many weeds and ob-
scure, insignificant plants; you would expect the weeds because the
family is so biologically successful, i.e., pushy, having colonized
every corner of the world with some genus or other. This combination of coarseness, weedy behavior, and lack of redeeming decorative value has given composites a bad name. Many of the genera will
be dismissed with a shudder by gardeners. Part of this piece will be
to point out a few plants you might want to grow in spite of the
name.

The family has been broken down into "tribes"; these can be
thought of as sub-genera. It makes for more digestible pieces, but
mere membership in a tribe will not be the determining factor for
whether you do or do not want to grow a plant. The unifying characteristic of Compositae is that the flowers grow in "heads." The
visible object that we casually call a flower, consists of several flowers. Each "petal" of an aster is a strap-shaped or *ligulate* (ray) flower
and the yellow disk at the center consists of a multitude of *disk* flowers or *tubular* flowers. These individual flowers may have pistil and
stamens, just a pistil, or neither. Dandelions have only ligulate

flowers while tansy has only disk flowers. Thistles and their relatives are composites too; their flowers are discoid only, though the outer flowers are sometimes enlarged and fluffed up camouflaging the disk effect.

First we shall look at those tribes that are daisylike, with both ray flowers and disk flowers for the most part.

DAISIES

The Astereae includes some of the best garden plants. The tribe takes its name from the genus *Aster*. You can buy many asters from a perennial nursery. Some of the named varieties of border plants have been derived from *Aster novi-belgii*, a plant from the eastern United States; the other main source is *Aster novae-angliae*, another easterner that has given us several beautiful forms. In our garden the most spectacular forms of *A. novi-belgii*, often called Michaelmas daisies, tend to get leaf diseases, mildew, and wilt, and do not seem to grow well in their own "native" soil, probably longing for the rich deep loam of the English and German gardens that bred them.

The species *A. novae-angliae* is itself a lovely sight on the highways of New England and New York; its strong purple is as good looking as any of its varieties. If it isn't living just outside your garden fence already you might want to grow this in the border. Asters in general suffer the same drawback as goldenrods; the plants you grow in the garden ought not to look like weeds however intrinsically beautiful. There are "red" and pink forms such as 'Harrington's Pink' and 'Alma Potschke' that are far removed from the wild beauty.

Aster tongolensis, A. subcaeruleus, and *A. yunnanensis* are almost the same middle-sized plant and have given us *A. 'Napsbury'*. They are close to a large *Aster alpinus* in general effect as are *A. farreri, A. forrestii,* and *A. soulei limitanus*. Grow any or all of these from seed or clones and keep only the good forms. They look best in a border, being a little heavy for a rock garden.

A. amellus is a European that has produced many garden

forms—the popular *A. X 'frikartii'* is one of its children. You can find pictures of many of the plants mentioned so far in a glossy catalog such as Wayside Gardens, and some of them are pictured in the R.H.S. *Dictionary of Garden Plants in Color.*

There are several mid-sized asters and it is worthwhile growing any of the species from seed to "take a look" at the plant. The ones to reject would have wishy-washy colors, too much leaf, a gawky habit, or be highly stoloniferous and very weedy. One has to hope that the person who collected the seed is a gardener at heart who knows a good plant and not merely an aster buff or a botanist with an inclination to split an already dull species into a hundred dreary parts.

Aster alpinus qualifies as a good rock garden plant probably at the upper limit of size for a small garden. After all it needs a couple of feet to ensure having enough room the second year. But it well deserves space for its attractive large flowers on fat 6" stems. It is variable, so smaller, neater forms exist. There are color variations too, including a white one and one called *A. himalaicus luteus,* which is indeed yellow but had rather poor, thin, curly petals when I last grew it.

A. kumleinii is an attractive species from the Plains states. A good form was found by Claude Barr and is now available as 'Dream of Beauty'. This is a little finer than *A. alpinus,* though just under a foot tall. On the other hand it spreads a little faster.

Aster ericoides is a sprawly shrubby plant, not unlike a heath in general aspect, with many small flowers, very promising in bud, and opening to a rather weak pinkish white. Nevertheless it is a great plant to grow because it blooms so late in the season and will flow down a wall in a solid cascade that outdoes even *Campanula carpatica.* Good forms exist, including one discovered on Long Island by Linc Foster. Linc found the plant, propagated it, and distributed it to other gardeners through nurserymen friends.

A. linariifolius is also called the Stiff Aster. It forms a tighter bush than *ericoides* and has brighter flowers. It doesn't wander quite so gracefully, but sends up its woody stems about two feet mostly inclined at 45° to the vertical.

A. dumosus is the name attached to many dwarf Michaelmas daisies; the species may be the parent of some of these. You can find names like 'Niobe' and 'Professor Kippenberg'. They are not rock garden plants. They take up a lot of space, they are a long time in coming to flower, and they look highly cultivated. They tend to be stoloniferous and need frequent division to get good flowers. Grow them in front of a border or around standard roses if you like that sort of thing. I am drawn to them in the same way that I am drawn to dwarf iris: nice names, nice colors, a substitute for the big plants I have no room for, but not very stylish. Somebody needs to invent a new garden environment for these plants that mope at the edges of a perennial border and are excluded from the rock garden aristocracy.

Machaeranthera is a genus of annual, biennial, or tender perennial asters. I suppose results depend on where you live, but *M. bigelovii* is a splendid "annual" for me, flowering, from seed sown in February, around the end of August and continuing until cut down by hard frosts in October. It forms a large tumbleweed bush of good blue-purple flowers that sprawls around but not very destructively, since its woody stems are airy. It is a good "filler" near species tulips; being a desert plant it won't need water in summer and, while not a ground cover, it fills a lot of vacant space by the time it blooms.

Close to asters are the erigerons. The difference seems to be in time of blooming—erigerons early, asters late—and in the bracts that form the cup where the calyx would normally be. In *Aster* there are several overlapping (imbricated) rows, which you can see in the shaggy buds of *Aster ericoides;* in *Erigeron* you might see only two or three rows (look at the two neat flat rows of phyllaries surrounding the heads of *Erigeron compositus*). Also the ray flowers of *Aster* form one row and in *Erigeron* more than one (but this can be confusing as many garden asters are "double"). None of these criteria gives foolproof identification and you will just have to look at the label if you want to improve your chances of being right.

There are border erigerons and many excellent rock garden species. The border plants include 'Foerster's Liebling' ('Forester's Darling'), a lovely pink form of *E. speciosus*. There are many cultivars or hybrids of this species; one strain (plants grown from seed collected from segregated plants) is 'Azure Fairy', a double mauve.

Among the plants suitable for the rock garden is *Erigeron glaucus,* the Seaside Daisy. This has short-stemmed, dumpy daisies on a rather solid mat. I am not sure it is completely hardy in my garden in the Berkshires.

E. aureus and *E. linearis* are two very choice yellow erigerons. The latter has finer leaves but it is a toss-up which is more elegant. *E. chrysopsidis brevifolius* is another yellow beauty. Grand Ridge Nursery sells a selected form of this that is especially floriferous. (You have to go to the nursery near Seattle to pick it up!) These three warrant a home in your second best trough, but in any case protect them from the rough and tumble of a large casual rock garden. *E. elegantulus* is another lovely plant, like a purple *E. linearis*.

E. compositus is a very carefree plant that is easy to establish and easy to keep. It is quite variable in size and color, varying from 2" to 4" tall and from good white to deep pink. This means you can safely accept another plant in addition to the one you already have, hoping it will be a different form. They can sow around too and perhaps need to be watched if you want to limit the number of plants. *E. trifidus* looks like a small *E. compositus* and *E. montanensis* a diminutive one. *E. humilis* is still smaller and could be completely overlooked in the wrong place.

There are a number of erigerons seen less often than *E. compositus* and the same size or bigger. They have individuality that is hard to describe without dry descriptions of leaf shape and approximations to measurements of parts. *E. thunbergii* from Japan is a good purple sometimes; the best bet is to try *E. leiomerus, E. peregrinus, E. asper, E. subtrinervis, E. glabellus, E. polymorphus, E.*

gracilis, and any others that show up in the seedlists. You can get anything from 4" to 30", several factors contributing to the variability. For instance *E. glabellus yukonensis* grew about 9" tall and is a remarkably good pink.

E. aurantiacus is a flashy, coppery orange about 6" or 7". It flowers in the summer so the intense color is appropriate and welcome. The times I have grown it, the plants lasted a full year but died the next winter. I see no reason why it should not be genuinely perennial; possibly it would not survive a really severe winter.

Another rock type is *E. flagellaris.* This plant sends out thin "whiplash" runners that root down lightly filling up plenty of space in one season with new babies each with its own umbilical chord. At the outset you are pleased to see it bouncing along but it can irritate a placid *Arenaria* unwittingly sitting in its path. The roots are shallow and can be pulled easily but the strings are in such a tangle there is usually a mess when a cleanup is attempted. It is virtually impossible to eradicate from tufa once it has become established. Another one with the same personality is *Erigeron mucronatus,* but this one sends runners underground. It is not much of a menace in Massachusetts as its home is Mexico and not much survives the winter. The flower stems are quite weak in both plants and they loll around delicately.

The third genus of the aster tribe important for rock gardens is *Townsendia.* The NARGS seedlist usually contains about ten names. The number offered has grown longer fairly recently as more collections of seed in the wild are being made and gardeners are showing their appreciation by growing them. The third edition of Harkness admits fifteen species. The big question is how perennial they are. Norman Deno on his Pennsylvania sand gardens has *Townsendias* selfsowing (and hybridizing?); I have never had this experience and only rarely had plants live to flower more than once. However all the species are worth growing. They look well with alpines even though they may not come from the high mountain tundra. Their form is alpine and Nature made an error allowing them to grow on the high plains. Their lifestyle is so close to being biennial that you would expect them to be dismissed by the gardening elite. In fact Clay and Farrer are less than enthusiastic but you are left feeling that they couldn't get hold of the plants. Now that we have them we know they are worth growing; if it turns out that one or the other of them is biennial we accept the challenge to grow it so that it reproduces itself each year. Until then we can collect seed and start afresh each year. *Townsendias* make a spectacular case for including plants that grow below 10,000 feet and for including nonperennial plants in the rock garden.

Townsendia parryi is the easiest to get going; keep saving the seed and resowing until you reach the happy Deno state of self-perpetuity. The first flower to form is usually a single large head on one stem rising 3" from a rosette of fine grayish leaves; before the head dies and forms seed, cut off the stem and several new buds will form as the plant enlarges. The plant can bloom at any time, including mid-winter in the alpine house. The head is 2" across and a pretty lavender color. *T. grandiflora* is similar but always white and the stems not as stolid as *T. parryi*. Some writers say with confidence that this one is really biennial. We found it growing in Roxburgh Park, near Boulder, Colorado. It was in short grass, not scree.

The flowers of *T. eximia* are not as large but it is more likely to form a clump that survives another year, so you can have a satisfying mass of large, strong-colored daisies the second year.

In *T. rothrockii,* the stems are shorter and the daisies almost sit on the mound with large disks greenish at the center and short ray flowers giving it a paunchy look. *T. sericea* may be the same as *T. exscapa* and again the large heads sit on the rosettes. I have never had a really good plant with either name but the picture of *T. exscapa* in Claud Barr's "Jewels of the Plains" is mouth-watering. He describes *T. hookeri* as a less glamorous *exscapa* but it is just as photogenic.

T. hirsuta and what I have grown as *T. formosa* are more like sumptuous erigerons with smaller flowers than *T. eximia*. The phyllaries (bracts) of townsendias are more like asters than erigerons and these two have an attractive hairy "calyx" (involucre) of shaggy bracts surrounding the base of the flower head.

These three genera of Astereae, the aster tribe—*Aster, Erigeron,* and *Townsendia*—are perhaps the most important to rock gardeners. They have been covered only briefly, since I only mention plants I have grown or plants that are otherwise well-known to gardeners, so remember that there are hundreds of good garden plants that will be passed over.

THE REST OF THE ASTER TRIBE

The "English daisy" is *Bellis perennis;* this is a weed in Europe and may well be in the United States, but curiously enough does not seem to have escaped in the Northeast. There are forms often cultivated in gardens here, especially the ubiquitous biennial double forms ('monstrosa') that appear in every nursery in April as ready-made color for a new garden or to perk up a border as the bulbs are dying off. They compete with pansies in their role as horticultural stimulant. If you are too proud to put them among your crocus leaves or next to the Red Emperor tulips, you could go for some of the small forms that even look well in a rock garden. Clones such as 'Rob Roy' should be divided in the fall and kept in coldframes until the next spring. They look fine with dwarf iris and other small plants that are less exalted than the alpine aristocracy.

A tender near-relative is *Bellium minutum,* which forms a tight mat of shiny green leaves and has 1" high stems with spidery white daisies on top. You could put this plant in a warm place protected from large neighbors but with enough room to spread a little. It will be killed over the winter unless kept in the alpine house (a cold-frame may not be adequate). If it is kept growing all winter it will be very tender in April and will not withstand any frost at all, so don't rush it into the garden with the first robin.

There are some yellow daisies in the aster tribe: the genera *Chrysopsis* and *Heterotheca* seem to be interchangeable although perhaps *Chrysopsis* is the better name to use. *C. villosa* is a variable plant with some good forms. It blooms at the height of the summer with heads an inch across, the leaves are thin and grayish and the stems slightly woody and dry, so although it can flop around it is less destructive than great mats of lush green foliage. There are some species of *Chrysopsis* from the Southeast United States—*C. mariana* and *C. graminifolia* and from further north, *C. falcata.* These are a foot or a foot and a half high and need an environment with other medium-sized perennials. My experience with the southern species is limited but I think they are hardy. If you get the daisy bug you will want to collect these plants and enjoy the never-ending variation of form and posture of yellow composites. And you can add *Grindelia integrifolia* to your collection. *Grindelias* have phyllaries that curl backwards giving the green cup under the flower head a nice ragged look. The plant is aromatic in hot weather and sports common names like resinweed. Also called "resinweed" is *Gutierrhiza sarothrae,* a roadside plant from Colorado. Here the individual heads are smaller but the plant makes a lovely hemispherical dome about a foot across and so has its own charm.

I don't find members of the genus *Solidago* charming at all. I have tried to like them and have planted several special species in the garden. The only effect has been that of a missed weed. I should explain that goldenrod grows in great profusion in the fields around us and no amount of conscious psychologizing enables me to distinguish the invited guest from the handsome prolific weed that threatens to shower my garden every fall with a million unwanted children. You may find *Solidago virgaurea v. minutissima* or *S. missouriensis extraria* to your taste, however, as I think I could if I lived somewhere where *Solidago* was exotic.

Haplopappus is a genus I find slightly baffling. They are described as usually yellow. There is one going around seed exchanges as *H. reideri;* this was pretty and blue and lived only a year; *H. clementis* was yellow but so like an arnica, I wonder if it was misnamed. Long ago I grew *H. coronopifolius,* which had dumpy blue daisies—it, too, "should have been" yellow.

The genus *Brachycome* comes mostly from Australia and Tasmania. *B. iberidifolia* is a well-known annual and seed is sold by the major seed houses. Some of the perennials are worth growing if you are willing to take cuttings over the winter or keep a plant in the alpine house. Occasionally a plant survives outside.

The last plant of the aster tribe I shall mention is *Boltonia asteroides*, a large plant covered with small pale daisies. One form is pink. If it is well grown and well placed it could be a feature at the center of a large island bed. It is a plant for people who would like *Gypsophila paniculata* on an even more extravagant scale.

SUNFLOWERS AND SNEEZEWEEDS

There are two other tribes most of whose members have both ray flowers and disk flowers. We could loosely call the helianthus tribe the sunflowers. Well, certainly *Helianthus* itself is commonly called sunflower, and we are all familiar with the gigantic annual *H. annuus* grown commercially for oil and birdseed, and grown with a passing nod to its decorative value in backyard vegetable gardens by every male chauvinist gardener in New England. *H. tuberosus* is Jerusalem artichoke. *H. decapetalus* is about 4' tall and is grown in borders, especially the double form and some of the hybrids.

Heliopsis helianthoides also has many forms for the summer border. I once read a warning against allowing a border to become "yellow sick." You have to resist other people's prejudices, for it is too easy to be turned off because some eminent authority is quirky about a plant or a color. However, if your yellow border turns out to be monotonous, you could introduce plenty of white or maybe mauve to cool it down. Or go in the other direction and make a really hot combination with reds and oranges. But by all means defend your love of yellow against the present day equivalents of Misses Jekyll and Sackville-West.

Medium-sized perennials are *Coreopsis grandiflora* and *C. auriculata;* both have plenty of cultivated forms. *C. auriculata* has ferny foliage and is pretty aggressive, but gives weeks of pleasure.

Some of the *Coreopsis* grown from seed are short-lived perennials but selfsow happily across a border. There are also good clones around, which have to be divided fairly often. The annual coreopsis are sometimes called calliopsis and are easily grown, shorter than the perennials and mostly warm browns and oranges.

Verbesina encelloides and *Viguera multiflora* are medium-sized yellow daisies for the border that come from the southern Rockies and Mexico. So does *Thelesperma filifolium,* which resembles single *Coreopsis* but is more graceful.

Ratibida columnaris has an elongated disk, cylindrical in shape (Mexican Hat) and diffident enough to grow near, but not too near, a rock garden. The Gloriosa Daisies are *Rudbeckia hirta* and these behave like *Coreopsis*—ineradicable because they have so many seedlings, but you find that by the time they bloom you really want them. In any case their generous droopy petals of browns, reds, and golds are the hallmark of a summer garden and nobody would want to ban them completely. There is also that familiar ten-foot giant, *Rudbeckia laciniata,* which New Englanders cherish as 'Golden Glow', a plant your neighbor will be glad to share and reverently describe as "old-fashioned."

Echinacea purpurea is a cone flower with a spectacular, hard, cone-shaped disk. The usual color is an unusual dusky red and the albino form ('White Luster') is a special kind of off-white that no other plant has. The white form is not so vigorous.

There are two plants that the rock garden can absorb. *Chrysogonum virginianum* is a well-known, slowly creeping plant that makes a solid mat of green and covers itself with broad petalled flowers of a rich yellow. There is a taller form less common but not more lovable. *Marshallia grandiflora* (Barbara's Buttons) is pink and has curiously shaped disk flowers and, unusual for this tribe, no ray flowers. It is native to the eastern United States from Pennsylvania to Tennessee. It is not an alpine, but you could grow it with *Campanula carpatica* or aquilegias. There are a number of other marshallias with similar qualities.

Some authors (Gray) place *Marshallia* in the helenium tribe. This tribe has two plants of similar size: *Gaillardia aristata* is also just under a foot in height (it is not as coarse as familiar *Gaillardia pulchella,* the mother of several strains of short-lived border perennials and biennials). The other is *Eriophyllum lanatum,* a cheery, vigorous yellow daisy with gray leaves that is content with part sun.

The tribe takes its name from *Helenium; H. autumnale* is the familiar but mysteriously named sneezeweed, which adorns the late August and September border with colors anticipating the fall foliage. Much earlier in the season is *Dugaldia (Helenium) hoopesii,* which is yellow and half the height of *H. autumnale.* It is a Rocky Mountain plant from a lowish zone. If you like plants that look natural or wild choose this one over the worked over Heleniums. If you like opulent color and lush growth try 'Moerheim Beauty', 'Riverton Beauty', 'Bruno', 'Coppelia', 'Butterpat', and on and on. The pretty little annual *Dyssodia (Thymophylla) tenuiloba* is also in the Helenium tribe.

Finally, and most importantly, *Hymenoxys* is a genus in this tribe. *H. grandiflora* is the 'Old Man of the Mountains', a 2" yellow disk on a 3" stem with leaves so fine and gray as to be almost invisible. This magnificent plant can be seen on Independence Pass and every Colorado alpine tundra; the flowers face east. In the garden, alas, the best one can do is to raise plants from seed and live in hope from one year to the next. The plants may take several years to bloom and the end result is usually a sad travesty of the mountain memory. But plants like these are the challenge of the rock gardener and one must keep on trying. *Hymenoxys acaulis* from Mount Evans is another gem. This has forms from lower elevations that are easy to please; they multiply and divide as easily as an aster. Other names for this plant are *Actinea herbacea* and *Rydbergia.*

AROMATIC DAISIES: THE ANTHEMIS TRIBE
The plants comprising the fourth tribe of the family *Compositae* are

mostly aromatic with leaves cut into intricate patterns. Their smells are varied and often evocative, sometimes disgusting. Chrysanthemums bring back memories of harvest festivals, an English equivalent of Thanksgiving. At least it was the custom in Congregational churches to decorate churches with apples, vegetables, and flowers. I have no idea what the Methodists, Anglicans, and Catholics did in October. We usually went to chapel reluctantly but without argument, but Harvest Festival was worth seeing and certainly worth smelling. And above the fruity smell of apples and the foody smell of cabbages arose the powerful aroma of massed chrysanthemums. For some people the association is funereal and not everyone likes the crushed leaves of *Anthemis, Chrysanthemum,* and *Achillea.* Often a chamomile lawn is planted to avoid boring grass and one of its points is the haunting scent as idiosyncratic as a thyme lawn.

Another member of the tribe is *Artemisia,* which gives some Western deserts their characteristic look and hot scent. For me Artemisia means "Lad's Love", which is the name we gave to *Artemisia abrotanum.* I do know what the Methodists, Anglicans, and Catholics were doing on Whit Monday—they were marching behind their own Sunday school banners, in the Whitsuntide procession along with the Congs on a five-mile walk to sing hymns in a muddy field. Everyone was wearing new shoes and a few, a sprig of Lad's Love or a carnation.

The genus *Achillea* has a number of frequently grown species. *Achillea ageratifolia* is often called *Anthemis aizoon* and is a spectacular foliage plant with good flowers. It is so good natured and well-known that you may take it for granted. It looks well in a border or a decent-sized rock garden with enough room to spread. Keep it out of a trough—it will swamp its neighbors. The flowers are white and daisylike with ray flowers as well as disk flowers. The individual heads are not very large, making you want to call it an *Achillea,* but the sprays of flowers are loose and the individual heads have some value, making it more like an *Anthemis.* Size of head is not a diagnostic test of the two genera though. The other main genera of interest to gardeners in the *Anthemis* tribe are *Artemisia* and *Chrysanthemum*. I shall group plants according to use in the garden.

First, some plants suitable for the border. Border chrysanthemums are probably to be treated like nursery bought annuals; we fill up empty spaces in late August and hope, usually in vain, that there will be something left for another year. If you want to take them seriously you must lift the stools and propagate them the next spring. This disrespectful attitude would be heresy to devotees of those glorious hybrids of aristocratic Oriental pedigree, grown and shown with meticulous flamboyance, especially in Japan. Two other standbys are *Chrysanthemum maximum,* the Shasta daisy, and *Chrysanthemum coccineum,* the pyrethrums. Both have named clones, sometimes hard to establish, that are propagated by division and both have ordinary forms that can be grown from seed. I have found that pyrethrums from seed are slow to get going but no other daisy has quite the same bold reds. *Chrysanthemum nipponicum* is a good white daisy with substantial leaves and woody stems, but it blooms rather late for the Berkshires. *Anthemis sancti johannis* is deep yellow and not very graceful. *A. tinctoria* is called Golden Marguerite, with excellent flowers for cutting, especially in the forms 'Kelway' and 'E. C. Buxton'. *Achillea filipendulina* is a tall yarrow with big flat tops ('Coronation Gold' is a clone); *A. millefolium,* the common yarrow, comes in many dirty colors; *A. ptarmica* is a better white with a goodlooking double form ('The Pearl'). *Achillea X 'Moonshine'* has *A. tomentosa* parentage, but is a better plant.

Some medium-large plants you could sneak into a rock garden or near the edges of a border include several *Achilleas: ageratifolia, clavennae (=argentea), chrysocoma,* and *clypeolata;* they are all good plants. *Anthemis barrelieri* (5", white with gray leaves), *A. cupaniana* and *A. marshalliana (=biebersteiniana)* are all a little lower, the last is a good yellow on deep gray. *Achillea abrotanoides* is a large ball of ferny leaves but not much flower. *Chrysanthemum rubellum* is a pink, foot high early chrysanthemum, probably a hybrid but more permanent than the fall monsters.

Shorter still is *Achillea erba-rotta rupestris,* which is charming
and white. *Achillea X lewisii* (the same as 'King Edward'?) is a 6"
high yarrow of a clotted cream color, with *A. tomentosa* as a parent;
a nice plant but not showy in the least. *Anthemis cretica* is a good
daisy about 8" high that sprawls wickedly in one season or sulks in
a small clump. If you have six feet of space to fill it can do the job
but there is no guarantee that it will. *Anthemis cretica ssp pontica*
forms nice mats and is worth growing in a scree area except that it
selfsows plentifully so you have to watch out for its neighbors' well-
being. *Chrysanthemum weyrichii* is a soft dusky pink and wanders
gently hugging a boulder. There are two taller forms, one of them
white, which are far less attractive. *C. alpinum* is a more polite *Anthemis cretica* and there are several other low white chrysanthemums such as *C. atratum* and *C. arcticum.* The real mat former is
Anacyclus depressus, which is hardy for us even though it comes from
Morocco. The flowers are at their best just before they open as the
reverse of the petals is a rich red. *Artemisia assoana* is also a mat until
the flowers start to ascend, but unless you want seed they can be
clipped to keep the silver carpet intact flowing down hot rocks.
Spectacular.

Other plants grown for the leaves include *Chrysanthemum
haradjanii, Artemisia stellerana* (Dusty Miller), and *Artemisia
schmidtiana,* which is more like a small shrub. This forms hemispherical mounds with no pruning and it can be used as comic relief in an otherwise humorless garden. The flowers spoil the shape.

There are other shrubby artemisias, mostly strongly aromatic.
Artemisia absinthium is a rather coarse plant, and there is a form
called 'Lambrook Silver' that is beautiful but also coarse. *A. cam-
phorata* is also not very refined and smells of camphor when you
brush it casually on a hot day. Similar in effect is *Santolina neapolitana* but here the flowers are yellow blobs making a better show
than the nondescript plumes of most artemisias. *Artemisia gnipi* is
much smaller but there isn't much reason to grow it unless it is the
exact gray you want.

There are a few annuals to try such as *Chrysanthemum coro-narium* and *C. carinatum. Anacyclus radiatus* is another I have grown but not highly recommended. Two tender plants well worth growing through the winter in the alpine house are *Chrysanthemum catananche* and *C. hosmariense.* These are borderline hardy and qualify as good show plants for the March show. You can plant them outside for the summer and make cuttings for the winter.

SENECIOS: ARISTOCRATIC RELATIVES OF THE GROUNDSELS
The fifth tribe of the daisy family is the Senecio tribe. These are mostly yellow daisies; i.e., the species have both ray flowers and disk flowers. The heads may be mean little nonentities as in the plants we usually call groundsel and ragweed, or large enough to claim the flower as the main feature of the plant.

There are several arnicas in the seedlists. I have grown *A. mon-tana, A. mollis, A. cordifolia,* and *A. acaulis.* They are a reminder of mountain meadows—the sort of plant you expect to see on a hike after you get your second wind but long before the snow line. Actually *Arnica acaulis* comes from the non-mountainous southeastern United States and looks more like a *Helenium* than the others. Arnicas have broadish "petals" and not very many, so when one of them has been munched there is a ragged look like a defiant urchin. If they like their location they will run about mildly and fill three to four feet comfortably.

Doronicum columnae (=cordatum) is one of the earliest perennials to appear, flowering with *Tulipa turkestanica.* If planted in a perennial border it would only be a brave promise of better things to follow, so it is usually used in combination with *Anemone blanda* and the main display of May bulbs. Besides, it keeps its leaves, more or less, mitigating the blank look after the bulb leaves have faded out. *Doronicum orientale (=caucasicum)* and *D. austriacum* are similar and there are a few hybrids. *D. glacialis* is shorter and later and can be grown in the rock garden with medium-sized plants.

The main members of the tribe are *Senecio* and *Ligularia.*

These are nearly all large plants for rich soil and damp areas. They can be grown in a border if you don't mind them looking a little unhappy in a drought. Or they can be used as accent plants, even in the middle of a lawn. The trouble with doing this is that the plants have little presence until mid-June, so you would have a circle of mulch to contemplate until the enormous leaves took over. These leaves are a joy and a problem as they suffocate every plant within two feet of the crown. These remarks apply to *Ligularia dentata* (some forms with spectacular reddish leaves), *L. stenocephala, L. przewalskii* (makes a lovely flower spike), and *L. hodgsonii.*

More easily placed in a border is *Senecio abrotanifolius,* especially the variety *tyrolensis,* which has a shower of yellow flowers in mid-June. Also *S. adonidifolius,* with leaves like an *Adonis,* which looks good out of flower.

An excellent rock garden plant is *Senecio leucophyllus,* a mat of gray, almost white, leaves. Others to be tried are *Senecios candicans, capitatus, congestus, doronicum, fendleri, incanus, korschinskyi, longilobus,* and *paulsonii.*

There are two other plants you may want to use if you are fearless and need to decorate a large wet area. *Petasites japonicus* has flowers very early in spring, curious but not beautiful, and large leaves in summer, beautiful but overbearing. *Tussilago farfara* is an even worse weed.

WOOLLY PLANTS: THE INULA TRIBE

The sixth tribe of the compositae takes its name from the genus *Inula,* but *Inula* is the maverick of the tribe. The others are woolly, hairy, felty, downy, nice to stroke. The flowers are often insignificant and have no rays. Sometimes the bracts take over as the objects of interest—chaffy balls of subtle colors. *Inula* itself usually has large yellow flowers with ray and disk flowers and the fruit stage is not noticeably different from many other yellow daisies. However, I have noticed whenever I have transplanted *Inula* seedlings that the young leaves are quite hairy and catch particles of Jiffy mix, so they probably retain this character as adults; it just isn't their most characteristic feature.

Inula magnifica has enormous gray-green leaves and can grow to five feet or more. It has a commanding presence in a border and needs a circle of clear space four feet in diameter to accommodate it. Unlike ligularias, it stands up to drought without wilting. Even taller and monumentally overbearing are *I. helenium* and *I. racemosa.* Give them a wild, rough place or let a single giant stand sentinel over a secret corner. *Inula ensifolia* is a very reliable and floriferous perennial that can be used in a large rock garden for July bloom or at the front of a border. Much more elegant is *Inula orientalis* with its very long petals having the decorative quality of spider chrysanthemums.

Two rock garden *Inulas* are *I. acaulis* and *I. rhizocephala,* the second being a condensed version of the first. These spend the winter as flat rosettes of soft green (dirty gray?) leaves. The flower buds form at the center of the rosette without a visible stem. As they open, the plants take on the appearance of a bridesmaid's posy—so flat it could be just a drawing. I think both of them are biennial—that's how they have always behaved. So collect seed and start again. Somewhere I read that *I. rhizocephala* needs hand pollination (I doubt it), but certainly there are enough of the right kind of insects around to pollinate *Inula acaulis.*

Other members of the *Inula* tribe are more obviously rock garden plants. The genus *Antennaria* contains some good species. You have to have the same sensitivity to color and shape that fern people have to be an *Antennaria* collector. A very vigorous species might be used to make a "lawn" to be walked on gingerly and rarely. Pull it out if it gets out of bounds, the roots won't be very deep. *Antennaria dioica* has some pretty forms where the bracts are pink and pass as flowers. *A. pulcherrima* has gray leaves that don't lie flat. There is a neat form of *A. neglecta* from Eastern Canada: *A.n. gaspensis.*

The genus *Raoulia* comes from New Zealand and contains

many gorgeous mat-forming plants. Some are hard mats with little gray or yellowish "daisies" sitting on them. It is bracts you can see and not ray flowers. Unfortunately raoulias seem to disappear after one or two seasons. I strongly recommend gardeners to grow them at least once; you can enjoy the variety of form and texture for a season, try to propagate pieces for the winter alpine house, win a few firsts at the shows, and if you are lucky even find the right place outdoors for a season or so. *Raoulia australis (lutescens)* is fairly easy. I once had *R. subsericea* not only survive two winters, but flower profusely and form seed. But nothing germinated and the plant died the next winter. Read this as a challenge, not as a warning. Of course New Zealand abounds with species of *Raoulia.* Especially ungrowable in Massachusetts and throughout most of the gardening world are the "vegetable sheep" *Raoulia eximia* and *Haastia pulvinaris.*

The most satisfying genus of the rock garden in this tribe is *Leontopodium.* Ignore all the Austrian-Swiss hype and all the subsequent debunking by indignant rock gardeners and come to the genus without prejudice. *Leontopodium alpinum* is very variable, the leaves are usually a pleasant gray and the "flowers" like floating iris beards. *L. nivale,* which is sometimes listed as a subspecies of *L. alpinum,* has exquisite light gray leaves and almost white beards and is usually only 3" tall. Another form of *L. alpinum* comes from the Dolomites and is shorter and neater than the standard form. Other leontopodiums come from Asia and are variants on the Edelweiss theme. Try any of them for a quiet, cuddly contrast to a green mat.

A larger member of the tribe is *Anaphalis.* The one you usually see is *A. margaritacea*—pearly everlasting—for a border or a wild garden. Also I have tried *Gnaphalium* now and then but never have I had a plant I wanted to keep.

THISTLES AND KNAPWEEDS: THE CARDUUS TRIBE

This tribe consists of plants with no ray flowers. The disk flowers are elongated forming a dense cushion. The characteristic of most species is the prickly nature of the leaves, the bracts of the individual flowers, and the involucre of bracts surrounding the head. The entire plant can be the apotheosis of hostility. In this lies part of their charm. A plant that sets out to defend itself against animal life with such directness and success becomes an object of admiration and respect. Well, respect at least, but some of them are in fact beautiful. Think of the statuesque quality of *Onopordon acanthium,* the Scotch thistle. Look at the marbled leaves of *Cirsium japonicum, Cnicus benedictus,* and *Galactites tomentosum.*

The nonhostile members of the tribe include *Centaurea.* These are usually called knapweeds. *C. montana* has rather meager, shaggy blue flowers. A better one is *C. dealbata* with good, reddish mauve flowers—this is one of the first border perennials to bloom and signals the last flourish of the late spring rock garden. *C. macrocephala* has large yellow bundles of fluff preceded by a bud with a metallic bronze look as good as the flower itself. Smaller and almost suitable for the rock garden is *C. uniflora,* a particularly good magenta. But there are some really fine rock garden *Centaureas,* many from Turkey. Look for *C. achterovii* and *C. chrysantha,* which have large heads sitting stemless on a rosette of lovely leaves. These are difficult plants whose culture is still a mystery.

Most of the *Echinops* are tall plants that belong in a semi-wild area where they can selfsow madly. *E. sphaerocephalus* has gray flowers and needs to be the foil of a brighter color such as *Liatris*—otherwise you hardly notice it; in *E. ritro,* the spiky balls are metallic blue. Dig up unwanted seedlings as soon as you notice them. If they pass the adolescent stage the leaves are already prickly and the roots headed for China.

There are a few members of the *Carduus* tribe that fit in well with a rock garden planting. *Serratula seaonii* is a quiet plant, 6" or 7" high, that blooms so late in the year—September, October— that its little purple brushes make a point. No prickles and the leaves are nicely cut. Then there is *Carlina acaulis,* a real thistle that makes a round mat of prickly leaves with the thistle head barely rising above the center. Much finer but with similar effect is *Carduncellus rhaponticoides.* This is a first-class plant with smooth etched leaves and no spines. It seems to divide easily but the seed can be overlooked as it forms a messy brown blob at ground level.

This covers the most interesting tribes of the Compositae as far as rock gardeners are concerned.

THE REST OF THE COMPOSITES AND SOME IMPOSTERS

Compositae is one of the largest families in the plant kingdom. Composites have tiny flowers grouped into heads. The circular platform on which they sit is called the receptacle. At the center of the platform are the disk flowers and around the edges are the ray flowers, where these exist. The Aster tribe is the group most like "daisies" with heads of both ray flowers and disk flowers. The Anthemis tribe contains mostly aromatic plants, the Helianthus tribe, sunflowers; the Helenuim tribe also has mostly both ray and disk flowers. The senecios are yellow daisies. The Inula tribe are the chaffy, felty ones mostly with no ray flowers. The Carduus tribe of thistles also has no ray flowers.

The Cichorium tribe has no disk flowers. The plants in our gardens are dandelions, hawkweeds, and lettuces. The only dandelions of horticultural interest are the colored forms. These are not easy to obtain and not in my experience easy to grow, but whatever success I have had has convinced me not to long for more. *Hieracium,* though, contains some plants worth considering. Many of them are grown for the decorative leaves that can be blotched *(H. maculatum)* or felty *(H. heldreichii, lanatum, welwitchii).* Perhaps the best is *H. waldsteinii,* which has nearly white leaves and bright lemon flowers and makes a ground-hugging mat. You could cut off the flowers of the taller kinds but you might enjoy the consternation that seeing a "dandelion" growing in the garden sometimes causes in a nongardening visitor. The gorgeous orange hawkweed, *Hieracium aurantiacum,* is a European import that you have to be careful not to introduce into the garden. The first forgetful season that you allow the seed to blow will begin years of regret.

Lactuca perennis is a blue-flowered lettuce, probably biennial despite its name. It isn't as good a blue as the roadside chicory, but then it isn't quite so weedy, and I have found it safe enough to have in the rock garden. It provides midsummer color and a little sowing around is desirable. I would like to recommend an annual too, *Crepis rubra*, a pink hawkweed that refuses to selfsow. But, I like it so much I collect seed and sow it every year. There is also a white form that is equally attractive.

This leaves only a few tribes unmentioned and really none of them are of much interest to a rock gardener. The Eupatorium tribe contains Joe Pye Weed of course for the wild garden and also *Liatris*, Gay Feather, which has a number of interchangeable species that can be used discreetly in a border. The Calendula tribe includes the annual pot marigold for a Herb garden perhaps. The arctotis tribe is mostly South African and not hardy, but there are plenty of plants here that can be grown as annuals. The mutisia tribe is mostly South American and ungrowable outdoors in Massachusetts. The vernonia tribe includes the beautiful *Stokesia laevis*, a good border plant with a nice white form as well as the soft blues. Also *Vernonia* (Ironweed) itself, with many similar species of tall, richly purple-flowered woodland plants that seem to be mourning the passing of summer as October progresses. *Elephantopus* is probably only useful south of New York.

Plants, not Composites, that look like Daisies

Of course you can hear the botanists sneering. But there are many of us who simply don't know what to look for or even how to look. So I want to confess to some of my errors, slipshod observation, and rank ignorance.

There are plants like *Phyteuma hemisphaericum* and *P. orbiculare* whose flowers form "heads," but each still has its own short stalk attached to the main stem; there is no receptacle. These are in the Campanulaceae family as is the genus *Jasione* with clusters of flowers reminiscent of a *Stokesia.* I was astonished too to discover that *Globularias* are not daisies either; in fact they are the name-bearers of a small family of their own, Globulariaceae.

Scabiosa, knautia, and *pterocephalus* are also genera trying to belong but in fact are members of Dipsacaceae, which are the teasels. And the teasels themselves look as though they ought to be thistles. True too of *Eryngium,* a member of the Umbelliferae. Another example more nearly daisylike is the whole mesembryanthe-mum family (Aizoaceae), where the petals really are petals and not individual flowers.

Recognition is a peculiar phenomenon. We don't measure nose length or count eyelashes in order to identify our friends, nor do we need more than a quick glimpse of a plant to recognize an iris, say. In our memory are stored hundreds of plant portraits like a photograph album; some are derived from a plant we have grown ourselves, some from plant shows and other gardens, some are from garden books and slide shows. A very few are from written descriptions. It should cause little surprise if we cannot recognize the genus or even the family of a completely new and strange plant. But there is a sense of accomplishment when we can put a name to a plant, especially one we have never seen before. These notes are not going to guarantee that you will always know a composite when you see one, but they might help you sort out the possibilities.

Finally, here is a list of composites that have been used at one time or another as herbs; i.e., medicinally or for food. I shall use the common name and leave you to look up the botanical name.

Agrimony, burdock, chamomile, centaury, coltsfoot, tansy (costmary, alecost), cudweed, dandelion, devil's bit, elecampane, endive, feverfew, chicory, mugwort, pellitory, spikenard, ragwort, scabious, blue simson, southernwood, sowthistle, starwort, tarragon, yarrow, fleabane, salsify, goldenrod, samphire, gosmore, groundsel, knapweed, hawkweed, lettuce.

What wonderful names with so many literary resonances, but of course many are weeds to strike fear in the heart of a gardener. I wonder how long it took the people that utilized them to decide that some herbs deserved cultivation and others were better left in the fields and hedgerows. Did ever a garden exist filled with such rampant vigor? The present day herb garden is only an effete descendant. A refinement? A compromise?

~ ~

Recognizing Conifers: Strictly for Beginners

CAN YOU DISTINGUISH one conifer from another? We grow many dwarf conifers in our gardens to give our miniature landscapes proper scale and interest in winter. There are probably full-size evergreens in your garden too, either wild or planted by you. Do you know what they are? I often have a problem with conifers, certainly with names of varieties but also with the species and even with the genus. There is no shame in not knowing a cultivar's name—there are so many, some forms have only slight differences, and their nomenclature can be as confusing as the common names of plants. Sometimes the same name is given to different plants and different names to the same or similar plants. However, a clonal name can sometimes be a simple device for remembering the genus and species. If you can recognize *Chamaecyparis* 'Boulevard' at a glance—and this happens to be a very popular blue, bushy plant with an attractive speckled look—then you can identify it first as a chamaecyparis, then connect the species *pisifera* with it and extrapolate the information to a more general recognition of other varieties of *Chamaecyparis pisifera*. You would have to remember that this soft-blue foliage is juvenile and the color a characteristic of the clone, not the species. This would be a first step towards the general recognition process, but how many of us see 'Boulevard' often enough to be sure of recognizing it in a strange setting? Besides, with so many clones in cultivation only a specialist is going to accumulate this kind of skill in any quantity.

Suppose you are in a garden surveying the landscape or in a car traveling at high speed through the mountains; how do you tell one conifer from another? In the second case it hardly matters what you guess since you are not going to be seriously challenged. Especially if all you saw was a single specimen. If you have a book of the local plants the choices will be very few, so selecting the correct genus will usually be sufficient to identify it completely. In a garden the situation is complicated by more possibilities and by being surrounded by friends who (you believe) know all the names, or at least more of them than you do. You could keep quiet and wait for your host to tell you the name or try out an arbitrary name, ready to correct yourself rapidly if there is no murmur of agreement. Keeping quiet is safe but not fun. Speaking out is fun but can lead to embarrassment. "What is the species of this pine?" may bring the reply, "That is a spruce," or worse, "That is 'Tiny Tim'," so you end up not knowing the genus or the species and even though you exposed yourself to possible ridicule you are no wiser. Usually you end up saying "Oh! I thought it was a pine, how silly of me." And then you are too shy to ask what it really is and don't dare take part in any further conversation that involves knowing the names of conifers. In the Northeast, the genera you are most likely to meet are *Abies* (fir), *Chamaecyparis* (false cyprus), *Juniperus, Larix* (larch), *Picea* (spruce), *Pinus, Taxus* (yew), *Thuja* (arbor-vitae), and *Tsuga* (hemlock). So let's go into the garden and take the first easy steps to identification.

The first mental questions might be the last: "Have I seen that clone before and can I remember its name?" If both answers are "Yes" everything goes smoothly—being able to talk about Boulevard rather than *Chamaecyparis pisifera* 'Cyanoviridis' is quite all right even though the second name contains more information. But what if you are not looking at Boulevard or any other plant in your meager memory bank with a comfortable pet name? Let's suppose it is winter. Maybe the first question might be: "Would it make a good Christmas tree?" (Be sure not to say this out loud). Are the boughs horizontal and firm enough to hang glass balls from? Are the branches in layers or whorls and is it the familiar conical shape with a nice leader for the star at the top? This much would reduce the guess to *Abies* or *Picea*. If you were close enough to see that the foliage was fan shaped without the needley look of Christmas trees you could bet on *Chamaecyparis* or *Thuja*. You could recognize *Pinus* by its bunchy long needles and you might recognize *Tsuga* by its drooping branches, neither one perfect for hanging ornaments from. *Larix* would be bare in winter since it is deciduous and so quite useless. This would leave *Juniperis* unaccounted for. This comes in so many shapes and sizes that it wouldn't be easy from a distance, but I don't know of a species that looks like a good Christmas tree. There are some well-known clones of juniper that you might easily recognize though. *J. communis compressa* is the rock garden dwarf column that looks like the toy trees from a 1920s Noah's Ark. *J. scopulorum* produces a tall, very slender blue column 'Moonglow' and *J. communis* a similar green column 'Pencilpoint'. Any shrub that covers yards of ground is probably a juniper too.

So you stall and reserve judgment until you are a bit closer; this might give you a chance to touch the branches and even sneak a sample of the foliage. By now you can certainly see whether the needles are in bunches. This confirms *Pinus* in winter. In summer you would have to consider *Larix* but the larch bunches are in a rosette formation with several to the bunch. Pines have two to five needles emerging together from a woody stub and almost lying side by side, like the tail of a horse rather than a feather duster. Nearly all the pines you normally meet have needles in pairs or in fives. The only doubtful situation is that a young tree could produce single needles and make you doubt your judgment. Better count several sets of needles to take care of accidents and anomalies. In any case pine needles are longer than other needled trees including larch.

You are now close enough to be fairly sure about *Thuja* or *Chamaecyparis*. Rule out *Thuja* if any of the leaves turn out to be needley looking; *Thuja* always have "scaly" leaves. Many *Chamaecyparis* leaves are scaly too but not so utterly flat as *Thujas*. If the branches are fanlike and fernlike but consist of soft needles—very short compared with *Picea* and *Abies* and minuscule compared with pine—it is probably a *Chamaecyparis,* although its leaves often are reduced to flat lumpy scales and the ends of the twigs can be like braided twine. Finally squeeze a swatch of leafy material and smell the result. *Thuja* has a rich, warm, fruity aroma, the essence of conifer. *Chamaecyparis* is much less aromatic. Junipers also produce scaly leaves when they are older but younger plants have pointed, sometimes prickly, needles. If it looks as though it wants to be stroked but rewards your attention with prickles it is probably a juniper.

You are also close enough to see the needles, if there are any. *Abies, Picea, Tsuga,* and *Taxus* all have needles scattered along the twigs. *Pinus* has long stretches of twig without needles. When you prune it, cut at a spot where there are needles growing, otherwise you will have a stub that can't produce more leaves. The two Christmas tree candidates can be instantly distinguished if they have cones. *Abies* cones stand upright while *Picea* cones hang down. Without cones you should look at the twigs where some of the older needles have fallen off. In *Abies* the fallen needles leave a circular scar on the bark, visible but not spoiling the smooth bark. In *Picea* the leaves drop, leaving a stub so the spruce twig is rough and lumpy. You can distinguish *Picea* and *Tsuga* because *Picea* (and *Abies*) needles hang on the stem by tiny curved stalks (petioles). People of my age would need to have very good light to see this but it is easily visible without a lens. If some of the leaves are dead but are still hanging on the branchlets, it is probably an *Abies. Picea* sheds its dead needles quickly when they dry out, and so it is less desirable as a Christmas tree unless you keep the atmosphere moist. And *Picea* needles are sharp. If you use the boughs as winter protection in the garden, by the end of winter the needles will have dropped, providing a useful summer mulch; however the needles are still sharp and will stick to your socks and sweater, at the same time piercing unwary fingers. *Tsuga* boughs are less hostile, the leaves being flat and less needlelike. This is true of *Taxus* also. Here the leaves are broad and flat. Neither one would make a good Christmas tree—*Tsuga* branches are soft and droopy at the ends (beautiful!), and *Taxus* isn't the right shape and is too precious to waste on frivolous decoration.

Suppose that the tree has fruit still on it. *Abies* has large upright cones, *Picea* cones that hang down, *Pinus* cones that are varied but coarser and woodier, *Thuja* cones smaller with woody overlapping scales in pairs, *Tsuga* cones that are small and pendulous, *Chamaecyparis* cones that are small too. *Larix* cones are small, round, and erect. *Taxus* has red "berries"—a cuplike aril that holds the seed. *Juniperis* has blue "berries" and so does *Microbiota*.

This is a rather halting first step toward recognition of conifers. The next would be to identify the species, a much more demanding task that needs an encyclopedia such as W. J. Bean's *Trees & Shrubs Hardy in the British Isles* to be even moderately successful. However knowing something about the species most often met with as dwarf conifers in rock gardens could be helpful.

The fir often seen is *Abies balsamea* 'Nana', a flat-topped spreading mushroom, quite low but a good spread after ten years. There are two very variable *Chamaecyparis* species that have produced several dwarf forms. *C. obtusa* has thick, fat, bluish scales and many varieties worth putting in a trough. 'Nana' needs a trough both because it is so tiny and because it needs a bit of protection in winter. *C. pisifera* has sharp-ended, scalelike leaves. In a young plant these may be juvenile and look like short, soft needles, as in those of *C.* 'Snow', a slow growing mound that I had in a trough for years then moved to a raised bed for another five or six years. Now it is getting a little large for its setting and should be moved again, perhaps to a conifer border. *C. lawsoniana* is a little more tender and less often seen. *C. thyoides* is often seen in the form 'Andelyensis', which seems to produce multiple tops and stiff branches more 'erect' than the other species.

The most interesting junipers are forms of *J. communis*. The silver-backed leaves are sharp and in threes spaced around the twig. One dwarf is 'Berkshire', 'Compressa' is a small column, and 'Pencilpoint' a slender tall column. *J. scopulorum* has brown-red bark that shreds and pointed scales for leaves. 'Moonglow' is a tall, thin, bluish column.

Picea abies is the dark green Norway spruce and a standard tree for Christmas. There are a host of dwarf forms with short leaves, such as 'Little Gem', and 'Nidiformis'. *Picea glauca,* the white spruce, also has some great dwarfs, 'Gnome' and 'Pixie' and also a very familiar form called by Hillier 'Albertiana Conica' (and variations of this name in other catalogs) that keeps its neat, pyramidal form and person-sized appearance for many useful years. *Pinus pungens* is the Colorado spruce and best loved in its blue forms, when you might call it a Colorado blue spruce, a stiff, smoke-blue pyramid. The leaves are sharp and square as you roll them in your fingers. Pungent can mean sharp, not aromatic, so the name applies to the needles and not to the smell.

Pinus aristata, the bristlecone pine, has leaves dotted with white spots of resin. It grows slowly so no special form is needed for a rock garden. The Swiss stone pine, *Pinus cembra* has a form 'Compacta'. This has erect blue cones and soft needles. *Pinus mugo* has stiff, curvy needles and a few dwarf forms: 'Mops' and 'Pumilio' are two names. *Pinus parviflora,* the Japanese white pine, has curved, blue-green leaves with light blue reverse that gives the tree its interesting look. It is the pine in the design of the willow-pattern plate. It grows slowly but you can keep it even more elegant looking if you cut the candles in half while they are still soft in June. Our own white pine, *Pinus strobus,* is universally admired for its graceful look and soft, long needles. We are at the southern edge of its range and probably provide it with more ice storms than it would have to endure further north. In any case many of our trees have lost enormous limbs and branches recently as thick ice and heavy snow sat on them stubbornly for days at a time. So far they have recovered their beauty the following season. There is a dwarf form

'Macopin', a dramatic pendulous form, and a fastigiate form.

Except for *Pinus mugo,* all the pines mentioned so far have five needles in each bunch so this is not a very good criterion for determining the species. The Scots pine, *Pinus sylvestris,* has two needles in a bunch so you would be off to a good start if you found this to be the case. The form you might find in a rock garden is 'Beauvronensis'; there is a 'Repens' too but it is not very pretty for as long as I have had it. Scots pine has twisted blue-green needles and red bark.

The arbor-vitaes have one variable species, *Thuja occidentalis.* Normally this is columnar with leaves in flat sprays. Dwarfs tend to be globe shaped, rather dumpy with spectacular bronze winter foliage. Be sure you like this before you get one, because some people read any shade of brown as dead and probably haven't realized the value of bronze and gold against the snow. In increasing order of size, you could find 'Tiny Tim', 'Hetz's Midget', and 'Rhinegold'. *Thuja orientalis* doesn't seem to have any dwarf forms.

Our native hemlock *Tsuga canadensis* also has many forms. The needles are not notched at the ends, which helps to distinguish it from other tsugas, but most hemlocks you see will be these popular dwarfs. 'Cole's Prostrate' is well-known and one of the best however it is trained. Many people collect forms—'Beehive', 'Cappy's Choice', 'Hussii', and so on. Many of them have white tips or streaks on the needles and such types can be found in the local woods. I have grown a golden form 'Aurea Compacta' for at least ten years and it remains about two feet tall.

Perhaps the garden in which you are testing your skills at recognition contains conifers not in this list of Most Often Found. These can be baffling if you are trying to get everything into one of the slots so far described. *Microbiota decussata* has been recently available. This has scales like a *Thuja* but is a shrub spreading across the ground and having berries like a juniper. *Cryptomeria japonica* has red bark with pointed leaves and long, thin branches. There are a number of dwarf forms. 'Knaptonensis' has white tips. *Pseudotsuga menziesii* is called Oregon douglas fir and has flat needles like a hemlock *(Tsuga)* and is not a fir *(Abies);* the cones hang down, the needles grow around the stem and don't have the flat look of *Tsuga canadensis.* 'Little Jon' is a dwarf form. You might also come across *Cunninghamia, Sciadopitis,* and other rarities that the owner will be delighted to show you and be rather disappointed if you know them already. If your host is obviously proud of his treasure, it is unwise and unkind to treat it as commonplace. Let him discover it for himself in your garden when he pays a return visit.

And then there are plants that look like conifers under certain conditions. These you must be wary of. It is reprehensible to mistake a *Picea* for a *Tsuga* but to mistake a *Hebe* for a *Chamaecyparis* would be ignominy. Yet there is at least one *Hebe* that could be mistaken for one out of flower. Beware of dwarf, tight forms of heaths and heathers—they too can fool you. *Hudsonia, Leiophyllum,* and other ericaceous plants can have needlelike leaves too, and if they happen to be the wrong shape, they can catch you off guard. This piece, after all, was written to save your face when you enter the occult world of conifer. To help you recover some of your self respect, it is only fair to tell you that names of conifers have been mixed up for years and are only now emerging from utter confusion. Linnaeus named common spruce *Pinus abies,* Miller in 1768 named it *Abies picea.* In the nineteenth century it was still *Abies* in England while silver fir was *Picea;* Linnaeus had called this fir *Pinus picea.* As Bean cryptically remarks: this explains why the name of the common spruce is *Picea abies.* As gardeners we try to give plants whatever name we believe to be currently accepted. We need to have more or less consensus if we are to have intelligent intercourse and isn't that what talking about plants is? When I first started planting dwarf conifers I decided to delay trying to learn their names until I was genuinely interested in them and not merely following fashion. Now my garden is full of plants that have lost their labels and it has become imperative to sort out from old records which plant is which. Reading all the books has helped a little and if what I have extracted from Bean, Hillier, and Wyman, and a host of others—as well as learning and lore gleaned from visiting gardeners—has helped you to join the semi-cognoscenti and leave the semi-illiterati, so much the better. But please don't put me on the spot when you visit my garden.

~ ~

Plants for Troughs, Small Raised Beds, and Crevice Gardens

ॐ ॐ WE USE TROUGHS (large containers), raised beds, and other specially designed mini-gardens for two reasons. The first is aesthetic: you can examine plants with greater ease and pleasure if they are above ground-level—between shin and elbow for instance—for some plants are so diminutive that they can be easily lost in a rock garden and only make a statement when the frame around them is also small. Troughs, raised beds, and crevice gardens are three distinct steps on a journey from the artificiality of growing them in pots in an alpine house toward more natural conditions. The second reason is horticultural: some plants are happier in troughs, where exposure can be changed or modified relatively easily, where soil mixture and watering are controllable, and where winter protection is more manageable. On the negative side, any care that involves actually moving troughs would have to be avoided by most of the gardeners I know. Raised beds and crevice gardens are fixtures so their site should initially be chosen as carefully as possible. Plants in them benefit from their isolation from weedy intruders, fallen leaves tend to blow off more easily, and drainage is taken care of automatically. In crevice gardens, the roots of plants nestle against their own personal rocks and many seem to benefit from this warm-in-winter cool-in-summer attention. I want to mention a few of the plants I have tried to grow in troughs and in their near relations, small raised beds and crevice gardens.

We might start with what not to grow. Of course there is nothing that you couldn't put into a trough if you really wanted to, but it would be perverse to want to grow a tree unless you were willing to make a 'bonsai' of it and that would be a different hobby. Nor would you grow border perennials. Actually even 8" tall plants look wrong unless you stuff the trough full of annuals and trailers as though it were any old planter. But if you want to grow alpine plants with the "right" scale (your judgment), you will want their nonflowering parts to be less than 6" tall and probably less than 2". And when the flower stalk develops, 6" will seem like a very tall plant unless the trough is really big. Also we want the planting to last a long time (i.e., forever). This is more of an ideal than a practical aim because mortality of plants in a trough is at least as high as it is on the slopes of the rock garden. In the case of crevice gardens it is much higher. This may be something to do with the difficulty of the plants I have tried to grow in special conditions rather than the actual conditions. What we must not do is plant a robust grower that will spread to fill the trough in one season. However beautiful it looks you will have a planter and not a trough. The graceful green waterfall flowing over the edges of the trough is also colonizing the flat spaces of the interior. Don't plan for this kind of disaster. A trough is a terrible thing to waste. Size is less of a problem as the growing space gets larger but must always be considered. It would be much worse to waste the physical labor and emotional stress of making a crevice garden on space-gobbling mats. You can, after all, buy another trough.

Unsuitable plants are most arabis, aurinia, alyssum, iberis (regretfully), aubrietia, *Phlox subulata,* silenes, violas, delphiniums, aquilegias, campanulas, thymes, antenarrias, artemisias... In fact most plants are not suitable for troughs. You know after one season whether this or that plant deserves a trough. The worst thing you can do is to plant a rare, expensive, but unsuitable plant, that hates to be transplanted, in a trough. *Arnebia echioides* for instance is far too big for most portable troughs and has a root that doesn't like to be disturbed (but it would be a good plant for a crevice garden). A dwarf conifer may have to be avoided for the same reason—you may lose it when the inevitable transplant operation is attempted at the end of the year. You could lose the trough too in the struggle. I consider plants such as ramondas, auriculas, *Lewisia tweedyi, Saxifraga longifolia,* etc., too large for a trough, but not for a crevice garden. You may be able to accommodate one specimen plant of this magnitude but if it is happy it will overpower a medium-sized trough and if it is miserable it will spoil the effect and die leaving a large gap that the eye refuses to overlook.

Another type of plant you may want to avoid is the too happy selfsower. Any new bed or trough will always look raw and freshly made until there is some selfsowing and even though a newly planted trough wins a popularity contest at a plant show it won't impress the cognoscenti. A mature trough has volunteer seedlings of good plants along with the inescapable mosses and lichens. But enough of a good thing is all you want and some species are far too generous. So it may be best to avoid annuals and biennials and plants such as *Chaenorrhinum origanifolium, Lewisia pygmaea, Erinus alpinus,* and anything else that looks cute colonizing the open rock garden too gaily. If I subsequently recommend a selfsower it will mean it hasn't yet exceeded its quota of offspring in any of my troughs or small raised beds.

Perhaps the most satisfying and satisfactory groups of plants for these locations are the androsaces and their near relatives: the douglasias and small alpine primulas. I will divide them into types in order to pigeonhole many other species. The first type covers those androsaces that are *ideal.* TYPE 1 plants can be further subdivided. TYPE 1A plants form *mounds* that grow slowly enough so that even after five years or more you still have a lovable hump about 5" across. *A. villosa v. arachnoidea* is the epitome of this group along with its soulmate *A. muscoidea.* These beautiful plants are easygoing too. Growing more slowly is *A. pyrenaica* and its hybrid with *carnea,* sometimes called 'Millstream'. These form harder mounds of less fuzzy foliage. You could also try *A. ciliata, hausmannii, hedreantha, hirtella, obtusifolia* and *pubescens. A. lactaea* is easier than any of them and selfsows generously so it might belong in TYPE 1B. The categories are not clear-cut.

Douglasias are the American cousins of androsaces. *D. laevigata, nivalis, montana* are all highly desirable plants for troughs. Some primulas would be at home with androsaces: *Primula minima, P. X bileckii* and *P. villosa* are low enough. Other plants with this ideal mound/bun growth pattern include many of the drabas. The very best for beauty and amenability is probably something from the complex of species found under the names *rigida, bryoides,* and *imbricata.* I have had various plants with these names and by now I tend to call them all *D. rigida.* The mounds are hard and tight and almost indestructable. Expect contented expansion for at least ten years, by which time there will be plenty of seedlings for the new trough you will have to make.(Troughs don't stay 'in beauty' for much longer and you usually have to empty and replant much sooner.) These drabas are TYPE 1A plants that perform all through the year. If you are one of those eccentric people who doesn't like yellow, just close your eyes in early spring—you can still grow *Draba rigida* with perfect integrity. Other drabas that fit into this mound-making group would include *D. caucasica* (like an even finer *rigida*), *D. rosularis,* which is splendidly hairy and totally impervious to winter wet, *D. paysonii, D. sierrae,* and many of the aizoides group (for instance *D. hispanica, D. hoppeana, D. parnassica, D. aizoides*). But every new draba should be tried. From genera whose other members might be dismissed as unsuitable are *Arabis bryoides, A. androsacea, Edraianthus pumilio, E. serpyllifolia, E. dinaricus, Jasione amethystina, Eriogonum caespitosum, Degenia velebitica, Gypsophila aretioides,* and the plant everybody wants— *Petrocallis pyrenaica.* Not all the thlaspis are worth putting in a trough but *T. rotundifolium* and *T. stylosum* are excellent. The best leontopodiums form mounds too, even though they don't seem to live very long. Perhaps *L. nivale* is the ultimate in white foliage and elegant form. The western cushion phlox, *P. pulvinata, P. condensata, P. bryoides, P. hoodii* are all exquisite plants perfect for a trough.

Treat dianthus species with caution but *D. pavonius* would probably behave well enough. One thyme, *Thymus 'Elfin'*, and one geranium, *G. argenteum,* are not too rampant for a trough. *Helianthemum bryoides* is a tight, tiny shrub that starts off as a bun. *Lesquerella tumulosa* is the best representative of that genus. Bryoides (mosslike), tumulosa (mound-forming), pulvinata (cushion-forming), and condensata are all encouraging specific epithets to look for when you are in doubt about using a plant in a trough. Nana (dwarf) also sounds good but you have to know what the regular size would be.

All the Porophyllum section saxifrages are excellent trough plants. You can also raise the species from this section from seed and get good troughophiles. Try *S. grisebachii, S. ferdinandi-coburgii, S. marginata;* amongst the easiest hybrids are *S. X apiculata, S. X elisabethae.* But any hybrid 'kabschia' is worth putting in a trough. Many saxifrage enthusiasts have troughs containing only saxifrages; since they all bloom at roughly the same time, there is a spectacular concentration of color in late winter or early spring.

TYPE 1B are also ideal plants and form small buns and rosettes that tend to selfsow. Clusters of individual plants rather than notable mounds would be characteristic. *Androsace carnea* and *A. mathildae* are the obvious representatives. Well, you could find a mat of *carnea* eventually, but mostly what you get is a lot of small plants dotted around your miniature landscape. These are growing from seed overlooked by the local ants. *A. carnea* has some lovely forms with large pink flowers and some indifferent leggy whites especially under the name *A. brigantiaca. A. mathildae* is always white with relatively big flowers sitting wide-eyed directly on quarter-sized, hard, deep green buns. Does a single rosette make a bun? As they selfsow such plants give spacial continuity to the planting and an escape from the tyranny of the even spacing you are forced to use when you first start the trough.

Other TYPE 1B plants include *Physaria alpina,* (not a bun, but it selfsows agreeably), the aizoides drabas, *Gentiana verna* (you have to be good to get this one going), *Primula scotica* (another minor miracle), and *P. modesta.* By now I would definitely avoid annual androsaces *(A. lactiflora, A. septentrionalis),* which quickly become a nuisance, taking up valuable space and smothering their betters. *A. armenum* is biennial and borderline acceptable, being prettier and less bountiful with its seedlings. *Papaver alpinum* in its many subspecies and forms is also dangerous without constant removal of seedlings. There are many composites that form buns, mats, or rosettes that will selfsow. *Erigeron compositus* is the most reliable, but only allow a really good form to remain (short stems, strong color, tight foliage, and it must have ray flowers). Most dianthus are willing selfsowers and a compact one like *D. freynii* might be tolerated, especially if you are willing to pluck out the larger, more splendid specimens. If you don't, the dianthus will take over.

TYPE IC are mat formers. These spread by stolons mostly, but by the time you have a decent mat there may also be some selfsowing going on. *Androsace chamaejasme* is a good example and *A. sempervivoides* an easy one. You may have to remove bits of plant if they encroach on other plants. For this reason I don't think *A. sarmentosa* is a good trough plant. It will fill the whole space in too short a time. If you plant a trough with other aggressives that can take care of themselves you can have a trough full of color for a couple of seasons. But would you want to use a trough in this way?

Every true mat that roots down as it expands has to be watched in a trough. Some grow so slowly that their tenure in the same trough lasts many years. Forms of *Iberis saxatile,* for instance. The plant may come as *I. pygmaea.* Some encrusted saxifrages will take forever to grow into large mats. *S. paniculata 'Minutifolia'* is one of them, but others grow too large to be in a trough for long. *Erigeron chrysopsidis brevifolius* and *E. aureus* make low mats of yellow daisies. Townsendias would also make perfect mats if only they would live a reasonable length of time. Sometimes you get a glimmer of possibility from *T. rothrockii* but you have to be content with a transient most of the time. *Petrophytum cinerascens* seems to be the easiest petrophytum. The mat is a tangle of fine gray leaves and the flowers are 2" "astilbes." Gentians of the *acaulis* group form good solid mats at varying speeds. Watch that their splendid, fat flowers don't steal the space of their neighbors. Many alpine primulas also form mats that look good in a trough. *P. clarkei, P. minima, P. wulfeniana* are low. Many of the auricula hybrids are too tall and too vigorous. *P. auricula* itself can form beautiful clumps of rosettes but in flower it may look top-heavy.

The small western United States heucheras form attractive mats with pretty leaves, as does *Telesonix jamesii*. Try *H. grossularifolia* or *H. pulchella*. Several good penstemons form mats or near mats: *P. laricifolius, P. aridus, P. linarioides, P. teucrioides, P. caespitosus*. Some eriogonums form mats without swamping other inmates: *E. douglasii, E. kennedyi,* and well-behaved forms of *E. ovalifolium* and *E. flavum. Helianthemum canum balcanum* forms a perfect gray mat and is a mild selfsower. There are many small alyssums such as *A. propinquum,* but in my experience most of the elegant alyssums either die after flowering or leave too many offspring.

There is another Androsace that needs its own pigeonhole. *A. lanuginosa* is a trailer. It sends out long stems that don't root down in any obnoxious way, but in a trough it needs to be planted at the edge and instructed to keep its stems outside the trough. If you want your trough to bloom into late summer, this plant is indispensable. For a similar trailing effect you might use a small summer gentian such as *G. grossheimii* or even a fall gentian like *G. sino-ornata,* but their many stems and substantial flowers could wreak havoc unless you allowed them plenty of precious space. In a raised bed or a crevice garden these desirable plants can be very decorative.

TYPE 2 are even "better" plants than those in TYPE 1; i.e., meaning more desirable, more beautiful, more rare, more difficult, and therefore less ideal. In an alpine house they may be easy—in a trough they may only merit the description possible, and in a crevice garden or a raised bed they would be a gamble. The trick would be to regulate soil and weather. One good first move is to

plant these prima donnas in a trough you can lift and move. At least
you would be able to regulate the amount of sun and in winter you
would be able to haul them into a coldframe for protection against
fickle precipitation. Everybody with such a trough should try *Androsace vandellii,* the queen of androsaces. After three or four years
you may achieve a perfect grayish mound two or three inches across
covered with exquisite white flowers. It will then probably die. But
it isn't monocarpic; there will have been a scattering of flowers in
the buildup years. And with skill and luck you could keep it much
longer. Those that can, do; those that cannot, weep. Close in god-
liness are *A. alpina, A. helvetica,* and *A. brevis.*

Non-androsaces that would fill you with joy but are more likely
to burden you with grief are *Physoplexis comosa* (not impossible in a
crevice garden), *Kelseya uniflora,* any dionysia, *Veronica bombycina,
Primula allionii, Aquilegia jonesii, Draba mollissima, D. acaulis, D.
polytricha, D. propinqua, Calceolaria darwinii (uniflora),* and a long
list of other southern hemisphere plants. Some of these plants
might be quite easy in an alpine house or in a climate less rigorous
than mine in Massachusetts. So try these plants patiently and only
admit defeat when you are convinced they are not worth the cost of
a controlled-temperature alpine house. I haven't yet succeeded in
raising an Acantholimon that was really happy, nor a Convolvulus
I could be proud of; but if I could they would go into a trough. *Eritrichium nanum* doesn't really like living outdoors, even for a summer, but *E. howardii* can live in a trough for two or even three years.
Another short list of failures includes: *Notothlaspi rosulatum,
Paraquilegia grandiflora, Anchusa caespitosa, Campanula piperi,
Centaurea achterovii,* and *Dicentra peregrina.* Difficult gentians for
troughs would include *G. froelichii, G. orbicularis,* and *G. pyrenaica.*
If you grow as many as five of these ultra plants in troughs you can
give yourself a ten for superior plantsmanship.

TYPE 3 are less good plants than those in TYPE 1, in the sense
that they are too vigorous for a long term sojourn in a trough. *Androsace sarmentosa* is the paradigm—an excellent plant in the rock

garden, it grows too fast for a trough. You could use it if you were very firm about not allowing it to spread further than you want. Use cuttings as propagation material. It roots very easily.

A list of similar plants would be endless but would include miniature mossy saxifrages such as 'Peter Pan'. A normal *Saxifraga trifurcata* wouldn't work though. By the time it has reached flowering time the mat billows over its neighbors, and hacking it back then is too late, and the beauty of some large mounds is ruined by indignant scissorwork. Even some encrusted saxifrages misbehave in troughs and don't take kindly to hacking. But if you don't mind growing plants that have to be disciplined, try *Aubrieta pinardii, scardica, canescens, thessala; Alyssum pulvinaris* or many other mat-forming alyssums; *Draba sibirica, Asperula gussonii, Vitaliana primuliflora,* and its many subspecies; *Campanula betulifolia, C. raineri, C. cochlearifolia,* and other mats; but not *C. carpatica, C. poscharskiana, C. rotundifolia,* or any other rollicking, happy-go-lucky plant, which should only be turned loose in a large rock garden.

TYPE 4 are types of plant with no Androsace example; i.e., trees and shrubs. Apart from dwarf conifers, which are almost a cliche in troughs, you could consider daphnes, which grow quite slowly in their early years. You would, however, have to find a permanent home in the garden after three or four seasons. *D. jasminea, D. petraea, D. retusa* (try this in a raised bed rather than a trough), *D. arbuscula,* and a dwarf form of *D. cneorum* are all possible. There are excellent, shrubby penstemons that can be used to add woody texture—*P. davidsonii* has many forms and you can find a small leaf, tight mat. Since you are going to give winter protection to some of your troughs you could try *P. newberryi* and *P. rupicola.* In the open garden these two are liable to get severe die-back. There is a tiny elm *Ulmus parvifolia* 'Hokkaido' that stays dwarf for a long time. Just be careful when you look for dwarf shrubs that the word means small in all its dimensions. You wouldn't want to put in a trough a plant like *Prunus pumila depressa,* which hugs the ground but spreads far and wide quite rapidly. Many mat-forming salixes are suitable for a time but eventually need a lot of spread room. *S. reticulata* is the safest, the hardest to find, and the hardest to keep. Some junipers would form mats too. But I think a list of dwarf conifers would be out of place here. There are so many and it would spoil your fun to single out any of the scores of beautiful possibilities. Other deciduous shrublets would include *Hypericum coris, Eriogonum thymoides, Fumana thymifolia,* and a few woody Alyssums, for instance *A. davisianum.* But the effect of these little shrubs is more moundlike than treelike and none of them takes the place of a daphne.

TYPE 5 are plants that blaze away for one season but cannot be relied on to do it twice. They are irresistible for a trough because of reason 1 above (the aesthetic reason) and if you can actually succeed with them, reason 2 (the horticultural reason) comes into play. *Dianthus alpinus, Phacelia sericea, Iberis candolleana, Calceolaria biflora* come to mind. Also the dwarf lupins from the Rockies: *L. breweri* and *lepidus lobbii* rarely stay a second year. Nor does *Mertensia viridis* or *M. alpina.* Even *Polemonium viscosum* is unreliable. You could call them the only annuals worth growing in a trough, except that there are genuine annuals I wouldn't exclude such as *Sedum pilosum.* Townsendias too are always welcome whether they are annual or biennial. *Inula acaulis* is a biennial and *Laurentia minuta* an annual and both are worth growing.

TYPE 6 are succulents and cacti, and they may need troughs or raised beds for themselves. We tend to have immovable prejudices about them, associating them with desert conditions. But many alpines are growing in desert conditions and many cacti are alpine plants. My reasons for segregation would be self-protection and possibly aesthetics. Anyway you can find room for *Coryphantha vivipara* and other *Escobarias* and *Echinocereus. Orostachys spinosa* would fit into any planting. Other succulents would include *Talinum okanoganense, Lewisia rediviva, L. rupicola, Spraguea (Calyptridium) umbellata,* and any other miniature example. *Lewisia cotyledon* is worth a monoculture trough. If well-grown to portly perfection it would use too much space in a small trough. Sedums, sempervivums, and delospermums are tempting as "groundcover" but even the smallest is too vigorous to be allowed near TYPE 1 plants. Better to try monoculture for them too.

Well, you could go on inventing types forever and there are many plants that are useful that don't fit into any of the categories so far. Where shall we place astragalus and oxytropis? We obviously don't want to put *A. gremlii* in a trough, but there would be nowhere else for *A. ceramicus*, which needs all the coaxing you can muster to produce its spectacular pods. Then there are the multiple rosette-formers such as *Jurinella moschus, Claytonia megarhiza, Carduncellus rhaponticoides, Crepis pygmaea,* and *Limonium minutum.* Shall we grow *Delphinium luteum?* You can answer questions like the last one by trial and error. If you like it, obviously you find a way to grow it. In time we form our own ideas about what a trough should be used for and ultimately what it should look like. The miniature "scene" becomes irrelevant. If you insist on a reduced version of Nature, you will think of a trough without rocks and miniature trees to represent the alpine tundra or even a woodland clearing. You can do and think what you like.

～ ～

Part Four

❧

THE PASSAGE OF TIME

The Rock Garden in Spring

✤ ✤ SOME TIME AFTER mid-March, one or more of the following significant events occur: Canada geese fly over, headed north; coldframes are left open all night; a snowdrop bayonet drops its head and opens; redwings, cowbirds, robins, starlings, grackles arrive; grosbeaks, juncos, red squirrels leave; a warm rain thaws the ground; the first windless 70° day since fall arrives; turkeys scratch the parking lot looking for leftover sunflower seed; raccoons quarrel after dark; chipmunks scrabble in the leaves looking for maple seeds; hawks circle high overhead looking for food; the first seedlings sprout; the grass greens. Some combination of these events signifies the onset of spring. There will be setbacks later— major snowstorms, heavy frosts, and floods—but we know that these tiresome delays cannot change the basic fact that days are becoming longer than nights, and the sun, given a chance, will get warmer.

Seed is still arriving by mail but is reduced to a trickle—stray packets from tardy friends or leftovers from a fellow seedaholic. Seed sowing has stopped except for the annuals and these will probably be done before mid-April. What do we do in spring? Garden work is mostly cosmetic—if you didn't weed in the fall you have to start right away (it may already be too late), if you didn't edge in the fall, the garden won't look right until you do it. It would be impossible to have picked up all the fall leaves so you can do that too, along with all the branches and twigs shed through the winter by windbattered trees. And you can pick up the bits of plastic pots you stepped on last November, the broken trays, plastic bags, styrofoam packing, and other detritus of the busy winds. As you weed and scavenge you can carry with you a bunch of fresh labels to replace the sad, shattered shards that litter the March garden. You will also need a pencil and a flat object to double as a writing desk. Labels written on your knee while you balance yourself on your heels in a stiff breeze with cold hands and a runny nose are seldom decipher-able later in the year.

By the beginning of April, the garden is mostly cleaned up and you are ready to receive the plants you ordered in so prodigally from the mail-order nurseries in January. Like buses in New York City, these ignore prearranged schedules and arrive in a cluster one day and then nothing for two weeks. On days you get a multiple deliv-ery everything has to stop except plant handling. First, though, you have to get into the box after guessing which side is up. Then you have to get rid of several cubic feet of newspaper, styrofoam, excel-sior, peat moss, and unravel several feet of sticky tape, rubber bands, aluminum foil, and plastic wrap. All this is part of an obstacle course to test your love of alpine plants and as partial penance for ordering more than you can handle. As you disinter and disentangle the plants one by one, you should pot them up. I use ordinary seed com-post. Never plant them directly in the garden. I used to do this and had many failures. The only exceptions are plants that are simply too big for the pots you have available. Then you must plant out whatever the weather, water in, and cover with a bucket. If it is ac-tually snowing you might want to sit each plant in shallow water until planting out is less harrowing. If a plant looks sickly or small, treat it as a cutting by starting it off in sand. If plants arrive in the pots they were grown in, you may feel that you can just put them in a cold frame until you are ready to plant out. However it is usually sound policy to repot. Replace their soil with your own mixture and comb out the roots. Potbound plants almost never establish if you just plug them into a big enough hole and firm down the soil. I have a little rake, 2" wide, designed for indoor gardening, that acts as a root comb. Heathers and other plants grown in a peat mixture need fairly rough treatment and of course a similar compost. Beware of woody plants with underdeveloped root systems; leave them in peace in the pot they came until they have a decent set of roots.

Buying plants is fun and the nurseries do us a great service in offering new plants, rare plants, well-grown plants, beautiful forms.

But any consignment can contain a disappointment. Expect this and try not to write endless complaining letters to nurserymen at shipping time. For reasons never fully explained there is always a nursery that ships in late May when you requested early April. This too requires patience. Once in twenty years I failed to get any order at all. Once or twice I have actually been enraged enough to call a dilatory merchant. This is not worth the cost of the call, for they have perfectly good excuses and you have to back down.

April is seed-germinating time. A few sprout in late March but April sees a steady parade of emerging cotyledons. Some break through tentatively in ones and twos, some spring up thick and green and uniform as though by consensus every one chose the same hour, some send up a 2" string of pale arching thread that looks doomed to collapse but usually doesn't. Peculiarities of timing make you want to ask profound questions about the vagaries of Nature. Why, for instance, did *Penstemons albidus, centranthifolius, fran-cisci-pennellii, fendleri, pallidus, palmeri, pinifolius, subulatus, su-perbus,* and *triphyllus* all germinate on April 27 last year, and next day nine more penstemons germinated? While eight *Dianthus alpi-nus* seedpots germinated respectively on April 6, 15, 17, 20, May 1, 7, 8, and 24, spread over a seven-week period! Looking is a daily event in April. I had sown about 1,700 pots of seed that year from different sources; if a species was very desirable, and there was enough seed, I sowed two pots at different times. These were placed twenty-four at a time in open lattice trays with a second tray on top to keep heavy rain, animals, and other accidents from disturbing the soil, then a hunk of wood to stop the trays from flying off. This meant close to one hundred trays to inspect each day. Sprouted pots are collected into trays, recorded for the computer files, and then left open to the sun and weather. They don't usually need care until they are ready for transplanting or until hot weather threatens to dry them out. This seed watch can be very exciting. Howard Pfeifer explains: "You have to get your kicks wherever you can." What seed freaks enjoy may not have universal appeal.

One of the biggest joys is to get germination from pots you kept from last year. It isn't worth keeping every pot that fails to germinate for a second year. I no longer keep ungerminated pots of composites for instance (though viable seed that you didn't sow will usually remain viable a second year), but androsaces must never be discarded until they have been given at least two years to appear. It is normal for *A. ciliata, cylindrica, villosa,* and *vandellii* not to show the first year, and the same with douglasias. Iris, hostas, lilies, and bulbs in general can be late germinaters. Some seed of course will never germinate—*Salix, Jeffersonia, Cypripedium*—while some germinates sporadically over weeks—*Astragalus, Oxytropis.* I usually transplant the first flush and discard the rest, which may mean finding a stray astragalus sprouting in a dianthus pot. The real treasures such as *Aquilegia jonesii, Physoplexis comosa,* and *Dicentra peregrina* seem to be oblivious to time and weather and try to surprise you in July or October.

In May you are still very much on the watch for seeds but by now fifty percent of them will have germinated and your attention is turning to transplanting and planting out. Transplanting is a very personal operation. I use the same compost as for seeds (fifty-percent coarse sand and fifty-percent commercial peat-based mix with a little fertilizer), but other opinions abound. Transplant "when they are big enough to handle" and "before the roots are too difficult to disentangle." Both rules vary from species to species. If it grows slowly enough *(Saxifraga)* and you have sown the seed thinly enough, you could leave these until September or the following spring. If growth is too thick *(Meconopsis, Primula)* but the roots are tiny and flimsy you may want to transplant small bunches intending either to thin down to one plant in each pot (I never do this) or separate them again when they are larger. They often grow better after separation and sometimes one or two vigorous plants take over and the rest die off mysteriously and without fuss. Nature makes the choice of which plants to save. Most of the time *(Anemone, Aquilegia, Delphinium)* there will not be much doubt about when the seedlings are ready to transplant—the first and possibly the second pair (not always a pair) of true leaves has formed and the root system has reached the bottom of the pot. Some plants *(Allium, Geum, Anemone)* will separate easily into singles without any great pulling or scrabbling; sometimes roots, leaves, or both (campanulas) will get entangled, and disengaging them one at a time is tricky. I like to comb out the roots before trying. The ideal wetness of the compost is also very personal. Some composts fall apart when dry so it is sometimes recommended to dry out the pot, then drop it on to the bench. The seedlings will then fall apart. I have not found that this method works for me, and in cases where the seedlings can be separated with soil clinging to the roots it is best to have the compost moist and separate into small plugs easily potted up. Anyway there are no universal rules and you have to find your own way. If your seedlings die within a week or so suspect that the compost is too airless, too soggy, contaminated, the seedling is underdeveloped, roots are damaged, slugs. If your seedlings dry out too quickly suspect that the compost is too loose, is not planted firmly enough, there's too little humus in the mixture. If you get moss and liverwort, stop using garden soil in your compost and keep your workbench clean. If your seedlings are stringy and weak they probably didn't have enough light after germination. This is usual if you try to grow seeds on a windowsill.

But ultimately spring is about the glory of the rock garden; our reward for the months of waiting and the years of preparation. The first wave of color is the yellow of drabas. I have a small raised bed devoted solely to drabas. They are really grown for their satisfying mats and buns in greens that range from the gray of *D. rosularis* to the deep green of *D. cuspidata.* The flowers have a narrow range of deep yellows plus a very few good whites, not many whites being worth growing. Nevertheless drabas are very welcome and as a group have a long period in flower with often a spotty preview in October and November. The easiest mats *(D. sibirica)* can be used to edge a border. Alongside drabas the bulbs erupt into a splendor

of yellow, purple, and white crocus, *Galanthus, Eranthis,* and *Iris.*
Connoisseurs and collectors see bulbs as precious individuals with
subtle differences in form and color and degree of rarity. Landscapers think in drifts and use *Crocus tomassinianus* or *Galanthus elwe-
sii* to cover large areas hoping eventually for selfsown seedlings.
Most of us grow bulbs in units of a dozen and think ourselves lucky
if we get two or three of that dozen flowering a second year. Chipmunks and mice take their toll but many a group decreases sponta-
neously without help from rodents. Because of this unreliability
and because maturing foliage adds very little beauty to the May-
June garden, it probably pays to plant very sparingly in a small rock
garden and keep your display "drifts" for the edge of a perennial or
shrub border. Or invent a place that seems conspicuous in April and
invisible in June.

In among these early birds are the tiny *Narcissus asturiensis*
and *N. juncifolius, Corydalis bulbosa, Anemone blanda, Muscari
azureum,* and two ravishing rock plants, *Eunomia oppositifolia* and
Jeffersonia dubia. The next wave creeps in before this first group is
exhausted but we are soon aware that the blue and gold of *Narcissus* and *Scilla* have taken over along with a scattering of early tulips.
The order of flowering varies from year to year and garden to garden. Compare last year's diary entry with what is taking place this
year. Somewhere along in early April, *Adonis amurensis* astonishes
us with enormous gold heads and ferny leaves that begin by fram-
ing the flowers and gradually overwhelm them as they fade. And the
earliest shrub that has been trying to flower even before the snows
left, *Daphne mezereum,* opens and fills the garden with a powerful
perfume. By the time the second wave of bulbs recedes, tulips come
into their own and complete the rainbow spectrum with brilliant
reds, oranges *(T. whittallii),* and an almost mauve *(T. humilis).* Fritillarias and erythroniums too; there seem to be a number of fritil-
laries that tolerate life outside an alpine house *(F. camschatcensis, F.
ionica, F. assyriaca, F. imperialis, F. persica,* etc.) but only a few erythroniums are permanent for me *(E. dens canis, E.* 'Pagoda', and

'White Beauty'). *E. americanum* has beautiful leaves but is native here and very weedy. If a clump gets established in good soil there may be flowers, but more usual are thick carpets of shiny, mottled leaves without flowers.

By this time the nonbulbous plants are in flower and the other crucifers take over from the drabas. These are *Arabis (sturii, ferdinandi-coburgii, caucasica, blepharophylla), Alyssum (cuneifolium, handellii, saxatile), Schivereckia (podolica, doerfleri), Kernera, Hutchinsia,* and later *Iberis (saxatile, pygmaea, sempervirens).* The *Erysimums* also start flowering and hardly stop the entire season. Particularly attractive are the low ones, *E. amoenum, E. nivale, E. kotschyanum.* Saxifrages start to open with the drabas, first the kabschias, then the silvers and the mossies. When they start to brown and die back you can fill in the gap with sandy soil and sometimes end up with two or three plants instead of one. Sometimes you are left with none at all, so you should take cuttings if you want to retain the mossies. There are usually a few seedlings too so be careful weeding. The kabschias will grow outside and flower well but you perhaps get better value if they are indoors or at least in a container where they can be admired at close quarters.

Troughs and containers are also an important part of spring. They are the best way to grow many androsaces and douglasias. In pots in the alpine house they are victimized by aphids, and since I am not prepared to fight pests with a spray gun all winter, I plant androsaces in containers and winter them in a coldframe. The easiest to keep are *A. villosa, A. mathildae,* and *A. carnea*; the most spectacular are *A. vandellii* and *A. aizoon coccinea* (for the color). Others that seem possible are *A. ciliata* and *A. hausmannii,* but all the ones that increase by rosettes *(A. sarmentosa, A. sempervivoides, A. chamaejasme)* are perfectly easy in the rock garden. So are all the forms of *Vitaliana primuliflora.* Don't despise the annuals and biennials; *A. albana* is delightful and some of the annuals *(A. lactiflora)* produce a gay haze when allowed to selfsow.

Halfway through May is probably the height of everybody's

garden. Lewisias, veronicas, aquilegias, *Gentiana acaulis,* and *G. verna, Iris pumila,* and more are starting. The shrubs are flowering—*Spirea, Malus, Exochorda, Cytisus.* The first cactus buds on *Neobesseya missouriensis* are forming. A Baltimore oriole has been spotted. Heaven!

Near the end of May the first *Paeonia* opens *(P. tenuifolia)* and this is an omen that the rock garden might soon have to take second place to the border. But early in June there is still a lot of interest left as the penstemons, arenarias, campanulas, dianthus, and lupins hit their stride. Ramondas are in bloom as are erigerons and edraianthus. But so is *Iris sibirica* and *Campanula glomerata, Centaurea dealbata,* and the first Oriental poppies. We are now torn between looking and doing. The borders have to be weeded so that you can actually see the effect of purples and oranges that demand our attention. We garden in Two Worlds—the World of subtle mauves and blues of *Penstemon aridus, P. eriantherus,* and fifty others that defy our ability to photograph; charming Dianthus and the rich purple of minuscule *Edraianthus serpyllifolius* and *E. pumilio,* and the World of the border with its robust forms and colors. Most gardeners have a Third World that is neither perennials nor rock plants. It may be woodland plants, prairie plants, succulents and cacti, rhododendrons, primulas, bog plants, ferns. If we have a woodland garden or primulas, our attention has already been diverted by hepaticas, anemonellas, trilliums, cypripediums, uvullarias, pulmonarias and dicentras, and the cowslips, oxlips, primroses, and polyanthas that carpet the edge of the woodland. It is a classic *embarras de richesse.* To complete our delight, the black fly have stopped. The deer fly have begun their piercing jabs, but they usually stay still long enough to dispose of them manually.

The end of spring brings us a feeling that is as close to contentment as gardening ever allows. We have put behind us the losses of the previous winter, the anguish of weather-related problems. If there has been a drought, the effects are not yet visible. More than likely the worst drought is yet to come but meanwhile the air is soft, the sun is warm, and the garden never looked better.

～ ～

The Rock Garden in Summer

꙳ ꙳ NEW ENGLAND SUMMER follows swiftly on the heels of spring. The magnificence of late May and early June is continued into July, as the rock garden remains colorful without apparent effort, and there are enough species that continue even into the hot days of August. Perhaps the garden ceases to be a blaze of color but it never loses interest completely. The genus *Dianthus* bridges spring and summer, and early June sees it at its height. *D. alpinus, callizonus,* and *glacialis* give up early but *D. erinaceus, freynii, nardiformis, neglectus, gratianopolitanus,* and *pavonius* grace the rock garden into July, and in the border or larger rock garden *D. lumnizteri, amurensis, gigantea,* and forms of *plumarius* will be flowering. At the edge of the woodland a few weedy ones are willing to oblige—*D. deltoides* and *armeria.* The bright colors of *D. chinensis* look best with other annuals.

Campanulas, adenophoras, symphyandras, and codonopsis give us whites, grays, blues, and purples. There are difficult scree plants *Campanula zoysii, piperi, raineri,* and *betulifolia*; standards of the rock garden and wall garden *C. garganica, tommasiniana,* and *cochlearifolia,* and scores of middling difficulty. If you grow campanulas from seed every unfamiliar name is suspect until proved not to be a version of *C. carpatica* or *rotundifolia* or worse still of *C. rapunculoides* or *persicifolia.* You need to be either hopelessly tolerant or anxious to fill your empty acres if you plant *C. punctata.* I sometimes think plants are called aggressive because that is the emotion inspired in the gardener who ultimately has to curb their invasions. Biennial plants such as *Symphyandra hoffmannii,* whose glorious display of enormous creamy white bells enchants us through the summer, can produce rosettes that casually obliterate their neighbors. You have to learn rosette recognition and ruthlessly pull out plants wherever they could be a nuisance, but leave enough plants in the right places to ensure next year's display. Some campanulas alas are perennial and in addition to producing vast quantities of seed speed underground coming up for air in the middle of a peony or a rhododendron. If this happens no amount of pulling out individual plantlets will rid you of this excursion center for further travel. You may have to dig out the hotel plant and remove every bit of resident root. *C. alliariifolia* and *C. punctata* are familiar adversaries. There are plenty of biennial campanulas everybody should grow at least once. Some are difficult, but can be a showstopper for impressionable visitors and give a long period of pleasure, some come back year after year but never become a nuisance. Try *C. sartori* in a scree, *C. lyrata* in a rock garden, *C. incurva* in a prominent place in a large rock garden, but give two feet of spreading room for its crowded crown of big bells. Grow *C. medium* for a border and *C. pyramidalis* for a patio pot (feed it heavily if you can bring it through the winter). Both are spectacular with luck and care.

Every gardener sooner or later specializes and you ought to have a collection of summer blooming species of one genus. How about delphiniums or aconitums? You could segregate them at the edge of the wood. The trouble with collecting one genus is that you sow the seed of a dozen different species in February, you get seven germinations, five of these give you plants ready to put out in the fall. Four survive the winter and bloom in the summer; of these, two are identical and you don't know which name is correct, one is misnamed, and the fourth has lost its label. You have to be prepared to build up your collection slowly—don't be discouraged by this gloomy scenario. Besides you should pin your hopes on several genera. So try also species peonies, composites, silenes, and gentians. If you can grow bulbs go in for liliums and alliums for summer bloom. *L. superbum* and *L. canadense* are our local lilies and among the best in the world. They grow in full sun or dappled shade and their only limitation is their edibility—from eight-foot high buds, to eight-inch deep bulbs, they are preferred food of deer, mice, and chipmunks. The latest protective device (after failing with hair, soap, urine, etc.) is tough plastic bird netting draped over the base of a clump. Anything that prevents access for deer also keeps people away and the physical inconvenience of uncontrollable netting is unattractive, as is the close-up view of this jumble of "invisible" plastic. But if you can grow lilies at all you could also grow *Nomocharis saluenensis* and *Cardiocrinum (Lilium) giganteum* and then you would be close to paradise.

A genus we all grow is *Aquilegia*. These are notoriously difficult to keep pure, so grow them from seed collected in the wild. And don't attempt to give positive identification to any unmarked plant in your or anyone's garden, especially if it is not in flower. An extremist would say that you should never grow aquilegias from garden-collected seed, but seed labeled *A. bertolonii* for instance will probably be on the small side, on the blue side, and on the elegant side, and probably would not disgrace your garden unless you had an impeccable reputation for being right about the names of the plants you grow. Aristocratic plants such as *A. jonesii* and *A. saxi-montana* provide endless hours of discussion about their authenticity.

But rock gardeners are more likely to leave their gardens in summer than in spring. This is a good time to visit other people's gardens. We visit before the memory of our own vivid display in May has faded so seeing a garden past its peak gives one a false sense of superiority. We are not influenced by any memory of its recent splendor. We repress these odious thoughts and immerse ourselves in the new garden's potential, subtly planning the owner's next move. "Why not move the larch to the center of the lawn?"; "Isn't it time to pick up and divide those overcrowded colchicums?"; "I'd make your next bog here," and other superfluous advice. Or we play the one-up-manship game: "I used to grow that," implying "I no longer think it worthwhile growing" and obscuring the true meaning: "It died." Or "I have the one with the variegated leaf," "I only grow the dwarf form." But most negative thoughts are

overshadowed by feelings of admiration and an incomparable feeling of goodwill generated by the shared experiences of rock gardening. The gardener by our side is showing his or her work of art
and the advice and commentary that we attempt is no more than a
coverup for our inability to verbalize the admiration we feel.

When we head for the mountains we usually leave the garden
for a week or a month at a time. Where do gardeners go in the summer? Washington folk have the Olympics and share the Cascades
with gardeners from Oregon, Montanans can go to Glacier, the
Denver crowd can climb around on Mount Evans. Southern gardeners go north, Easterners go west, the British go to France and
Spain, the Czechs go to Romania and Russia, New Zealanders go
to the Rockies, the Japanese go to North Carolina. Seed collectors,
photographers, and botanizers from all over the gardening world go
on uncomfortable treks to Turkey, Kashmir, and Hokkaido. Native
plant groups fan out in Nevada and Montana. The Scottish Rock
Garden Club journal reports that seventy-five percent of the people you would meet on a certain ridge near Wengen would be rock
gardeners. It is safe to say that anyone above 10,000 feet in Colorado
looking down rather than up is probably a rock gardener.

How can these people leave their gardens?

Well, to go anywhere requires weeks of preparation. You obviously can't leave a weedy garden and you have to see that the
seedlings are safe. That much is minimal. If you have an automatic
sprinkler you can arrange all the pots of transplants, the sprouted
pots not yet transplanted, and the unsprouted pots within the orbit
of the sprinkler. Program for a daily sprinkling and then you can
leave them without a care. Or can you? Your ears are glued to every
forecast hoping for rain the day you leave and intermittent showers
for the following two weeks. If this is your hunch it would be wrong
to overwater and return to drowned plants in soggy soil. If there is
no rain at all while you are away then once a day for fifteen minutes
isn't quite enough. The situation is tense—shall you cancel the trip
after all?—or shall you lose face and ask a friend to look in?—you

bought the computerized water regulator just to be independent of your friend's unreliable favors. If you don't have an automatic system the worry is unbearable; you might just as well bid your seedlings (and six months of anticipation) a fond goodbye and resort to all-purpose prayer. If you are in the habit of watering the garden too, the problem is that much worse and no matter what you do a good prayer will come in handy.

And when you return you find chaos. As you drive up to the house you see long grass where lawn used to be—the relief at finding the house still standing passes quickly into anxiety about the nonvisible part of the garden. A quick run around confirms your worst fears. The garden has been engulfed—mostly oxalis. That is the most pervasive and showy of all the summer weeds. Later you find that enormous flat mats of euphorbia and portulaca have gone to town on every path and in every bed, and wherever grass meets earth there is a dense band of rumex. The whole garden is uniformly green. Did you leave a plant in the greenhouse? It is now a brown twig with a few shrivelled leaves lying on the soil. The pots in the coldframe look dry and a few of the leafier plants are wilting. The ground around the automatic sprinkler is sodden; under the first pot you lift is a large slug. A more careful look around the garden reveals dead buns and browned mats. It takes a week or so to recover your sangfroid and accept your losses gracefully. That first glimpse was the worst; once the weeds have gone, and the dead things have been removed and the shrubs and mats trimmed you can put your losses into perspective. Five *Dianthus alpinus* died but there are still three left. And not all the transplants of *Penstemon rupicola* dried out. The only things gone completely are the campanulas, codonopsis and phyteumas, the oxytropis and the delphiniums— every one eaten by slugs. Don't throw the pots out though, sometimes there is enough left of the stub for it to sprout again—the roots are okay.

Anyway your car or your suitcase is loaded with plants pressed on you by kind gardeners from distant parts. Or you have returned with eighty packets of seed collected on the trip. Most of them say *Aquilegia ?jonesii, Silene sp., ?composite,* or sometimes just "?" You even forgot where you collected it. If you brought back cuttings or plants they are probably a soggy pudding in a plastic bag—you rush these into a first aid sand bed even before you check the house for burglars. A week after you return and the balance sheet is complete you are glad you went on the trip. Not only for the precious souvenirs of Mount Hood or the Bighorns but because seeing plants in the wild gives you an insight into your own garden. Seeing somebody else's garden gives you encouragement and new ideas. Bringing back seed gives you the best reminder of the mountains—the pleasure will last one full year minimum and maybe a lifetime. You can also share that pleasure with others in the seed exchanges and have perfect strangers all over the world bless you for having been to Idaho and having brought a new physaria into cultivation.

Summer is seed-collecting time in the garden too. Every dry day you go the rounds with scissors and plastic containers to collect the bounty. And of course summer is the time you are grateful for the annuals, for reliable, slowly changing color—the curse and the blessing of annuals. Grow even the fickle ones that collapse after the first flush of flowers. Too few annuals come back a second year. Perhaps they miss the desert conditions they have in nature. But their seed production is usually sufficient to let you repeat the ones you want a second year. It is always the homeliest that selfsow. Big exceptions are *Nigella, Iberis,* and an annual delphinium. A few others come back but rather stingily.

Summer is the time to put into effect all the ideas that were churning through our minds last winter. The original plan will never mature, but some parts of it will be set in motion, adapted to the realities of space, cash in hand, and availability of materials. Perhaps a bog, a path through the woodland area, or a new bed. Maybe a collection of containers, a bulb frame, or even an alpine house. Summer is also planting out time. There is no chronologically best time for this. If the earth is dust dry of course planting out is taboo, but often August sees a series of thunderstorms or the remains of a hurricane. So when the ground is moist enough and if no major drought is imminent you can plant out all the plants from the mail-order nurseries that had to be put into coldframes for the summer. And there will be plenty of seedlings from seed sown in February just ready to put out—look for roots coming out of the bottom of the pot and trying to grow into the sand in the coldframe. If your July has been spent making a new bed you will have the extraordinary pleasure of filling a large blank area instead of the usual difficulty of trying to fit forty plants into twenty unsuitable places. If you have the right plants you could even restrict the bed to plants from one geographic location or plants of one color or one genus or family. Usually these great ideas go overboard as soon as you have plants with nowhere to put them and you discover a little vacant space in your special bed. In succession we have first polluted and then abandoned a cactus bed, a primrose bed, a silver and gray bed, a blue and white garden, a lily bed, and a bog plant location. Eventually they all became just rock gardens.

Late summer is when colchicums start blooming but that event is part of a complex series of changes in weather, air, and trees, and in the gardener too that is usually thought of as fall. Before that happens we see the heat of summer retreating and a group of plants in bloom that are by no means left over from spring. *Silene schafta* spreads its magenta riches; alliums come out in profusion (*A. tchaihachewii, caeruleum, cyathophorum, flavum,* and at the very end *Allium thunbergii*). *Caloscordum neriniflorum* and *Lycoris squamigeri* share the stage with the alliums. The mint family produces some good summer bloomers—*Origanum pulchellum, Teucrium webbianum,* and *T. subspinosum.* There are composites from the Southeast—*Marshallia mohrii* (pretty) and *Echinacea pallida* (quaint). *Linum flavum* makes a fine show and *Erigeron glabratus* has been blooming since June. Gentians, mostly the larger ones, proliferate in August—*G. septemfida, asclepiadea, fischeri* are lovely. Some of the others are welcome only because we think we need anything we can get at this time of year. *Eryngium bourgatii* flowers late and there are prickly spheres of seed on the other eryngiums. *Cassia marilandica* and *Santolina neapolitana* are pretty large for a rock garden but make good background plants for this season.

As summer slides by even the mosquitoes leave us and New England luxuriates in sensual days and gentle nights. *Oxalis* may be a nonstop pest but there will be a day near the middle of August when we sit outside under the maples and say "Forget the oxalis."

⤙ ⤚

The Rock Garden in Fall

⤙ ⤚ AT THE VERY end of summer through the first half of September, the soft orange flowers of *Kniphofia galpinii* light up the garden. They bloom well into fall, lasting with the lilac and white goblets of *Colchicum speciosum* until a really heavy frost spoils the flowers. During September the leaves of the trees surrounding the garden are changing color and no modest rock garden plant can compete effectively against them. Occasional flowers on all kinds of alpines go on and off like Christmas lights in slow motion—a primula here, a delphinium there. A draba has a flurry of a dozen flowers opening on the sunniest of cold October days. But these are anomalies—a free bonus, unplanned and unplannable.

The flowers you can depend on for September and fall bloom are the aster family. One really has to discount the garden center chrysanthemums (mums) as anything but the fall equivalent of garden center petunias. If you use them it is to fill a blank spot with strong color. If you are a savings bank or a university you could make a whole bed of them in the space that had tulips in spring and marigolds in summer. There are chrysanthemums that are good perennials and one or two around the garden is a good idea, for instance *C. rubellum* 'Mary Stokes' (peach X ginger) or *C. r.* 'Clara Curtiss' (raspberry X lilac). The really large "decorative" chrysanthemums look out of place anywhere in the open air. There are some useful species too; *C. morifolium,* some of the plants labeled *C. weyrichii* might still be in flower, and *C. lactea* and *C. nipponicum,* which are late bloomers.

There are four or five kinds of plant that bloom in the garden in the fall. First there are the leftovers of late summer. An adenophora or an inula. *Lobelia siphilitica* and *L.cardinalis, Zauschneria (Epilobium) californica* and a few penstemons might still be in bloom. These are remembrances of things past, not always lovely here but further south they could be in full beauty. Other "leftovers" are annuals. These are more satisfactory on the whole than perennials if all you want is a splash of color. Annuals are having a last fling in their efforts to make seed and close down for good. *Phlox drummondii* goes on and on for instance. So do *Psilostrophe tagetina, Erysimum capitatum wheeleri,* and *Machaeranthera bigelovii.* Then there are the flowers of spring—alyssums, saxifrages, and primulas that half open a few almost misformed blooms. These are always reassuring but never spectacular. Also we can count on a few of the seedlings we sowed in February to produce their first flower, and unless they survive the winter it may be their only flower. Townsendias, for instance, are often good for a few fall flowers.

Finally there are the plants that bloom naturally in the fall. There are enough of these to design a fall garden with, but few of us have the space to realize such a luxury. Perhaps in North Carolina or Oregon it would be worth the effort. Mostly we are satisfied with a patch of color here, a well-placed clump there, or a section of the woodland garden to show off a *Cimicifuga simplex* or a *Sanguisorba canadensis.* What your fall plant list is depends very much on where you live—how long you can fend off the first killing frost, and then the second. Two 4" high alliums, *A. thunbergii* and *A.splendens,* look good in a raised bed. The late gentians *(G. farreri, sino-ornata, scabra, andrewsii, crinita)* are variable in first blooming time and there is a limit to how much frost the flowers will withstand. A large group of heathers, forms of *Calluna vulgaris,* are still flowering in

October. These are worth grouping into a special bed. Some kniphofia hybrids may want to bloom so late that they are not worth the trouble of growing even if they are hardy plants, but *K. galpinii* has always bloomed for me through the end of September and it only succumbs to the hardest frost. *Physostegia virginiana* blooms well into November. *Cyclamen hederifolium,* a glorious standby on Long Island and southern Connecticut, tries hard in Massachusetts but is hardly worth the effort. Nor is *Sternbergia lutea.* Nor are the autumn crocus (*C. speciosus, ochroleucus,* and *sativus*) worthwhile in our part of the country. They are buried by leaves in mid-October before they open; by the time you move the leaves to expose the flowers the first hard frost doubles them over. Anyone living south of middle Connecticut should count themselves as blessed to be able to grow a few sweeps of these fall beauties. *Colchicum speciosum* is a different story. It is easier, earlier, tougher, taller, and its color is highly visible among the falling leaves. Even after heavy rain or frost when the heads have wilted and sprawled over each other, there is a startling patch of color to titillate the senses. And of course *Silene schafta* may be lingering on.

But in the Compositae is the genus *Aster* itself. Apart from the ubiquitous *Aster novae-angliae* forms and hybrids and the *Aster 'dumosus'* dwarf hybrids, there are *Aster ericoides, porteri, caeruleus, oblongifolius (kumleinii), linariifolius, patens, paludosus, ptarmicoides,* to name a few of the fall flowering species. These are all most welcome unless they happen to be your local weeds and unless they clamor for too much space or forget to flower. Running asters are easy to pull up; unfortunately you forget which are the wicked ones until you notice in October a large green mat with hardly a flower to be seen. Other composites in bloom in the fall include most noticeably and regrettably *Solidago* species but also in areas with late first frosts there are species of *Helianthus (salicifolius)* and *Helenium (autumnale* forms and hybrids) worth growing. These are all big plants for a border or a prominent clump. Include also *Sedum spectabile, Aconitums (carmichaelii, uncinatum), Anemone japonica,* and *Boltonia asteroides* if you have that kind of room. Vernonias, too, in the woodland are extravagantly tall and of a piercing purple that you notice only when you are really close.

The glory of the fall is the change of color of the leaves; until Columbus Day flowers have to compete with the oranges, reds, and yellows of the maples, oaks, and sumacs while after the fall of the leaves they must be tall enough to be seen through them or placed well outside the canopy of every tree and shrub. After cleanup and a few frosts, flowers are secondary to evergreens. So, for mid-October think about leaf associations—*Euonymus alatus, Rhododendron vaseyi* against the yellows and bronzes of *Chamaecyparis pisifera* or *obtusa* forms. Place a larch where it will shine in November and a *Pinus densiflora oculis-draconis* where you can see the yellow bands on the needles in late November. Use grasses and artemisias to contribute grays, silvers, and subtle browns in contrasting shapes and textures. Some of the flowers will have to be cut off to keep them respectable.

By mid-November there have been many light and a few heavy frosts, the first snow flakes have fallen, the first snow to accumulate has melted by noon the same day, heavy rains dispel our obsessive fear of drought and we can believe the rhododendrons will survive the winter. At least if they don't we can't blame lack of rain. Daylight starts noticeably later even after moving the clocks back and if you get up at your habitual six o'clock you have to fill in time indoors until well after sunrise—the sun, late and low, lacks warmth and it could be ten o'clock before gardening outside seems attractive. These are the days to rake leaves, pull brambles and goldenrod at the edges of the woodland, construct a new bed, make a new path, install snow fences. All the jobs that use energy. The hideous paraphernalia of winter is dragged out—gloves caked in March mud, long johns and old sweaters, boots to replace the sneakers, which now seem so flimsy. These garments are reassembled from their summer hiding places with reluctance. We wish winter would delay its arrival but cold knees and frozen toes demand a change of costume. Our macho alter ego puts up a struggle, but cold wins. Once dressed for it, making a raised bed with cinder blocks is an exciting game instead of an ordeal. The gardener looks around for other creative jobs with a godlike feeling of "I can do anything now I am in winter underwear—provided I can find the hammer and the staple gun, start the leafshredder and the chainsaw, and provided I bought enough black plastic, roofing nails, burlap, and cinder blocks." Some jobs may have to be merely sketched in and left for the merciful snow to obliterate. Some may remain forever unrealized, churning in our minds like guilty thoughts. Like making a large bog or a below-ground irrigation system. Have you ever started on a project after months of premeditation and bullying yourself into the right frame of mind only to find that the hardware store is out of tee joints or angle irons? Even hardware has seasons and if you fail to construct at the proper time what the rest of America is constructing you may well never construct it at all.

Fall is letter-writing time. We can no longer postpone those bread and butter letters thanking other gardeners for garden tours, longed-for plants, and overnight stays. If you postpone until December no one will believe your excuse that you "only just got back." But the real reason for most mail in the fall is seed. Many packets change hands each year. Plants admired in gardens have to have their seed harvested and sent to the admirer. Seedlists have to be supplied. Widely separated plant friends exchange their own seedlists. It is an easy way to give plants, not a straightforward gift but more like a kit for making a harpsichord instead of the instrument itself. The pleasure will involve work and care and a two year wait for the first flower. Seeds are less a gift than an opportunity. And what do you do with seeds you don't want? If you do nothing you will have a sense of willful waste and uneasy feelings of guilt. If you get seed of a plant you already grow you feel obliged to find another home for it. If seed is choice or if it comes from a famous garden or a dear friend I sow a little even if I already have the plant. So

I usually sow everything I get. My rationalizations are: I want to compare the plant I have with this one; it may be a new form; I can verify the name. My reasons are: My plant may die; I want more seedlings coming along; somebody will want the seedlings; I just can't dump it.

I sow seed in fifty-percent coarse sand, fifty-percent peat-based soilless mix and a handful of slow-release fertilizer; cover with a sprinkling of sand; place in lattice bottom trays; place the trays outside on tables exposed to the weather except for the protection of an inverted tray. Since I have had no systematic failures I continue with this method, though I am certain there are better methods for other people. I cannot claim any success with *Cypripedium, Acantholimon, Salix, Soldanella,* or *Rhododendron* among others. One thing you need is room for the tables. You need tables because stooping over a coldframe to inspect pots for germination in March and April is backbreaking, and because a table is easy to keep clear of snow when you want to add trays in January and February. Also mice like to inspect coldframes and the height of a table is an extra obstacle.

October and November are not too late to turn the compost heap unless it is already unpleasantly wet. My compost is mostly sod, and the green stuff gets absorbed fairly rapidly so turning a heap is rather like digging a bed once the top layer has been dragged off. By the time you get to the bottom two feet of a four-foot high heap that has been sitting for two years, the soil is mellow and crumbly enough to be used to fill a hole in the garden or plant a tree in the arboretum (meadow).

In November you have to assume that every day in the garden is the last. It could freeze, snow, etc. You could be dead before the next workday. So at some point the barn must be cleaned out so that each day all the tools and carts can be stored there in case it really is the last day. When that last day comes, it will snow hard and you will have forgotten what you were doing by the time the snow has gone. Of course the last day concept is an illusion, there are always days in mid-winter when something seems possible, but it is never the unfinished work of November.

October and November are animal months. In October the chipmunks are still storing food, some of it is from your garden. As you cut down plant remains you may notice the hole of an animal actually living in the garden—even in a raised bed. You can stuff an oily rag into the hole—two attempts is usually enough to discourage a chipmunk, more for a woodchuck. Equally devastating are the footprints of deer in newly planted beds. Whole plants can be wrenched out, chewed on, and left high and dry. Armerias are very susceptible to this treatment, but nothing is exempt. So there is a constant rescue operation going on through mid-November. None of the aromatic deterrents seem to work satisfactorily and I am now covering precious raised beds with a spun polyester "blanket" or polypropylene netting. Beds with good drainage suffer most as the surface is loose sand and stone. Woodland suffers less from clumsy hooves than from careful teeth. From mid-November until the ground is frozen hard there are hunters around and the damage seems to decrease. Snow makes the garden even safer so a heavy snowfall has a calming effect on the nerves. There is a lot of anger and anxiety generated by animals but very few gardeners actually shoot them. We seem to live at the edge of success—never really free of unpredictable outside agents that mindlessly arbitrate what will and what will not succeed. Is there some character building in all this that compensates for the tribulations of fall? Perhaps our pride is subdued and our vanity disciplined while each small success becomes an occasion for thanksgiving. But how irritating to have to thank a deer for not eating your *Dianthus alpinus.*

Some time in November you have to roll up the hoses and put them away—if you leave it too late you will be stuck with several yards of intractable hard plastic that would rather break than roll. Empty water pipes. Don't leave buckets upright to fill with water and freeze solid bulging the bottoms. Bring in the shovels from the compost heap, the sand pile, and the woodchip pile. They all freeze solid. Turn on the greenhouse heat. Close the doors and windows at night, open them in the day. It will heat up to 80° in November on a sunny day. Everything is common sense. Everybody knows these things and everybody forgets at some time to do them.

The leaves are down and the sun is about as high in November as it is in February, but what a difference! November grass has a warm, ripe look and the lawns are lush. There is no snow to echo the sky, the earth is still earthy and accepts moisture. And November is blessed and cursed with strange and beautiful lights, mists, and fogs. The garden is both clarified and mysteriously trans-figured. As we wander through the woodland garden, paths are blurred with leaves; where the landmarks in summer were lilies they are now sharp-budded rhododendrons and piles of freshly cut logs waiting to be hauled up to the house. The larches have had their brief fortnight of glory and have shed their bronze needles. Pines, spruces, and hemlocks now assert themselves through fascinating variations on the conical theme and rhododendrons attempt varia-tions on the hemisphere. In the raised beds and containers the buns and mats mutely explain survival in a hostile climate. The gray and silver mats of *Artemisia assoana, Antennaria dioica, Arenaria tetra-quetra,* and anonymous hieraciums show off and douglasias, an-drosaces, and asperulas are at their most lovable. Crucifers form soft, fat, neat pillows after a summer's untidy sprawl. Iberis, aubri-eta, and variegated arabis combine into a gleaming gladness of greens. One or two drabas are brash enough to open a few flowers and we gratefully accept this token that true spring will follow in four months or less.

⁓ ⁓

The Rock Garden in Winter

ॐ ॐ WINTER PUTS ROCK gardening on hold. We spend three months of the year preparing for it starting with the first chilly night in September. An alarm goes off inside the brain and muscles: we start thinking cleanup, plant out, edge, turn compost, and the muscles react to this sense of urgency. When winter arrives—let's say around Thanksgiving—there is a sense of fulfillment alternating with a sense of resignation, a feeling that what wasn't done doesn't matter, that snow will soon be here to hide the sins of omission.

The garden itself is at rest even when howling winds sweep down from the northwest to set the stems of *Calamagrostis epigejos* shivering and genuflecting to the tyrant from the Arctic. If there has been a silent powdery snow, the remains of *Sedum spectabile* sit crowned with a powder puff. Some plants are as beautiful in death as they are in life. I don't choose plants specifically for this reason though, I just accept the serendipitous when and where it happens. There are very few days of winter when you look at the details of the garden. Winter is the time to look at the overall effect, the paths, the rocks, the placing of shrubs and conifers. There isn't much you can do except dream and plan and promise, and threaten and boast about what you will do once the ground thaws. It is the best time to cut down the trees that you carefully banded in the summer. When spring arrives you will be delighted with the new light and the extra space; you never want a tree back that you decided to remove.

After the first serious snowstorm—probably in early January—even tidying up stops and anything loose has already been blown away and buried. A coldframe, its lid broken and crumpled, is embalmed in ice and shrouded with a white, winding sheet. I try to forget which plants are buried under the debris, there being no point in anticipating a special calamity, as there will be plenty of losses to bemoan in April.

All this is winter in a rather high, exposed patch of New England. It may be happening in Minnesota too. But many gardeners have very different winters. One of the pleasures of winter travel is to visit other peoples' gardens and experience vicariously what it would be like to garden in a different part of the country. Of course a visitor only gets a snapshot of what a garden is like. Trying to place a one day visit in context of a 365 day cycle is almost impossible, so we ask a lot of questions about what goes on the rest of the year. Even if a garden is under snow you can enjoy this activity. As far south as Pennsylvania gardening stops for snow and cold. They seem to have a longer, hotter, stickier garden season than Massachusetts but it comes to an end around Thanksgiving as ours does. Further south in Virginia, even at the beginning of January, we saw a shoreside garden that was quiet but not frozen and not completely dormant. *Narcissus bulbocodium* was already in bloom and the first crocuses had already opened. Later that winter there were bad storms but at the time we saw it, the garden was a patchwork of the maturity of fall—the berries and lingering foliage of a shrub garden—winter hiatus and spring promise.

In North Carolina at the southern end of the Blue Ridge Mountains, a hilltop garden enjoys a winter totally unlike ours. Gardening continues throughout the year and stops only for an occasional fleeting snow. This is as far south as you can do rock gardening with alpines and you need to be high in order to succeed. But this is real success and this garden is the closest I have seen to a facsimile of high Colorado tundra. Nothing much in bloom in mid-December but the mats and buns are content and a healthy size. Nearby coldframes are open to the sun. They only need cover on a few days of the year. Living in North Carolina means the owner, Ev Whittemore, can sow seed as soon as she gets it and leave it outside to germinate. Well, so can I, but there is no added value to sowing seed in November over February for me except not to fall behind. Ev gets the added pleasure of getting germination throughout winter. Inspecting and transplanting never stop. I looked at her setup with a little envy but remembered too that I wouldn't have left my own garden if I had had so much activity and it was only because my garden was immobilized that I was there at all.

Even the subtropical gardens of Florida are "dormant" in late December. There are flowers of course, but they appear stationary, waiting to be joined by all the others in a spring rush that I shall miss. But are the gardens of Florida ever a blaze of color? The most enviable aspect of these gardens is the bountiful fruit trees: oranges, lemons, and avocados.

In February in San Diego you can also eat oranges from your own tree. We saw gardens there like a greenhouse without walls. Gardeners all over North America seem to push plants to their limit of hardiness and even in San Diego use protected places and glass to grow the ungrowable. But there are probably no rock gardens this far south. In San Francisco, on the other hand, there are rock gardens of many styles. One steep garden combines scree, bog, sand garden, and rocky slope in an enclosing curtain of shrubs and climbers. Another small garden seems to flow out of the house, or is the garden invading the living quarters? The trellises and structures and the intensive use of every inch of ground creates a boxlike bower. That is until you go out to the front of the house and see a rock garden that almost overflows on to the sidewalk. In February these gardens are full of action.

In one beautiful and original garden close to the water but perched on a hillside, the summer weather is so friendly—enough fog—and the winters are so mild that the rock plants are orchids and the ground cover echevaria. In California too you can grow Calochortus and South African bulbs. California gardens force you to reassess your view of what a rock garden is and stir up vaguely disturbing feelings that one is wasting one's time in the East. We think ourselves very clever to grow a few rhodohypoxis or an occasional gladiolus, but California gardens have a feast of color in late February that matches our May display.

Even in Seattle and British Columbia, rock gardening in winter is a different story from the bleak prospect of the Northeast. But here you have the feeling that growth has slowed down and there is a static quality to the landscape. People seem to be waiting just as we are in the East, but they have nonstop pleasure watching their charges. They can do the cleanup in a leisurely way. So it seems. Fall in the Northwest must be a very relaxed time. You know that nearly anything can be put off until February! But the Minnesotans must share our rush into winter. Their gardens in winter are like ours— on hold.

Still there is plenty of interest in a New England or Midwest gardening life from December through grim March, and we are always glad to return to the snowfields. The seedlists and catalogs have to be read and order sheets rushed to the mail. Seed has to be sown when it arrives and the pots put out in trays in the snow. Have you noticed what happens when you give a plant to a visitor? There is a sudden change of attitude towards the plant. When the visitor arrived the plant was standing in the sun waiting patiently for the next rain; it had spent the past two months in this position and, as the visitor must have observed, was flourishing. Now you give it to your friend and instantly they want to water it and remove it to a shady spot. They reverently but censoriously remove a little moss growing in the pot and ask a torrent of questions about size, color, flowering time, hardiness, and so on. A similar fit comes over me when I receive seed. It must get immediate attention—listing, labeling, sowing in 3" pots, mulching with sand, overnight immersion in an inch of water and not until it is safely out in the snow ready for its first overnight freeze and its name entered on the computer as well as in my log book can I relax. This is true even though I know the seed has been sitting in an envelope in a shoe box since August. The sooner the seeds imbibe and start on their long journey from dormancy into planthood the better. I do restrain myself from sowing annuals too early though. Nothing is more vexing than to have to transplant seedlings into individual pots in March when there is no room in the greenhouse to spare and all the coldframes are full. So it is probably a good idea to sow fast germinating annuals in April or even May. In New England you don't want to plant them out until the beginning of June at the earliest; even the hardy ones don't really like frost. You may be thinking why even discuss annuals in this context. I will merely mention *Lupinus lepidus lobbii,* which behaves exactly like an annual, though I don't believe it is annual on Mount Hood. Anyone would be happy to see it blooming its first summer after sowing and overjoyed to have it set viable seed.

Nor is winter an unbroken period of steady state. There are warm days as well as those glorious frigid blue days. On warm days there is pruning, sawing, and trash burning. If there is an extended period of warmth or, heaven forbid, a warm rain, the snow may vanish for a few days and the top inch or so of the soil unfreeze. You rush for a spade and jar your knee as it hits the frozen subsoil. How about weeding? A claw seems possible. Well, you have to be lucky to hit on a good place to start—most places the roots are firmly iced in and the best you can do is behead a few weeds and maybe sprain your wrist hitting hard ground.

Mostly winter is making lists, organizing slides, reading, writing, and remembering. Gardening is still a process—a mental process. We can sometimes escape into other people's realities—those people who live where frost is rare and snow ephemeral. There is little point in debating which location is best. Gardeners make gardens anywhere plants will grow.

◡ ◠

An Ideal Day

ॐ ॐ I GET UP at six. It must be late May or early June because the sun is just about to rise above the hills on the east side of the house. It rained during the night; there is no need to worry about watering the seedpots. Nobody is visiting; there is no need to shave. I'm downstairs exactly in time for the weather forecast, avoiding the Dow Jones average, baseball scores, rock music, and ads—it will be dry and sunny with a high of 70°. I drink my orange juice while waiting for the kettle to boil, then slice a perfectly ripe banana on cereal. In the greenhouse, after breakfast, last night's transplants are sitting in water soaking. I put these pots into trays and carry them outside to sit on a table until I am ready to move them to a coldframe. The air is cool after the rain and the grass wet so there is no urgency to cross the lawn and look at plants; in any case 6:30 is a favorite mosquito time.

This makes potting in the greenhouse very attractive. I remembered last night to bring into the greenhouse several pots of seedlings ready to transplant. All of them have between ten and twenty well-spaced seedlings, each with two good leaves and some with more. All of them are very desirable, being new to cultivation, new to me, or things I want to either try again myself or give away to friends. All of them have pretty leaves and strong stems. There is enough compost ready mixed from last night to get me through the first three or four species, but I have to mix up another batch to finish off all the pots of seedlings waiting to be done. Wood pigeons are cooing, robins are making assertive noises, a white-throated sparrow sings my favorite song. The potting goes well, the roots separate easily and I end up with four kitty litter trays of transplants soaking in an inch of water. By now it is 8:30 and I retire to the kitchen to drink hot chocolate, write labels, and record the transplant activity in my seedlist.

At 9:00 I have finished putting the labels in the pots, the sun has warmed up the air and the grass while still damp is no longer soaking wet. It is gardening time. There is a tray of plants ready to be planted out, they are all big enough and require the same growing conditions, so I carry them to a suitable bed that needs refurbishing. I return for tools: buckets, claw, trowel, spade, scissors, kneeling pad, fertilizer. I weed the area, plant the whole batch, go to the pump for water, water them in, go back to the parking lot for buckwheat hulls (or gravel or whatever mulch seems right) and mulch the planted area. It is now 10:15; a good time to take photographs. The camera is loaded and I get some brilliant shots of a new plant flowering for the first time. I check the label for the name. The label is there behind the plant and unbroken. The name is visible. I write the name in a little notebook where I shall find it when the slides come back. I take other pictures and find I can remember the names of the plants or find a legible label. On the way around the garden I take note of all the plants in bud, admire the ones reaching full beauty, say goodbye to the ones going over and take note of the ones going to seed. It's 10:45 and time to open a can for lunch. Norman gets the mail. Over lunch we read the mail, which consists of letters from other gardeners containing fresh seed of short-lived viability, a few checks, and a notice that my pension will be increased next month.

After lunch is the best time to look at seedpots for germination—excitement without exertion. Since it is late in the season I can't really expect too much but end up with over twenty, including some pulsatillas (these seem to germinate erratically) and iris (which usually germinate late) and an unexpected kniphofia. I arrange the pots alphabetically and enter the germinations in my seed record. It is now noon and the weather delightful so I decide to edge a bed. Once wielding a spade I am overcome by an impulse to make the bed larger. I start cutting sod and laying it upside down where the extension is to be. This is so absorbing I swiftly lose all sense of guilt about doing something I shall be later asked to explain and justify. By 2:00 I can see the new bed taking shape and I feel I can leave it and take time out for tea. At 2:30 tea is over, the sun is strong and a spell in the wood is indicated. I find a shady bed to weed and it seems a good opportunity to finally learn the names of a few ferns. Instead I barely glance at the labels, admire the varied patterns of the ferns as I weed around them, mulch them to make them look pretty, and face up to the reality that I shall never remember any name with four parts for more than a minute. After the ferns I visit the bog and note that *Cypripedium reginae* has six shoots coming up, the Dodecatheons look marvelous even though they are going over, the *Lobelia X vedrariensis* is still alive, and the mimulus is coming back. I start the return trip back to the house, weeding the ornamental grasses on the way. I am back in the kitchen by 4:30 and think about dinner. Fortunately there are leftovers, so it means microwave and not real cooking. By 5:30 the eating process is finished for the day and I relax watching the weather on TV. At 6:00 it is time to go out again. The mosquitoes are still quiet and I can get in an hour's mowing.

At 7:00 I am back in the greenhouse and go on transplanting until sunset. After sunset I write labels. Finally at 8:30 I have a shower and read or write until 10:30, with maybe a half hour of TV trash sandwiched in there. An ideal day would be followed by a night of sound uninterrupted sleep. But there are very few days like this; most of the time I have…

≈ ≈

A Less than Ideal Day

ॐ ॐ IT IS 6:00, already hot, and a bit sticky. It hasn't rained for days. A New York friend called last night threatening to visit so I have to shave so as not to appear uncouth. Breakfast is spoiled—the orange juice ran out. This means going in to town—what a waste of time. I go into the greenhouse, the screen door was left open, and I hear the buzz of a wasp and the low scream of a mosquito. I forgot to bring in any pots of seedlings so I have to go out to the frames to find something ready to transplant. The pots feel clammy and as I search for half a dozen pots I get bitten. The Jiffy mix bins are empty. I go to the barn and carry back a forty-pound bag to the greenhouse. Sand too is low so I bring in four buckets from the sandpile. By now it is 8:00 and I feel I haven't even started.

There seems to be something wrong with each of the pots I brought in. One of them is crowded with seedlings too closely sown, but when I knock it out the roots are obviously not long enough. The compost it was sown in was too sandy and the mass starts to fall apart. I rescue a few clumps but the tiny single seedlings are not worth potting. The first drop of rain would annihilate them. The next pot has three large seedlings and several small ones. Shall I do it and risk losing all the little ones? I ponder the alternatives and decide to wait until they are a little bigger. The next pot is *Alyssum saxatile.* Why on earth did I sow these seeds? My own garden has a rich variety of yellows and I don't really need any more plants of this useful but commonplace species. I remember the plant sale and what a good plant this is for beginners so, a little grudgingly, I spend time potting six of them. I try a campanula next but the leaves have become entangled and extreme care is needed not to break them off. The roots too have grown together and are hard to pull apart so I take an unconscionable length of time to get just a few plants potted. By now it is 8:30 and time for hot chocolate. Today it tastes sickeningly sweet and I resolve never to drink the stuff again.

The forecast promised thirty percent chance of rain tomorrow so we use this as an excuse to postpone marketing. So no orange juice tomorrow either. At 9:00 I am ready to go outside. I decide against changing into rubbers. The grass is still wet with a heavy dew and my sneakers and socks are soon soaking. I carry a tray of plants to a bed ready for a planting-out session. The black fly are back and I feel something bite my ankle while another gets me behind the left ear. I put down the tray, swipe my ear, and bend down to tuck my pants inside my socks. Too late—and the bottoms of the pants are wet through. I deliver the tray and go back to the barn for planting tools: a claw and a trowel. I go back to the bed and realize I shall need a kneeling mat so back to the greenhouse. Now I see that the open space I had my eye on has a label—*Roscoea!* Is it still alive? Shall I risk digging it up? I remember roscoea comes up late and decide to try another bed. I find room for one plant. But now insects have gathered into a small cloud around my head and I have to retreat in haste and discomfort, leaving the tools on the ground. I go back to the barn and pick up a spade to do some edging. The bed I choose is on stony ground and the spade soon hits a big one. The next half hour is spent getting it out. Wet grass, turned soil, and human sweat attract the maddening hum of deer fly. Usually you can let one land on your wrist and give it a biff with your other hand. With hands covered with mud this turns out to be unpleasant and ineffectual so I leave the rest of the edging for another day.

It is lunchtime and we are reduced to peanut butter. The mail is junk and bills. There is no newspaper. I remember a plant I have to photograph—*Eritrichium howardii*—and grab the camera and go out looking for the raised bed I think it is in. Eventually I find it placed about a foot away from the edge. The raised bed has a border fully planted and there is nowhere to kneel without doing serious damage to at least one plant. If I stand I am too far away, if I sprawl with my wrists on the bed I have no control. I settle for kneeling.

There are an infinite number of ways a day can be imperfect and this day has been discouraging. It could have been an accident with a clumsy hose, a broken spade, an elaborate attempt to collect seed that turned out to be unripe. The worst category of mishap is the kind that forces an action you really don't want to do. The mowing machine breaks down, an animal digs a large hole in a bed or digs up a plant and leaves it on the surface with exposed roots, you run out of sand, Jiffy mix, pots, labels, or something else vital, you notice a plant wilting in the coldframe and have to stop whatever you are doing to water, a bird gets caught in the chipmunk trap, UPS arrives with twenty bags you have to help unload, a kind neighbor brings bales of hay and dumps them in the wrong place, visitors arrive just as you are transplanting a pot of tricky *Eriogonum* seedlings, a storm breaks a few branches that crash down on one of the beds. These are major events that seem sent by Jehovah to test the patience of the Jobs of gardening. But most of what makes a day less than perfect is lack of planning, forgetfulness, willfulness. In other words it is your fault. But there is also…

∿ ∿

A Third Kind of Day

ঽ ঽ You may have to spend the day in bed ill, you may have to go to a mall to buy clothes, you may have to take a visiting relative to an art gallery, or you may have to go to the dentist for a root canal job, or attend a birthday party, you might win a lottery, you may have to leave for a vacation. These are the experiences of a third kind that novelists and movie script writers celebrate, along with sex and crime, as the fabric of life. I suppose they are right in a way. Gardening is nothing compared to a major operation or a declaration of war. But essentially the novelists are wrong. The dramas of life certainly affect its course, but unless your life is in fact a soap opera of sex and crime these catastrophic events are few and far between. How often do you go to a mall? Uneventful living takes up most of our time. Gardening is part of it, possibly a trivial part to the rest of the world, but by no means less important to the gardener than the big events.

A perfect day for anybody is most likely one of the in-between days when nothing happens. For nongardeners it may mean a smooth commute to work with a great Danish pastry at coffee break and the boss in a good mood. For gardeners it may be not misplacing your secateurs. On a day when something *important* happens and no gardening is possible I turn off. As I drive down Norfolk Road I stop thinking of seedlings, botanical Latin, mulches, and mowing. The resentment at having to leave paradise has already been lived through as part of the anticipation and has tempered the pleasure (or annoyance) that doing something important might have promised. As I lie in bed with flu, surrounded by boxes of Kleenex, or sleep off the pain of an operation, the garden hardly exists. Not even making garden design doodles has any magic. By the time gardening intrudes itself on my consciousness again I know I am nearly well.

A garden can be very accommodating in this way, especially if you have to leave it for an extended period of time. The garden exists even though you ignore it and when you finally get back to it you have to not only catch up with the obvious cleanup chores, you have to rethink your whole plan. Is this patch of weeds a place you cleared in order to plant or has everything died? It takes a full day of this disorientation to grasp the situation and recollect what the garden is all about. When you do you are horrified at the gross changes a few days away from the garden can bring about, and then pleased that even weedy, you love it and are glad to be back. Even if you are only away for a day some alienation takes place and it isn't until you have picked up a spade and made a few false starts that it all comes back to you and you take possession of your domain once again. On an ideal day you don't lose touch; you belong to the process and everything you do seems right.

∿ ∿

Gentiana subindex

Gentianella subindex

Gentianopsis subindex

ABOUT THE AUTHOR

GEOFFREY B. CHARLESWORTH is a retired Professor of Mathematics who received the 1987 American Rock Garden Society's prestigious award of merit for "outstanding plantsmanship," and the Carlton Worth Award for "distinguished writing on rock gardening and rock garden plants." Former Chairman of the Connecticut and Berkshire Chapters of the North American Rock Garden Society and co-founder of the Berkshire Chapter, he is a frequent lecturer at regional and international meetings. He has been described by Pacific Horticulture Magazine as one who "demonstrates that literate and entertaining writers on gardening are still to be found." His previous book, *The Opinionated Gardener,* is also available from Godine.

COLOPHON

A Gardener Obsessed was set in Adobe Garamond.
Garamond, one of the most popular of all typefaces,
was originally designed for metal type by French engraver
Claude Garamond in the sixteenth century. While
preeminently a fine book type, Garamond gives
great distinction to display forms in which a
refinement is desirable.

The book was designed and typeset by Ken Wong
and has been bound and printed by Maple-Vail Book
Manufacturing, Binghamton, New York. The color insert
has been printed by CS Graphics, Singapore.
The paper is 55# Sebago Antique Cream.